A FRONT ROW SEAT

NICHOLAS ROOSEVELT

A
FRONT
ROW
SEAT

UNIVERSITY OF OKLAHOMA PRESS : *Norman*

BOOKS BY NICHOLAS ROOSEVELT
A Front Row Seat (Norman, 1953)
A New Birth of Freedom (New York, 1938)
The Townsend Plan (Garden City, 1936)
America and England? (New York, 1930)
The Restless Pacific (New York and London, 1928)
The Philippines: A Treasure and a Problem (New York, 1926)

Library of Congress Catalog Card Number: 53–8809

COPYRIGHT 1953
BY THE UNIVERSITY OF OKLAHOMA PRESS
PUBLISHING DIVISION OF THE UNIVERSITY
COMPOSED AND PRINTED AT NORMAN, OKLAHOMA, U.S.A.
BY THE UNIVERSITY OF OKLAHOMA PRESS
FIRST EDITION

T O

M. M. N.

in appreciation of thirty years of friendship,
hospitality and help in the making of books

FOREWORD

A COMBINATION of circumstances gave me a front row seat at numerous important international and national events during the last forty years. About most of these I wrote at the time, often in diaries and letters, occasionally in books, usually in newspapers and magazines, and for several years in diplomatic dispatches to the Department of State. The resulting files form the basis of this volume.

If to some it may seem that disproportionate space is given to the Oyster Bay branch of the Roosevelt family, the reason is that, having been brought up at Oyster Bay, I saw much of T. R. Furthermore, it is to him that all Roosevelts in the twentieth century owe the initial wide fame of the name, and to whom I, in particular, am indebted as a dominant influence in my life. The passage of decades has not dimmed my admiration and affection for him.

Work on the *New York Times* and the *New York Herald Tribune* at various periods between 1921 and 1946 gave me opportunities to study history in the making and to meet persons active in national and international affairs. So also did my service as a young attaché in the American embassy in Paris in World War I and as United States minister to Hungary from 1930 to 1933. In this latter post I had the duty of reporting to Washington about the economic collapse of Europe and the rise of Hitlerism.

The interrelationship between journalism and history is closer than many newspapermen—and nearly all historians—admit. Much of today's news will be history tomorrow. As a newspaperman, I appreciate the importance of a thorough background of history for any journalist specializing in national or international affairs. At the same time, as a lifelong student of history, I am struck with the fact that most American historians lack the newspaperman's schooling in the use of clear and simple English and are handicapped by not having had the training in evaluating the importance, as well as the credibility, of material which is basic in good journalism. It is significant that to most historians the term "journalistic"—usually referring to something which is readable and concise—is one of reproach.

It is the world's—and historians'—loss that highly trained newspapermen were not present at great historical events before the twentieth century. What would we not give for a day-to-day, eye-witness account of the Congress of Vienna in 1814–15 by Anne O'Hare McCormick, or a daily column by Arthur Krock, detailing from his own first-hand observations the proceedings of the convention which met in Philadelphia in the hot summer of 1787 to draft the Constitution of the United States, or an analysis by John Gunther of Julius Cæsar as he knew him in 45 B. C.—even if its title was *Inside Cæsar?*

This volume cannot promise such rich fare, but it is offered as a newspaperman's reactions to some of the historical events—and the actors in them—which he watched as a recording observer.

NICHOLAS ROOSEVELT

Big Sur, California
June, 1953

CONTENTS

ILLUSTRATIONS

A FRONT ROW SEAT

CHAPTER ONE

A RUGGED BROOD

FEW PERSONS not born or wedded to a Roosevelt know the magic in that name. Other American families have been prominent in successive generations, other presidents famous in their day besides Theodore and Franklin. But members of these other families have not aroused such strong reactions as have Eleanor (Franklin's wife) or Alice Longworth, or Corinne Roosevelt Robinson, let alone T. R. and F. D. R., in our own times. Even a century ago it was the same, for in 1840 Philip Hone, onetime mayor of New York, noted in his famous diary that James J. Roosevelt, then in the State Assembly in Albany, was "the leader of the blackguards, in whose person our poor city is disgraced," and said that he "resorts to every species of vile, disgraceful conduct and language." According to Hone, this Roosevelt was the "chief of a most unworthy delegation of a misrepresented city" and "a small man, very conceited and inferior." The two most famous Roosevelts, Theodore and Franklin, were hated with a bitterness rarely equaled in American public life. At the same time they were worshipped by millions.

The extent to which devotion to T. R. persisted after his death is illustrated by an incident which occurred in 1933, when I was writing a series of articles about farm conditions in the Middle West for the *New York Herald Tribune*. Dean Burr of the School of Agriculture at the University of Nebraska had taken me to a farm near Lincoln. We found the daughter of the house in the kitchen.

"Is your father around?" the Dean asked.

[3]

"Yes," said she, "Pa's upstairs. He's sick."

"Oh, I'm sorry to hear that," said Burr. "I brought Mr. Roosevelt from New York and hoped he could see him."

"What name did you say that was?" she asked.

"Roosevelt," said Dean Burr.

"Roosevelt," she repeated incredulously, and, again, "Roosevelt?" She paused, as if making a decision, and then said:

"Well, Pa's sick, but he'd be a durned sight sicker if he knew anybody of *that* name had been in this house and he hadn't seen him."

So she got "Pa" out of bed, and "Pa" told me how he had heard T. R. speak in Colorado in 1905 and had followed him into the Bull Moose party in 1912, and how he had voted for F. D. R. in 1932 because he thought that anyone of that name ought to be a good bet.

The haters of T. R. included many businessmen who later looked on Franklin as equally destructive of the American way of life. Among these was the younger J. P. Morgan, who shared his father's bitterness toward Theodore Roosevelt and reacted so violently to Franklin that his family discouraged visitors from even mentioning the name of Roosevelt in his presence lest it raise his blood pressure to the bursting point.

Shortly before his death in 1943, Mr. Morgan had to act as temporary chairman of the board of directors of the New York Public Library. When the meeting was over Mr. Morgan said to the librarian, Franklin Hopper:

"By the way, Hopper, I'm thinking of putting on an exhibit of political cartoons in the Morgan Library. What do you think of the idea?"

Mr. Hopper, who told me this story, replied that it was an excellent plan and added:

"But you know, don't you, Mr. Morgan, that the best collection of political cartoons in the city has to do with the life and times of Theodore Roosevelt and is at the Roosevelt Memorial Association on 20th Street?"

Mr. Morgan angrily shook himself into his coat and deep from his heart said:

[4]

C. V. S. ROOSEVELT
His exceptional ability at making money proved a boon to future
generations

"God damn ALL Roosevelts!"

"Oh, come now, Mr. Morgan," said Mr. Hopper soothingly. "Surely you don't mean ALL Roosevelts. You were very fond of T. R.'s sister, Mrs. Douglas Robinson, weren't you?"

"Just another Eleanor, just another Eleanor," Mr. Morgan growled as he stamped out of the room.

For the first five or six generations in this country the Roosevelts had been respected but inconspicuous in the little town of New York, where the Dutch progenitor of the family had settled in 1649. Occasionally one of them served as alderman. In 1730, John Roosevelt (a direct ancestor of Theodore and of my father) was a member of a committee of five to receive twenty-one cases of books to be placed in the City Hall, which became a part of the first public library in New York. A Nicholas Roosevelt at this time was a silversmith of enough ability to produce pieces which are still coveted by collectors and museums. During the Revolution a few Roosevelts served in the army. Isaac Roosevelt, great-grandfather of F. D. R., possessed either more than average ability or a higher sense of responsibility to the community, or greater ambition—or a combination of these traits—than his forebears and relatives, for he not only was a leader in business and banking but was a member of important groups in the Revolution, including the Constitutional Convention which, in 1777, drew up the Constitution of the state of New York. Eleven years later he was a delegate to the convention which ratified the Constitution of the United States. He was state senator for four years, and was fourth president of the Society of the New York Hospital, the first important hospital project in New York. He was also president of the first bank organized in the city.

A cousin of his, Nicholas J., was prominent in the development of the application of steam to navigation. About him a good deal has been written, but not enough to clear up the century-old contest as to whether or not to him, rather than to Robert Fulton, belongs the credit for the invention of the vertical paddle-wheel, which inaugurated successful steam navigation. There were lawsuits, claims, and counterclaims involving charges of downright trickery and deception on the part of Chancellor Robert R. Livingston and Robert Fulton. The scarcity of available records makes it hard at this time to support or deny the charges. Undeniable is the fact that this Roosevelt had an inventive mind; that, at the same time that others in this country and in England were seeking means to propel a boat by steampower, he devoted many dreaming hours to this search; that he built and experimented with various types of steam engines for use in boats; and, finally, that he built and operated the first steamboat ever to make the trip from Pittsburgh to New Orleans on the Ohio and the Mississippi rivers. He thus belongs among the pioneers of the industrial revolution, combining the capacity to imagine with the ability to create and the energy to put his inventions to practical use. Had he, in addition, possessed in a higher degree the acquisitive instinct so strong in others of his tribe, he might have become a powerful figure in the industrialization of America. Instead, others reaped the financial rewards of inventions which he had helped to develop. Born in the age of stagecoaches, sails, and backbreaking manpower, he lived to see the use of steam successfully applied not only to river navigation but to transatlantic shipping, as well as to factories and mills and to railroads crossing the country as far west as the Mississippi. He was forty-four years old when he built and took the *New Orleans* down the Ohio and Mississippi in 1811, and lived almost as long thereafter.

By the time of his death various Roosevelts had acquired sufficient prominence for the *New York Sun* to state in 1841 that "no family shines more honorably in the Dutch annals of this province than the Roosevelts—the venerated burgomasters of their day." These early Roosevelts may have been venerated. They may even have been as self-assertive as their descendants. But they left few records of their achievements. It was not until the early nineteenth century that an increasing number of Roosevelts became as voluble as they were energetic. In my youth, whenever two or more Roosevelts met, each talked vociferously and ceaselessly, paying no attention to what anyone else tried to say. Today most family gatherings develop into a symphony of concurrent monologues, in which stout lungs are at a premium.

[6]

CHAPTER TWO

A PASSION FOR BUSINESS

WHILE NICHOLAS J. was still devoting his restless mind to the problem of driving a boat by steam, a nephew of his was born and christened Cornelius Van Schaaick Roosevelt. Because his descendants include so many unusual characters, of whom Theodore (the president), Theodore's daughter Alice Longworth, and his niece Eleanor (wife of F. D. R.) are the most famous, it would be interesting to know more of him than is preserved in scraps of family tradition, a few newspaper clippings, and a handful of his letters. His brood included writers, lawyers, bankers, inventors, poets, politicians, parasites, and even a few alcoholics. Nearly all of these had an exceptional amount of energy. Many of them left things undone which they ought to have done. Some did things which they ought not to have done. But what they set their hands to they did with gusto, and even those who, metaphorically speaking, went to hell, did so with zest and vehemence.

Nineteen of them are listed in various volumes of *Who's Who in America*, including his last surviving son (Robert B.), three grandchildren (Theodore, Emlen, and Corinne Roosevelt Robinson), ten great-grandchildren (Theodore, Jr., Alice Longworth, Kermit, Archie, George E., John K., Philip J., Nicholas, Eleanor, and Theodore Douglas Robinson), and five of his great-great-grandchildren (James, Elliott, and Franklin Roosevelt, Jr., and Joseph W. Alsop, Jr. and Stewart Alsop). Few, if any, of his contemporary Americans have such a record of distinguished progeny.

Business was the overmastering passion of C. V. S., as he was commonly called. His father had maintained a prosperous hardware shop in New York during the Federalist era, and left to C. V. S. what has been described as a "modest fortune." Even during the time of his engagement to Margaret Barnhill, of Philadelphia, whom he married late in 1821, his letters were full of his consuming interest in his work. "Business calls me with its imperious beckoning," he wrote his wife-to-be in August, 1821. "That business has become to me now a matter of more consequence than ever, and that too in the hope that it may be the means of promoting those finer feelings which others sacrifice at the shrine of avarice." The next month he set forth what was to be his lifelong goal with even greater clarity and brevity: "Economy is my doctrine at all times—at all events till I become, if it is to be so, *a man of fortune.*" (The italics are his.) That this was not mere moralizing may be seen from the fact that, in this same letter, he gave his fiancée the benefit of his ideas on how they should live in New York: "You know," he wrote Margaret Barnhill, "that I hate extravagance in young folks, and the only things in which I shall be extravagant will be carpets for the two lower rooms, a sideboard and a *sofa. Our* chairs," he added smugly, with a clear underlining of the pronoun, "*our,*" "will not be mahogany. My idea is that of little or nothing for ornament alone, but of that which is useful to be also ornamental if possible." When it came to the buying of a wedding present of silver for his bride, he prudently waited till after the wedding, and then made his Margaret do her own selecting.

C. V. S. lived in a large house on Union Square, which at that time was the edge of the city. Life in this house must have been exciting and gay, despite his absorption in business. He and Margaret Barnhill had six children, all sons, five of whom grew to manhood, and who, with their families, were a closely knit group. It is a measure of the activities and personalities of these five sons that all of them were elected to the Century Club, which has always chosen its members on grounds of achievement rather than because of their social connections. In their youth they were apparently full of vigor and fun, and the despair of a Mr. Mac-

Millan who served as their tutor. My grandfather, S. Weir, was the oldest, and Theodore the youngest. In a letter to the latter, at the time (1851) doing a "grand tour" of Europe, Grandfather gives a sidelight on life at Broadway and Fourteenth Street when all but Theodore already had families of their own. Telling of a mutual friend who had paid the house a long visit, Weir wrote Theodore that this man "seemed to comprehend the various styles of manner and peculiar dialects in use among us. This, you know, requires a good deal of versatility; for a stranger must be somewhat bewildered by the sudden fits we take of irony, cordiality, conceit, affection, nonsense and sense; which succeed each other without any apparent connection or warning approach."

The close association of the winters in and about the Fourteenth Street house was carried to the country in summer, when the clan migrated, usually en masse, to some place in Jersey or on the Hudson, and after the Civil War to Oyster Bay. Till then they usually picked a boardinghouse, or, as in the summer of 1855, what Mrs. C. V. S. described in a letter to her son Theodore, Sr., as a "Water Cure Establishment." "The girls," she wrote (referring presumably to those of her daughters-in-law who were to accompany her), "call it nothing but the Lunatic Asylum, and as it will be quite new to us we expect to enjoy it very much!"

The letters from these various summer places are full of references to "symptoms" and to "dyspepsia"—unquestionably a reflection of the lack of refrigeration and of the unsanitary conditions of the time. When, at last, they rented houses at Oyster Bay, life, at least for the younger generation, was healthier and happier.

As early as 1837 C. V. S. had begun to transmute his modest inheritance into a large fortune. In that year he bet on the future of New York when the whole country plunged into the worst panic it had known prior to 1930. Businesses failed, banks closed, unemployment was widespread, and property values collapsed. But C. V. S. acted upon the sound business principle that the time to buy is when others are eager to sell. Accordingly he bought lots in different parts of Manhattan Island, convinced that the country would pull out of the panic and that paralyzed and starving New York would revive and prosper. What he did not know, and knew he could not know, was which lots in Manhattan would become the most desirable, and hence the most valuable. So he bought hither and yon, sure that some would be highly profitable and that others would probably never yield any gain.

In 1842 the *New York Sun's* "Wealth and Biography of the wealthy citizens of New York" listed C. V. S. as worth $250,000, and three years later increased this figure to $500,000. As his success mounted his interests broadened, and by 1850 he had dropped hardware for plate glass. Before his death the family business had gone into private banking, thus further extending its activities.

In 1844 C. V. S. Roosevelt joined with several others in the reorganization of the Chemical National Bank, of which he became a director, and with which he was associated until his death in 1871. It is a measure of his business success that in 1868 he was listed with ten others in a number of newspaper articles in New York as being among the largest holders of taxable property in the city. The list is interesting today because of the names and the amounts attributed to them:

Wm. B. Astor	$16,114,000.
Wm. C. Rhinelander	7,745,000.
A. T. Stewart	6,091,500.
Peter and Robert Goelet	4,417,000.
James Lennox	4,260,000.
Peter Lorillard	4,250,000.
John David Wolfe	3,997,000.
M. M. Hendricks	1,690,000.
Rufus L. Lord	1,500,000.
C. V. S. Roosevelt	1,346,000.
Total	51,405,500.

Between them they held about 10 per cent of the total taxable property of the city, which at the time was valued at more than $500,000,000. Whether accurate or not, these figures reflect only the relative holdings in taxable real estate and do not include stocks and other productive property. By the time of his death C. V. S. possessed a fortune substantially larger than the real estate holdings listed above, and was referred to as one of the five richest men in New York. His doctrine of "economy" had indeed brought him the great wealth which he craved.

It would be interesting to know, however, whether in his successful old age he ever recurred to the doubts about this concentration on business which he had expressed to his fiancée Margaret Barnhill just before their marriage in 1821. "I sometimes say to myself," he wrote her on September 1 of that year, "oh could I tear myself from that absorber of every gentle and every noble feeling of the soul, business, and fly away and be at rest in the midst of the more enchanting pursuits of the mind. It seems to me sometimes that here I could revel . . . ." But looking at those who had tried this, he found that they "complain of ennui, of want of occupation, and speak enviously of business." He concluded that he would not be a happier man if he were so circumstanced.

A crayon portrait of C. V. S. still exists. It shows a little man with a large head, an unusually high and broad brow, keen twinkling, light blue eyes behind little square glasses, a somewhat thick nose and large mouth—obviously a man of energy and quick intelligence, shrewd, sure, and tenacious. What the face lacks in fineness of line and feature is made up in alertness, vigor, and determination. George Templeton Strong, the New York lawyer and diarist, noting the death of C. V. S., remarked: "his appearance always suggested to me a Hindoo idol, roughly carved in red porphry."

If C. V. S. was so concentrated on business that he seems to have lacked the lighter touch and so concerned with his private problems that he had no time for public affairs, his brother James J. made up for him. He was the assemblyman at Albany who had aroused the resentment of Philip Hone. He was an ardent Jackson man and a lifelong Democrat, who, after his term in the Assembly at Albany, was a member of Congress—the first of the Roosevelts to be elected to the federal legislature—and later was named to the Supreme Court of the State of New York.

The Judge, as James J. was commonly called, married the daughter of Governor Van Ness of Vermont, a lady who early abandoned the frugal life of that state for the more sumptuous social activities of Washington, Paris, Madrid, and New York. A volume of "Queens" of American society, published in 1867, has as its frontispiece a lithograph of her—a buxom beauty bedecked with jewels, with an elegant coiffure and an appearance of replete self-satisfaction. Certainly, if she read the adulatory account of her social talents and achievements in that volume, her already ample bosom must have come near the bursting point.

The Judge apparently delighted in his wife's social pretensions and, unlike most of his relatives, enjoyed the fashionable world. In his youth, while still in local politics in New York City, he had disported himself in Paris with calling cards describing himself as "membre du Conseil de New York et Attaché à l'Ambassade des États-Unis," which caused the New York diarist Philip Hone, who was the recipient of one of these visiting cards while himself in Paris, to note that "this is one way of bringing a New York assistant alderman into notice and transforming a minister plenipotentiary into an ambassador." But it appears that in time his wife's fondness for ostentation ran afoul of his inherited Dutch sense of thrift, for family tradition has it that she had a private arrangement with A. T. Stewart and Company, the forerunners of Wanamaker's, by which that store would give her the pocket money which her husband denied her and then include corresponding charges on the bills it sent to him. In this way she is said to have acquired $30,000 of spending money.

Two other Roosevelts of this generation are of interest because of their prominence in different fields. One is James Henry Roosevelt, grand-nephew of Isaac. The other is Clinton, a second cousin of C. V. S. James H., born in 1800, inherited a modest fortune and set out to be a lawyer. But in his early twenties he was stricken with paralysis and was so impressed with the inadequate medical and nursing attention available, even to persons with means, that he made up his mind to establish a hospital for the benefit of his fellow citizens. Crippled by his paralysis, he never married, and he devoted forty years before his death in 1863 to the management of his affairs with such skill that when he died he left about a million dollars—at the time a large fortune—with which the hospital that bears the family name was endowed. This was one of the earliest large charitable bequests in New York. The hospital which he founded, and in the management of which his relatives have been closely associated for eighty years, was and still is one of the leading institutions in the city.

Quite different, and in many ways more picturesque, was Clinton Roosevelt, who was born in 1804, became an economic radical and political reformer in the days of Andrew Jackson, and lived to see his young kinsman lead the Rough Riders in the war with Spain. Recent historians have described Clinton as the "leading theorist" of the Locofoco movement, as the then left wing of the Democratic party came to be known. It is doubtful if an economic thinker who had been ignored so long would have thus been assigned a role of influence had it not been that his name was Roosevelt and that he was, in a sense, an early nineteenth-century New Dealer. His books and pamphlets have a clarity, vigor, and simplicity unusual for economic tracts. He advocated controlling prices by regulating the volume of currency in circulation. He insisted that not even gold was a stable measure of values, and he even used the "rubber dollar" simile that his distant kinsman a century later was to make famous. He indicted the bankers as oppressors of the people and brakes on progress and urged that their powers be curbed. Largely as a result of the support of the early leaders of labor in New York, he was elected to the state Assembly at Albany in 1835. Later he advocated a form of national socialism more totalitarian even than Rexford Tugwell's proposal in his article on the Fifth Estate.

In 1860 Clinton Roosevelt was again in print, urging the American Association for the Advancement of Science to set up a sort of national planning board, and attempting to solve the paradox of want in the midst of plenty and to devise means for preventing the recurrence of panics, which he picturesquely described "as in fact the delerium tremens of trade, arising from that stimulant, bank paper, by the credit system." In August, 1898, at the age of 94, unmarried, he died, apparently the forgotten Roosevelt, for I could find no account of him in the obituary notices of the *New York Times* in that month.

[13]

CHAPTER THREE

CIVIC RESPONSIBILITY

O F MY GRANDFATHER'S generation only three survived into my own lifetime. One of these was the wife of C. V. S.'s son James A. Roosevelt. She was a Philadelphia Quaker, Elizabeth Norris Emlen, known as "Aunt Lizzie" and regarded as the head of the family. Outspoken, blunt, and austere, she was treated by all of us children with fearful reverence, which was intensified by the fact that she looked and dressed like Queen Victoria. At her summer place at Oyster Bay, every Sunday morning after church, the clan gathered to exchange family gossip. Not even the fact that she always served delicious lemonade and never sought to limit our consumption lessened the awe in which we stood of her. I am sure that at heart she was kindly, simple, and gentle, but to us she seemed a survival from an early era when the earth was peopled with giants, a living proof that there was something even more powerful in the world than a parent or a mere president of the United States.

Her husband, known as "Uncle Jim," was a formidable man with a sandy beard and shrewd, light blue eyes. Doubtless he was kind, but we children had either sensed or been warned that his displeasure was easily aroused and much to be avoided. From his father, C. V. S. Roosevelt, he had inherited a consuming passion for business, and successfully transformed the old merchant's plate-glass and hardware enterprise into one of the most profitable small investment houses in the country.

One of Uncle Jim's four brothers, Robert Barnwell, also lived long and acquired considerable fame as a stalwart Democrat. Rob was too full of animal spirits to be a true conservative, which may explain why he reverted to the Democratic party when his brothers, like nearly all other respectable Northerners during the Civil War, joined the Republican party. If Uncle Jim ever had any thoughts that were not conventional he carefully kept them to himself. Uncle Rob, in contrast, cared little for the conventional and broadcast his thoughts to all who would read or listen to them. Although Uncle Jim and, later, his son Emlen served the very best fare (though plainly cooked), they looked upon the joys of the flesh as snares of the devil. Uncle Rob welcomed them as gifts of the gods. Jim could occasionally chuckle discreetly. Rob loved laughter and to make people laugh. While Jim lived prudently, Rob lived with open hands. The former looked upon business as something always to be taken earnestly. The latter had fun in public life and met with a large measure of success. He led the Citizen's Committee in New York which put the Tweed ring out of business. He was elected to Congress, served as United States minister to Holland, and was treasurer of the Democratic National Committee in the second Cleveland administration.

In Rob, the restlessness inherited from his father, C. V. S. Roosevelt, took the form of a passion for fishing and hunting. His common sense told him that the rapidity with which the country was growing and becoming urbanized would result in the extermination of the country's wildlife. His sense of the practical led him to fight for the first measure for conservation in this country. A century ago it was unthinkable that a man should be restricted in the number of birds or animals he might kill on his own land, or the fish he might catch in his own streams. True, many landowners sought to keep city trespassers and others from shooting or fishing on their property. But only an occasional voice was raised against the wholesale slaughter of game and fowl on public lands in various parts of the country, and only a few ardent fishermen objected to the pollution of streams by the dumping of sawdust, sewage, and industrial refuse into them. Rob was one of these, and he objected publicly, frequently, and loudly. In time he was appointed New York State fish and game commissioner, and was able to shape various movements in behalf of the con-

[15]

servation of fish and wildlife. At least three of his books dealing with fish and game are still highly regarded by conservationists, for Rob had inherited the family fondness for self-expression and wrote with relish and ease.

Vigorous, lusty, vital, he was an Elizabethan survival in the Victorian era, an unconventional member of a society and family in which the prudent mores of a provincial mercantile class viewed with disapproval any departure from the accepted norm. Although I met Uncle Rob only once—at the inauguration of his nephew, Theodore, as president of the United States in 1905, when Rob was nearly eighty and I was only eleven—my impression, formed probably from what various relatives did not say about him in my youthful presence, is that he was a salty old bird and that he got more fun out of life than many of those whose silence about him failed to hide a prim distaste for the manner in which he insisted on living his own life in his own way, instead of theirs.

More conventional than Robert, and yet not as austere as Jim, Theodore, the father of the President, was in many respects a more important figure in the community than any of his brothers. He had a strong sense of obligation to society. If he became convinced that something had to be set right, he shouldered the burden himself and enlisted the aid of his friends. When, as in the case of the injury to the spine of his eldest daughter, he discovered that New York had no hospitals and medical men to cope with spinal injuries, he set about establishing the New York Orthopaedic Hospital. It was significant that when he died, the *New York World*, which so bitterly reviled his son and grandson named after him, headlined the account of his funeral as the "Funeral of Him who was Eyes to the Blind, Feet to the Lame, Good to All." Such a characterization would never have been given him if he had not fully deserved it. He loved the good things of life and enjoyed horses, pretty ladies, and dancing; yet, besides his charitable activities which took much of his time, he was a leader in the establishment of the Metropolitan Museum of Art and the American Museum of Natural History, as well as in the administration of the Children's Aid Society and the Newsboys' Lodging House.

Apparently out of deference to his Southern wife, whose brothers were active in the cause of the Confederacy, the elder Theodore Roosevelt did not enlist in the Union Army. Instead, he drafted a scheme for the allotment of a portion of the soldiers' pay to their families and was largely responsible for its acceptance by Congress and the President. Later he was appointed by President Lincoln as one of the three commissioners of allotments from New York State. His work in this connection took him from camp to camp and to the battlefields. He spent months in the saddle and personally interviewed thousands of men and officers and arranged for them to send home part of their pay. Later he joined in forming the Protective War Claim Association to help the crippled soldiers and the families of those who had fallen obtain the back pay and pensions that were due them.

The first-born son of C. V. S. Roosevelt was S. Weir Roosevelt, my grandfather. He was graduated from Columbia College in 1841, and took up law as his profession. Family tradition, reinforced by the few of his letters which I have come across, is that he was a merry soul, full of fun and whimsy, and ever ready to twist a phrase or win a smile. He enjoyed playing with words, whether in prose or verse, and became a persistent writer of letters to the *New York Times*, *Tribune*, *Post*, and *Sun*. Many are preserved in his scrapbook—as tedious as most other letters to the editor, and lacking the sprightliness for which he was famed, and which runs through his letters to his family.

A dozen years after his graduation from Columbia, Weir led a revolt of the alumni of that college against its trustees when, in 1854, these gentlemen refused to appoint Professor Wolcott Gibbs to the chair of chemistry at Columbia on the sole ground that he was a Unitarian. Weir's position in the community is attested by the fact that the papers of the day reported at length his withering denunciation of the trustees for making religious prejudice a test of fitness to teach chemistry, and they reprinted the resolution of censure which he drew up and which was warmly upheld by the alumni body.

[17]

Public interest in Weir Roosevelt rests in the fact that he became a member of the Board of Education of the City of New York towards the close of the Civil War, and that, until illness rendered him so crippled that he was house-bound, he devoted almost all of his time to the work of this board. He attended all the meetings, visited as many schools as possible, learned first-hand the problems of the teachers, and fought for better pay for them and for fuller support from the pubic.

Contemporary with my grandfather's generation was James, the father of Franklin. He was brought up in affluence and carved out for himself a highly respectable career. He married a rich relative, Rebecca Howland, as his first wife, invested his inheritance shrewdly and successfully, enlarged his acreage at Hyde Park, bred trotting horses, drove four-in-hands, had his private railroad car, made frequent visits to Europe, joined the most fashionable clubs in New York, and was a perfect example of the Hudson River variant of the English country gentleman who is not above taking an active part as a director and stockholder in business enterprises. He was distinguished looking, kindly, conservative, popular in society here and abroad, and highly respected in the business world.

James's wife died in 1876. The careless author of a superficial volume entitled *The Amazing Roosevelt Family* states that in the early spring of 1880 Mr. and Mrs. Theodore Roosevelt, senior, gave a dinner party to which James was invited and at which he met for the first time the youthful and beautiful Sarah Delano, daughter of a wealthy neighbor on the Hudson. Others have speculated on what passed between these two fathers of presidents-to-be. The scene is romantic, and somehow fraught with historic significance, except for the fact that Theodore Roosevelt, senior, had died two years before it was said to have taken place. If, as family tradition states, James met Sally Delano at the Theodore Roosevelt house in 1880, only the elder Mrs. Theodore and her children could have been present. Sally was a contemporary and friend of the oldest of these, Anna (Bamie).

Despite the twenty-five years difference in age between the handsome and charming Miss Delano and the well-groomed and distinguished looking widower James, they were greatly attracted to each other and were married later in the year. It is interesting to note that their son, Franklin, had as his godfather, Elliot, a son of the elder Theodore Roosevelt, and soon to be the father of the girl who was to become Franklin's wife.

CHAPTER FOUR

OYSTER BAY OLYMPIANS

FROM THEIR DUTCH ancestors the Roosevelts inherited the concept that the family embraced forebears, living and dead, as well as cousins to the fifth degree. We had impressed on us a strong sense of obligation to live up to the name. We learned that the "family" personified loyalties, ideals, and standards of conduct, and that it also imposed obligations. Our elders obviously had a serene confidence that the family was—or at least must appear to the world to be—above reproach.

In practice this meant that at no time should any member of the family depart from the strict code of conduct inherited from Dutch Reformed ancestors and sanctified by transplanted Victorianism. The few individuals whose excess of vitality took unconventional forms were ostracized. If ever their names were mentioned in the presence of the youngsters the conversation was quickly turned, and our parents, when pressed, explained that every family has its black sheep, of whom the less said the better. Later we learned that these deleted relatives happily survived the frigid blasts of family disapproval, brazenly enjoying their waywardness and, as a rule, charming all whom they met outside the family. One, whose extramarital relations added to the populations of four continents and whose business ventures were largely at the expense of new acquaintances hypnotized by his name, his dreams, and his promises, continued to lead a vigorous and exciting life at an age when most of his more conventional relatives had grown fat and stodgy in bored retirement. When not flying over erupting volcanoes or fishing for sharks, he was absorbed in new and alluring schemes which he was sure would bring him fame and wealth, enabling him to repay generously his latest creditors. As in the case of his father before him, who lived handsomely and joyously in Paris for decades on borrowed (and never repaid) money, it was hard to tell whether his success in dunning his friends and relatives or his pagan enjoyment of life gave greater offense to the "family," who viewed his every appearance in New York with apprehension and his hedonism with asperity.

The completeness of the family's disapproval of wayward members was a reflection of its loyalty to the members in good standing. The successes and honors achieved by any Roosevelt were welcomed with pride by the others—at least until the break between the Oyster Bay and Hyde Park Roosevelts in the early nineteen twenties. Even thereafter the lines were never tightly drawn, and various Roosevelts from Oyster Bay supported certain of Franklin's objectives even when they disapproved others. The Roosevelts would suffer grievously in a police state, for freedom of expression is one of their most cherished privileges, including, specifically, freedom to criticize their relatives, whether asked to do so or not. The mere fact that one of them occupies the White House has never been a deterrent to cousinly candor.

The family life of our branch of the Roosevelts centered at Oyster Bay, where Theodore (the president), Emlen (the banker), and my father (Dr. J. West Roosevelt) had built adjoining summer homes in the early eighteen eighties. These three were first cousins. Their fathers before them, S. Weir Roosevelt (my grandfather), the elder Theodore, and James A., had spent the summers at Oyster Bay since the end of the Civil War, living in rented houses. My grandfather died at Oyster Bay in 1870, followed, a year later, by his own father, C. V. S. Roosevelt.

The Oyster Bay that we knew and loved was a place of water, woods, and semi-wilderness, in which the cousins lived a life so self-sufficient that few non-Roosevelts took much part in their affairs. Cove Neck was an isolated community, with dirt roads, split-rail fences, cedar-dotted fields, and sandy oak and chestnut woods. The hot summer haze of the North Shore blanketed the countryside with tropical humidity, the air vibrant with the buzzing of locusts and crickets and the humming of bees, flies, and other insects. Children naturally took to the water and spent as many hours of each day on or in the bay as parents would allow, while the elders stayed at home and rocked on the porch, complaining of the apparently never-ending heat. Living was simple and, according to modern standards, primitive, with no screens to keep out the insects, kerosene lamps for light, water piped into the single bathroom which served even a large family, and a daily trip to the "village" by horse and carriage to purchase the day's supply of food. It was not till the turn of the century that such extravagances as a bathroom on every floor were countenanced. Electricity and the telephone did not reach the more remote Roosevelt summer homes till the early nineteen hundreds.

It was only natural that T. R.—"Cousin Theodore," as he was known to those of us who were not his own children—dominated our life at Oyster Bay. We worshipped him—not because he was president of the United States—but because he was one of us, a leader in many of our games, full of fun, deeply interested in each of us, and constantly setting us an example of fearlessness, fairness, and fineness. Here were brains, brawn, charm, energy, courage, and a positive passion for what was right and decent, all rolled into one. We took it as a matter of course that he was also president, and we accepted as our own such perquisites of the presidency as the Secret Service men (most of whom we adored) and the presence in Oyster Bay of the naval yacht *Sylph* and, occasionally, the *Mayflower*.

There was something torrential about T. R.'s nature, a great upwelling of interest in people and ideas, and a steady outpouring of love and affection for those close to him. His gaiety—a quality which his old friend Fanny Parsons (Mrs. James Russell Parsons) told me in 1946 was an outstanding characteristic when he was young—remained with him till his death—or, perhaps I should say, until the death of his beloved son Quentin, only a few months before his own. To be with him was inevitably to have fun, because of the humor, cheerfulness, and warm affection which he radiated. We loved nothing better than the family picnics, the overnight camping trips on Lloyd's Neck, and the games of hide-

and-go-seek in the old barn on his farm at Sagamore Hill, because in all of these he was the dominant figure. No matter how much sand was in the clams or how lukewarm the ginger ale or how burned the steaks, he enjoyed each picnic more, even, than the youngsters did, and certainly much more than the harassed other parents who preferred their clams without sand, their ginger ale iced, and their food properly cooked and decently served at a table.

The camping trips to Lloyd's Neck—about six miles away by rowboat—followed a fixed ritual. Cousin Theodore rowed, taking with him one, two, or three of the youngest and lightest children, usually Archie and myself. The older boys (the girls did not go on these camping trips) teamed up in other rowboats or, occasionally, in sailboats. Immediately on arrival the provisions were unloaded, camp was made, and each youngster picked the place for his blankets. Then all adjourned for a dip in the Sound, conveniently (and with T. R.'s silent consent) forgetting their mothers' last warnings not to go in if it was too cold. After this (we usually arrived in late afternoon), T. R. would fry steaks and bacon for all, and after a desultory cleaning up of the eating utensils, we would gather round the campfire, as night fell, and demand that he tell us ghost stories. This he did, interrupted by corrections sternly interjected by the younger members who, having heard the stories often, called his attention to any departure from his previous rendition. When he had told two or three ghost stories our active imaginations began to translate any unusual night sound into something spooky, which added to the delight of the occasion. We would be up early the next morning and, after a greasy breakfast of bacon and fried eggs, reluctantly start the journey back to the respectable confines of Cove Neck— a reluctance which he never expressed, but surely must have felt when he realized that he must plunge at once into affairs of state.

The games of hide-and-go-seek in the old barn were for rainy afternoons. In this barn was stored the hay from the meadows at Sagamore, and through this hay—usually under some of the giant, hand-hewn oak beams—we youngsters had pierced tunnels, most of them only just large enough for fairly small children. Our particular delight was to get Cousin Theodore—or, better still, a member of his cabinet or some other visiting dignitary who had been bamboozled into taking part in these games by the exuberant President—to follow one of us into these tunnels and then watch his antics trying to get out. As T. R., even in his early days in the presidency, was inclined to stoutness, and as many of his official family or visitors were ample of girth, short of wind, slow of leg, and quite unaccustomed to forcing themselves through haymounds on their hands and knees, we children had many opportunities to gloat over the discomfiture of our elders. I do not remember if Elihu Root ever took part in one of these games—the picture is almost inconceivable, despite his leanness—but Attorney General Moody always joined in when the opportunity offered, and he did so with good humor, even though he would not have chosen such a diversion had it not been thrust on him by the President of the United States.

The other great family institution in which T. R. was the leading spirit was cross-country walking. The rule was that you followed the leader—who was, of course, T. R.—and that everyone went through or over obstacles, never around them. If we came to a pond and he plunged through it, we followed, even though we got soaked to our necks. If he climbed the roof of a barn, we did likewise, and whoever flinched or failed to abide by the rules met with T. R.'s disapproval and with the scorn of the other children. His sister, Mrs. Robinson, acquired great respect among the children by accompanying the family on one of these obstacle walks, and, when confronted with the problem of how to climb over a bath house at Eel Creek, she tackled it head on with such vehemence that she made it as successfully as her younger and more sprightly relatives.

These obstacle walks had a double purpose: to obtain exercise, which he dearly loved, and to give the children lessons in physical and moral courage. His teachings were the simple fundamentals—to overcome fear, to finish what we set out to do, to do well whatever we undertook, to play the game well and hard, to shun excuses, to be loyal, and to be truthful. He had no patience with cowards, slackers, leaners, or whiners, and his disapproval was as blunt as it was crushing. Always good natured, quick to laugh, sympathetic, and ready to do more than his own share, he was the kind of elder the children adored, and a constant example for them to remember as they grew up.

While T. R. naturally dominated our life at Oyster Bay, other elders also loomed large in family affairs. Of these, Mrs. Theodore Roosevelt, known to us as "Cousin Edith," was a special favorite. Gracious, a *grande dame*, a voracious reader, she was a wonderful wife for T. R., a perfect First Lady of the Land, and a devoted mother to their children. We sensed her strength and dignity, and, like Cousin Theodore, we shunned her displeasure. From her famous forebear, the austere and domineering Jonathan Edwards, she inherited a stern sense of duty and a conviction that her ways were the right ways. She had a quiet determination that those whom she loved should conform to her principles. To us children she represented law and order, perhaps because she was herself so perfectly disciplined. Through storm and calm, in dangerous seas or placid waters, she held the helm of her personality with a firm hand and a sure knowledge of where she was and whither she was bound. Nothing daunted her. Nothing diverted her from her chosen course. It is remarkable that as positive a character as T. R. should have had as his wife an equally positive character and that the marriage should have been as happy as it was. I have never seen a more devoted couple, and never heard an unkind word spoken by either.

There were occasions when Cousin Edith viewed T. R. as merely another of her wayward offspring. In fact, he once said to my sister: "Your Cousin Edith sometimes treats me as her oldest and rather worst child." Certainly he knew that he would be held to account by her if, in putting us through some of the games that we adored, he permitted anything of which she disapproved. Cousin Edith had a way of disassociating herself from the more reprehensible acts of her family or friends which was as chilling as it was charmingly courteous. At times her patience was sorely strained, as, for example, when Cousin Theodore had taken all the children on a cross-country walk on a cold day and had marched them through a chilly pond. When they got back to

Sagamore she seized her shivering brood, dosed them repeatedly with liquid quinine, and apparently told T. R. just exactly what she thought of his conduct, for, when Kermit, about twelve years old, came to him to complain about the bitterness of the quinine and to ask him to intercede with his mother not to give him any more, Cousin Theodore, according to the story which he used to tell us, remarked wryly and with asperity: "Kermit, I'll be lucky if SHE doesn't force ME to take some of the stuff too."

On this particular occasion Cousin Edith's exasperation with T. R. was shared by my mother. When my sister made an attempt to defend herself as one of the walkers and, by implication, to defend Cousin Theodore, my mother said to her tartly: "Just because your Cousin Theodore behaves like an idiot is no reason for YOUR behaving like an idiot."

On another occasion Cousin Edith's sense of the appropriate was again deeply outraged. It was in the summer of 1905, when T. R. was trying to bring about peace between Russia and Japan. Part of the Navy was in Oyster Bay, preliminary to a review, and Archie and I decided that we wanted a glimpse of the fleet. It was anchored in the outer harbor, and as we had been warned not to go out there we were driven to the expedient of borrowing a flat-bottomed rowboat from neighbors (permission not asked!), and we set out to row the mile or more to the *Mayflower*. Archie was eleven and I was twelve. It was a bit rough and windy, but we made it without mishap.

On the way we passed one of the launches from the *Mayflower* and were recognized by an officer. Knowing there would be trouble if we were reported, we begged him not to tell on us. When we got back to Sagamore we were met by old Mame, who had been nurse to Cousin Edith as a child and had brought up the Theodore Roosevelt children. Mame, usually our friend and ally, was stern, and she severely told me that I must go home at once and told Archie to report to his mother. We suspected, and soon discovered, the worst—that the naval officer had "squealed" on us and that our mothers were frantic and furious. We were sent to bed without supper and were forbidden to see each other for a number of days. The incident might have ended there had not

T. R. learned from Archie that we had asked the naval lieutenant not to tell. He was so indignant with the man for giving us away that his sympathies were enlisted in our behalf, for which he received hail columbia from both mothers. Up to the time of T. R.'s death, when Archie and I were already officers in World War I, we could arouse a quarrel between my mother and Cousin Edith on one side, and Cousin Theodore on the other, by reminding them of this incident.

The picture of the Oyster Bay of my childhood would not be complete without the inclusion of several other members of the clan. Among these was my mother, who was born in New York City in 1858, the daughter of an American army officer of French origin, Théophile d'Orémieulx, and Laura Wolcott Gibbs. Her father had been for years professor of French at West Point, and her mother was the daughter of Colonel George Gibbs, of Rhode Island, and Laura Wolcott, whose father had been secretary of the treasury in Washington's cabinet.

Mother spent the first two decades of her life in the house of her grandmother Gibbs on Green Street, just off Washington Square. Mrs. Gibbs, herself the granddaughter of one of the signers of the Declaration of Independence, had seen Washington, Hamilton, and their associates at her father's table. She passed on to her descendants her own passionate interest in public affairs and her sense of responsibility to the government which her father and grandfather had helped to create. It was only natural that she should have taken the lead during the Civil War in the formation of the United States Sanitary Commission, which was the forerunner of the Red Cross. The need for such an organization was obvious, and to her it was equally obvious that she must do something about it. With other men and women of New York, she organized the women of that city and of the North to help care for the wounded and the sick.

Despite my father's death only thirteen years after their marriage, Mother continued to spend her summers at Oyster Bay, where she felt completely at home. She had known the Roosevelts from childhood and had been from the age of three an intimate of Christine Kean, who married Emlen Roosevelt. Mother's sprightliness and cosmopolitan interests appealed to T. R., as did her fondness for teasing him and for differing with him vehemently on many things. She and Cousin Edith had many tastes, interests, and problems in common, not the least of which was how to manage a household of Roosevelts. But Cousin Emlen and his father and brother were puzzled by the nonconformity which she inherited from her French father and by the spirit of independence which came from her Wolcott grandmother. They accepted her because she had married a Roosevelt and because Christine was deeply devoted to her. But they never quite understood or forgave her liking for a broader life than they had known, or her insistence on giving her children a thorough grounding in foreign languages and an appreciation of the arts. Mother loved theaters and concerts and dances and gaiety. Society meant much to her. The contrast between the life which she enjoyed and the Emlen Roosevelts' idea of a good time, in those early days, was marked. She often described to us how, after a dinner at the Emlens' summer home, punctuated with laconic remarks about business by the men and observations on the shortcomings of the children by the women, the relatives would adjourn to rocking chairs on the porch, where, with blankets over their knees to keep off the mosquitoes, they would rock in silence for an hour. Then the cousins would disperse, bringing to an early end their jolly evenings. No wonder that Mother, who had studied music in Europe, and who had the French fondness for conversation and amusement, sometimes found life with her in-laws constricting.

Another cousin who flitted in and out of our background at Oyster Bay was Leila, a sister of Emlen's. Her usual costume resembled that of a Greuze shepherdess, and she always carried a tall cane, not unlike a shepherd's crook. A strong-willed individualist, she went her independent way and said her caustic say with a wit and a grim humor which sometimes must have galled her relatives as much as did her weakness for the family's black sheep. She had compassion for sinners and sympathy for rebels against the strict conventions of the age of innocence, which probably stemmed from the fact that she herself had shaken the family by divorcing her distant kinsman, Montgomery Roosevelt Schuyler,

[28]

courtesy Harvard College Library

T. R., MRS. ROOSEVELT, KERMIT, AND ARCHIE ON A HIKE
Mrs. Roosevelt sometimes doctored excess zeal with quinine

back in the eighties or nineties, when nice people didn't get divorces. She took as a second husband an amiable but innocuous gentleman who bored her almost as much as he did her relatives, but who possessed the great virtue of silence—a useful attribute for anyone who marries a Roosevelt.

Leila's sprightliness is preserved in the account, attributed to her, of the wedding of a member of the family (who shall be nameless) to a lady whom I shall call Mrs. Jones, who had a brood of children commonly believed to have been fathered out of wedlock by this Roosevelt. Because of this departure from convention, Leila's mother, a stern Quaker, refused to attend the wedding, although she was sufficiently curious to be glad to have Leila go and make a report to her about it. This report, according to other members of the family, was brief: "Donald [this was not his real name] stood near the head of the aisle," said Leila to her mother, "when up the aisle came Mrs. Jones, followed by all the little Joneses, nés Roosevelt. Then they were married."

Next to T. R., my favorite cousin in that generation was his sister Corinne, who married Douglas Robinson. Brilliant, widely read, as insatiable in her interests as she was overflowing in her sympathy and understanding, she had an explosive sense of the ridiculous at the same time that, deep in her heart, she was a poet and a dreamer. Her friends could be counted by the hundreds in all parts of this country and the world. As in the case of Theodore, these friends came from all walks of life—politicians like Henry Cabot Lodge, poets like Edward Arlington Robinson, historians like James Bryce, and quantities of others. Wherever she went she was received by kings and princes, sought after by authors and poets, flattered by society leaders, and adored by those who served her. The thoughtful gesture, the grateful word, the friendly smile, the eager and sympathetic ear—these were the outward expressions of her warm and understanding nature. She loved living, and she loved people. Life, in turn, was good to her, and people requited her love.

As a hostess Corinne was skillful in directing general conversation, and in drawing out any guest who had something particularly interesting to say. This, be it noted, was only possible when there were not too many members of her own family present, for the Robinsons (in addition to the Roosevelts' passion for all speaking at once with no regard for what others might be saying) were so noisy that guests had difficulty in making themselves heard. Her husband, Douglas, had a voice like the bull of Bashan, and her sons Teddy and Monroe each in his own right could outshout the father. The two Corinnes (Mrs. Robinson and her daughter, Mrs. Joseph Alsop) and other relatives had early acquired the art of talking loudly at table as the only way to take part in a Robinson party in any other capacity than as audience. Mrs. Robinson's close friend Fanny Parsons told me that when she (Fanny) brought her second husband, James Russell Parsons, to his first meal at the Robinsons she warned him: "Talk as loudly as you possibly can, and answer your own questions!"

Corinne had to a high degree her brother's irrepressible energy. Nothing tired her, not even the endless round of social activities which were forced upon her wherever she went. Nothing —not even dull people—bored her. In Washington, when T. R. was in the White House, she reveled in the contacts with official and social life. When she went round the world in 1910, her husband, writing to their daughter Mrs. Alsop, ruefully described himself as being under the guidance of "the strongest, and keenest female sightseer living today. I can think of nothing we have left unclimbed, unseen, unvisited above and below ground or by river or by sea, in our route since we left New York. Your mother is stimulated by every musty smell of an old temple or mosque, and as for towers of Victory 300 or 400 feet high—why they are like cocktails—mental and physical stimulants—and away she goes, and the rest (what is left of us) after her. I climbed so many stairs and towers after Bombay until we reached Benares that at Agra I had a sort of tower-palace-temple knee. It refused to bend any more for nearly a day. We visited the Taj Mahal by daylight, by morning light, by afternoon light, by sunset light and by moonlight. Your mother said she was made drunk by it, and I think she was right in her statement."

Corinne's passion for politics, originating in her interest in Theodore's career, grew after the latter's death, and she was much in demand at Republican rallies. A good speaker, her vibrant personality and her close association with her brother made her a popular campaigner. She had his moral courage, especially when annoyed by the pussyfooting advice of political leaders who preferred to see her play safe and not risk offending possible backsliders. At the same time, she had T. R.'s sense of humor and some of his sense of the dramatic. I remember her telling me about a rally in the Metropolitan Opera House towards the end of World War I, which was obviously nonpolitical and at which she had been asked to make a nonpolitical speech. This she did, and when she was through she announced that she would be glad to answer questions as long as they were not of a political nature. Several proper questions were addressed to her. Then someone rose and asked in loud tones, clearly heard throughout the hall:

"Mrs. Robinson, will you tell us why President Wilson refused to send your brother, Theodore Roosevelt, to France at the head of a division of troops?"

There were murmurs, hisses, and boos from the audience. Corinne jumped to her feet and held up her hand, and when there was silence, she replied:

"I *said*"—and she paused to underline and emphasize the word —"I *said* that I would not answer *political*"—and again she paused as she raised her inflection to emphasize "political"—"questions."

Being a good actress she remained standing in an attitude of expectancy. Some of her friends, getting her meaning, chuckled, and then, as the audience caught on, delighted laughter spread through the house, followed by prolonged applause.

Mrs. Robinson had seconded the nomination of Leonard Wood for the presidency in 1920; later she was a strong supporter of Mr. Hoover. But it was characteristic of her that, in the 1932 campaign, when F. D. R. ran against Mr. Hoover, she announced that she could not take part in the campaign because of the fact that her favorite niece, Eleanor, was so deeply involved in the outcome. She lived to see F. D. R. elected, but died a few days before his inauguration. One of F. D. R.'s last acts as a private citizen was to attend Corinne's funeral, not only because she was his wife's beloved aunt, but because she was one of his cousins who had never allowed political prejudice to dampen her personal affection.

I never knew T. R.'s oldest sister Bamie (Anna Roosevelt Cowles) as well as I knew Corinne and Theodore, but, like all who came in contact with her, I was fascinated by the vitality of her mind, her picturesque and often caustic speech, the breadth of her intellectual interests, and her truly remarkable courage in the face of constant pain. I visualize her in a wheel chair, her hands twisted and almost deformed by what, in those days, was called rheumatism, her back arched, her face deeply lined from suffering, almost deaf, and yet full of humor, vitally concerned about people and ideas, and always the center of attraction. She lived in the beautiful old Cowles house in Farmington, surrounded with books and with lovely furniture that had belonged to the family of her husband, the Admiral, and there held court, not only for her close neighbors and friends, but for those who came from the ends of the earth.

Owing perhaps to the fact that she had been crippled as a child and, in later life, was in almost constant pain, she did not show the great physical vitality of Corinne and Theodore and was driven more into the life of the mind. But she was never a recluse, for she loved people, and they loved her, and she had taken her full share of responsibility for others. At the age of fourteen her father virtually turned over to her the household and the supervision of the children (she was the firstborn in that family) because her mother, as she grew older, seemed even less inclined to be practical than she had been as the spoiled "Missy" on the slave-tended Georgia plantation in her youth. Bamie later helped look after her nephews and nieces, including Alice (later Mrs. Longworth) who, before Theodore married Edith Carow as his second wife, was motherless. In the nineties she took over the care of Helen Roosevelt, daughter of "Rosey," who was F. D. R.'s half-brother, when Helen's mother died.

In London, where "Rosey" was secretary of the American legation, she acted as his hostess—which, in a diplomatic center, is a position of responsibility bringing wide social contacts. There she made many friends, including the naval attaché at the legation, Captain William Sheffield Cowles, whom she married when she was forty years old, and by whom, three years later, she had a son, to her unending pride and satisfaction.

In some ways Bamie was less of an extrovert than Theodore and Corinne. She was also more subtle and diplomatic, capable of thinking and planning far ahead and of working unobtrusively towards the achievement of her ends. Had she been a man in seventeenth-century Europe it would be easy to imagine her as a successful and highly capable minister of state or perhaps a cardinal, unquenchable in zeal and effective in guile. She charmed all by her wit and astonished them by the wide scope of her knowledge of men and affairs and by the acuteness of her intellect. In many ways hers was the best mind in the family, and her personality one of the most dominant and fascinating.

The manner of her death, as recounted to me by her daughter-in-law, was in keeping with her way of life. She had been weakening for days, confined to her bedroom on the second floor at Farmington and had been often only semi-conscious. But one afternoon she awakened, fully conscious, and directed the nurse to have Hopkinson (the family butler) prepare tea downstairs in the little front room to the left of the entrance where, in colder weather, she was used to having tea served. Then, overriding the protests of nurses and family, she had herself dressed and carried downstairs and placed in her accustomed chair behind the tea table. She checked the kettle and the little plates of sandwiches and cakes and looked about the familiar room which she knew so well and loved so much, with an air of expectancy as if an important visitor was coming. Then, satisfied that everything was in order, she sat back to await the guest, closed her eyes, and died.

[33]

CHAPTER FIVE

A GALLERY OF YOUNG COUSINS

Sᴇᴠᴇɴᴛᴇᴇɴ ʏᴏᴜɴɢ Rᴏᴏsᴇᴠᴇʟᴛs of my generation were brought up together at Oyster Bay, with frequent visits from several other cousins, including Eleanor (Franklin's wife). The detailed history of these cousins does not belong here. Most of them, like their relatives in earlier generations, were vital and energetic. A few were brilliant. Many were self-centered and intolerant. All of them (myself excepted) were highly vocal. They read profusely and widely, expressed their opinions vehemently, played vigorously, and lived zestfully. They quarreled with each other with gusto and offered each other—or anyone else—the frankest criticism, usually unsolicited. The extent to which they were rugged individualists may be gauged from the fact that, at the family picnics, each built his or her own campfire in the conviction that no one else could broil a steak or fry a chicken properly. Despite their capacity for ignoring the points of view of other members of the tribe, they preferred their relatives to all outsiders. It used to be said at the Harvard Club in New York that whenever two Roosevelts happened to be in the club at the same time they automatically gravitated towards each other and soon were lost in dissertation, as oblivious of, as they were indifferent to, the presence of any non-Roosevelts.

When not taking part in such family affairs as picnics, camping, games in the old barn, swimming, or tennis, the youngsters were more or less inclined to run in pairs. Ted (Theodore, Jr.) was likely to be with George (Emlen's oldest son.) Kermit was much with Phil (George's brother), although in college and after

I saw much of these two. Kermit had to a high degree the dynamic energy which was so characteristic of the family, and an insatiable curiosity about life. At the same time he had a devouring restlessness—one of the factors that later made him a successful explorer and led him to the ends of the earth. He was at home anywhere—in Africa or India shooting big game, in Brazil in the banking business, in the Near East as an officer in the British and later the American army, at the River House or the Knickerbocker Club in New York, in the world of shipping, or as a frequent week-end companion of F. D. R. in the latter's first years in the White House. Wherever he went he could be depended upon to discover a particularly beautiful view, an inconspicuous but interesting bit of architecture, or a little restaurant that specialized in a rare delicacy. He knew enough of Romany to get along with Gypsies in various parts of the world. He enjoyed the Greek classics in the original and read widely in French and Portuguese, as well as in English. He had even delved into Arabic, Urdu, and Hindustani. His interests covered folklore, animals, hunting, politics, military affairs, the arts, literature, and history. In many of these fields he was sufficiently well versed to be at home with specialists. His was a fine and eager mind.

Ted (Theodore, Jr.) was six years my senior—enough to set him apart as one of the older cousins in our Oyster Bay childhood. In later years I worked with him occasionally on political matters and confirmed the impression formed in my youth that Ted had not inherited his father's flair for politics. To the extent that he held three administrative posts with distinction—assistant secretary of the navy, governor of Puerto Rico, and governor general of the Philippines—his record belied my estimation. Yet I am of the opinion that, despite his fine work in these posts, it is primarily as a valiant, able, and unselfish military officer that he will be remembered. In all things he was a good soldier, both actually and metaphorically. Fearless, brave, tireless, with a strong sense of responsibility and a truly great gift of inspiring his men, he was at his best in war. General Duncan, who had been in command of the First Division in World War I, told me in 1936 that Ted had been the best officer who had ever served under him—with-

[35]

out any exception. In World War II Ted lived up to this reputation. Beyond the draft age, he went back into the army and literally killed himself in the service of his country. He made no pretense at being a great strategist. As an administrator he was experienced and able. But it was as a personal leader of troops under fire or in difficulties that he was at his best. It is said of him that he knew by their first names more than a thousand men in his division. Even those whom he could not thus name derived strength and encouragement from the knowledge that, where other generals might be busy in the rear, Ted would pop up in the front lines at any moment—especially if things were not going too well—and would have a word of cheer and praise for his men and set an example of endurance and fearlessness. No wonder that the wiser among the general officers regarded him as worth a division himself, because of his great gift of leadership and his rare capacity for heartening a whole front line.

It would be presumptuous for me to say that I knew Ted's sister Alice Longworth well. Yet through the years I had frequent glimpses of her, heard much about her, and, in the course of my newspaper work and my interest in politics, often crossed her trail. She was a great figure in America—joyous, sparkling, outpouring, vital—a woman who delighted in living life to the full, and who for half a century enlivened the usually drab Washington scene with her caustic comments and pulled strings to make political puppets dance. Brilliant, politically shrewd, but intensely partisan, Alice Longworth had her father's zest for living, his great interest in people, and his gift of flattering them by remembering about them things which even they themselves had forgotten. At the same time she was a bitter hater, and seemed to derive stimulation from thwarting those whom she hated—more even, than she did from helping those whom she loved.

The center of her affection was, of course, her father, and when he died she became the jealous guardian of his ghost and made up her mind that her brother Ted must follow in his footsteps. The careers of these two men were her passionate concern. She appraised everyone with an eye to his possible utility to them. Weaned on the milk of politics, and living for half a century in

SAGAMORE HILL

The summer home which T. R. built and loved

the very center of American political life, her political enmity was not something to risk lightly, nor was her aid to be belittled. She had known well and had praised or fought with every American prominent in politics since her father's appearance in Washington as assistant secretary of the navy—Elihu Root, Mark Hanna, John Hay, Taft, Lodge, Cameron, Penrose, Crane, Harding, Borah, Coolidge, Hoover, Curtis, and a host of others. She was a frequent visitor in the House and Senate galleries. She knew all the leading Washington correspondents of the last fifty years by their first names. Her husband was speaker of the House of Representatives—in itself one of the most powerful offices in the country. She played poker with these men, made fun of them, entertained them, encouraged them, thwarted them, used them, and discarded them. They, in turn, were fascinated, amused, and angry, and their wives never forgave her for the biting things she freely said to and about them. Alice never hid her comments under a bushel. On the contrary, she delighted in making or passing on *bon mots* about people, the more barbed the better. Those who came in contact with her left with their brains tingling, even though she might have been scathing in her attack on the persons with whom she had been talking.

The contrast between Alice and Eleanor (Franklin's wife) is interesting. In youth Alice had everything—an adoring family, good looks, independence, many admirers, and great popular adulation. Eleanor lost her parents when still very young, was brought up by relatives who were fond of her but never gave her a real home of her own, was made to feel that she was a sort of ugly duckling, and was not particularly popular in her circle. Where Alice, though launched upon her career through her father's position, soon made a place of importance and influence in her own name, Eleanor was largely eclipsed by her relatives. Even at her own wedding, interest was greater in her Uncle Ted, who "gave her away," than in her as the bride. She moved almost at once into her mother-in-law's house—the house, be it noted, of a great lady, but of one accustomed to rule her household with an iron hand, and who continued to rule the house in which Eleanor lived. It was not until Franklin was elected governor of

[37]

New York that Eleanor began to have a chance to be herself and to live her own life as she wished it, and not until they moved into the White House did she become a national figure in her own name.

As Eleanor grew in influence, the basic differences between her and Alice became more apparent. Alice was brilliant, picturesque, vitriolic—passionately absorbed in the day-to-day plays of the political game. Eleanor was sympathetic, fundamentally kind-hearted, believed in reform, and looked on politics as a means rather than an end. Where the steely quality in Alice made her an indifferent humanitarian, Eleanor, who had known more personal suffering than Alice, was quickly responsive to the troubles of others—so much so, in fact, that her sympathies frequently led her to support people and causes without stopping to look into their motives or to ascertain whither they were pushing her. Of the two, Eleanor was the more liberal, but it took her twelve years in the White House to discover that the pursuit of liberalism does not consist in merely expressing sympathy for the underdog but involves clear thinking and hard fighting against those forces of reaction which, in the guise of humanitarianism and security, are subtly attempting to shackle freedom. Eleanor's heart was in the right place from the beginning of her public career, but it was not until 1946, when she came face to face daily with the Soviet representatives to the United Nations, that her public utterances showed that at last she understood the true nature of the struggle for freedom. In her years in the White House she often supported poor causes when her heart got the better of her head.

However much people may have criticized her judgment or deplored her lapses of good taste while First Lady, or regretted the slowness of the process of her maturing politically, there is no denying the fact that her broad sympathies, her obvious sincerity, her tireless energy, and her personal graciousness brought her great popularity and made her into one of the dominant figures of our time. Certainly she stands out as one of four truly remarkable Roosevelt women, the others being her aunts Corinne and Bamie and her cousin Alice. Like all of them she has lived zestfully, and wherever she goes, she makes friends. I suspect—though

I do not know—that, like the others, she has enjoyed many of the jokes and quips aimed at her. Some of these, of course, have been mean, but others, like the "Song of the Maori Woman," make fun of her foibles in a genial and inoffensive manner. This "song," written by an author whose name I have not been able to discover, refers to the instance when, visiting one of the South Sea Islands while on a Red Cross tour during the war, she rubbed noses with a Maori woman. The incident provoked a certain amount of amused and indignant comment, especially on the part of her relatives when Eleanor was quoted as saying that nose-rubbing was "an old Roosevelt family custom." The effect on the Maori woman was described in the following lines:

> My nose was just a common nose,
>   Though somewhat plain and bent,
> But now it is a nose no more,
>   It is a monument.
> . . .
>
> So tourists, take your place in line
>   And for a modest fee,
> You may rub the nose that rubbed the nose
>   Of Mrs. Franklin D.

To another of the cousins of my generation, George, who became head of Roosevelt and Son when his father, Emlen, died, is attributed a story which is characteristic of the Roosevelts' irreverence for each other. For years Roosevelt and Son had been administering the estates of numerous relatives, including a part of some funds belonging to F. D. R. In 1933, shortly after F. D. R. had entered the White House, George sent F. D. R. a list of proposed changes in his investments, including the purchase of some stocks which at that time were very low, and asked, as a matter of routine, for F. D. R.'s approval. Franklin, according to this tale, returned the letter and list, having written on it in longhand: "The responsibility is *yours*." George was a little nettled, but said nothing and bided his time. The following year, when F. D. R. had taken the country off the gold standard and there was uncertainty as to the future market value of government bonds, and

[39]

as to what further experiments in economics the New Dealers might attempt, George reported to F. D. R. that he had sold various stocks in F. D. R.'s trust account and that with the proceeds he had bought government bonds. Then, underlined, George added a postscript to his distant kinsman in the White House, with particular reference to the government bonds: "The responsibility is *yours!*"

Quentin, the youngest of the Theodore Roosevelt children, died in World War I, as did his brothers Kermit and Ted in World War II. He shared the family characteristics of gaiety, energy and curiosity, and had his father's passion for reading—poetry, history, novels, detective stories, anything and everything. Like his father he remembered much of what he read. In addition he was fascinated by machines and spent happy hours taking wrecks of automobiles apart and putting together something that would run. He collected and dissected old watches and made clocks that would work. He loved people, old and young, and had his father's gift of making whomever he talked with feel that his interest in the individual was sincere, which it was.

It was Quentin who, when Archie was desperately ill of diphtheria at the White House, took Archie's Shetland pony, Algonquin, upstairs in the White House elevator to visit Archie and cheer him up. It was Quentin who, on being approached by a reporter when scarcely ten years old, and asked a more or less intimate question about his father, replied guardedly that he saw his father occasionally, but that he "knew nothing about his family life." I have always understood that it was to Quentin, also, that the famous characterization of T. R. is attributable: "Father always wants to be the bride at every wedding and the corpse at every funeral."

The next to youngest of the Theodore Roosevelt children was Archie, only eight months my junior. He and I were inseparable during the summers of our childhood at Oyster Bay. Our parents knew no more severe punishment to mete out to us when our conduct seemed to them beyond parental endurance than to forbid us to see each other for a number of days. Much of the time we were in or on the water, usually at Eel Creek, on the

west side of Cold Spring Harbor, where the Theodore Roosevelts had their bathhouses and float, and where Archie and I spent
hot, muggy, sunbaked hours on long two-by-twelves exploring
the winding recesses of Eel Creek, sliding off every few minutes
into its warm, fetid waters.

On rainy days we frequently adjourned to the somewhat awe-
inspiring "gun room" on the top floor of Sagamore Hill, where
T. R.'s hunting rifles (and later his children's) were put away in
glass cases. We treated these weapons with respect not only because we knew that we should be punished if we failed to do so,
but also because T. R. had instilled in us the idea that a gun was
to be handled with the greatest care and was, under no circum-
stance, loaded or unloaded, to be pointed at anyone. T. R. took
us out periodically for target practice, which further enhanced
our awe of weapons and gave practical occasions for him to drive
home the folly of ever being responsible for a situation in which
the excuse would have to be "I didn't know it was loaded." In all
such matters he was a strict disciplinarian. He regarded carelessness with weapons as being worse even than cowardice, for by
the latter a child would endanger only himself, whereas through
carelessness with a gun he might injure or even kill someone else.

One of our perennial occupations was to hitchhike the three
miles to the village of Oyster Bay in search of ice cream sodas at
Snouder's drugstore. I remember one such occasion. It was a steaming day in the summer of 1905. We started back to Cove Neck
on foot, overloaded with cold sodas, hoping for a friendly de-
livery man to relieve us of the penance of walking the three miles
home. Glancing back at the sound of horses, we spied Charley
Lee, the colored coachman of Sagamore, and saw that he had in
the back of the phaeton two little men in high hats and frock
coats, obviously Japanese. Barefoot and dusty, clad only in shirts
and knickerbockers, we hailed Charley, knowing that he would
befriend us. He stopped and we climbed up on the driver's seat
beside him and were driven to Sagamore, happily indifferent to
the impression that we must be making on Barons Kaneko and
Komura, the members of the Japanese peace delegation, who were
making a formal call on the President of the United States.

[41]

There were, of course, periodic visits to the White House. One of these was during the inauguration in 1905, when Archie and I covered ourselves with Roosevelt campaign buttons with the exception of the seats of our pants, on which we wore large buttons of the defeated candidate, Alton B. Parker. For a while during the inaugural parade we sat in the presidential box (presumably having first removed the buttons of Judge Parker), but I have no particular recollection of the details of the parade other than the appearance on horseback of some Indians, including, I believe, the famous Apache, Geronimo. In the evening we looked in on the inaugural ball, but to boys of eleven or twelve such pastimes had little interest.

On another visit, Archie and I explored the White House at midnight, apparently as the result of a casual remark by T. R. We were caught by one of the White House policemen, but we induced him not to tell Cousin Edith (knowing that this would bring severe punishment upon us) and, instead, to await the return of T. R., who had been away for a few days, and then report to him. Convinced that if we won Cousin Theodore as our ally we would avert at least a part of Cousin Edith's displeasure, we wrote a brief report of our actions in verse and waited at the front door of the White House on his return and thrust it upon him. I remember his receiving it with a combination of good humor and reserve, doubtless because he knew from experience that we were seeking to enlist him as a confederate, and he was not sure whether our case deserved his support or was strong enough for him to espouse it without himself being put in the doghouse.

T. R. kept the "poem" and sent it to Kermit, who was in school at Groton, explaining that it referred to a "bit of unhappy advice" he had given us, because of which he fell into "merited disgrace" with Cousin Edith. The "poem," which he attributed largely to my pen and which is thus the earliest writing of mine in print (and scarcely a promise of a successful career as a writer!) follows:

Good morning Mr. President,
How are you today,
We have obeyed your orders,
We're very glad to say,

We went around the White House,
Araisin up a row,
And if you want to know about it,
Then we'll tell you now.

We went into the East Room,
We went into the Red.
And frightened everyone,
Who was not in his bed.

We want to have a pillar fight,
With you this very night,
And if you do not play with us,
We'll squeeze you very tight.

(*signed*) Archie Roosevelt
Nicholas Roosevelt

Archie was, as a rule, the leader in our escapades, having a great love of adventure and being completely fearless, whereas I was more timid and more given to the contemplative. In later life Archie's initiative and fearlessness led him to distinguish himself for exceptional bravery in two wars. He was never one to spare himself or to leave to others the doing of disagreeable or dangerous tasks which were his to perform. A quick mind, saved from impatience and intolerance by a tumultuous sense of the ridiculous, further strengthened his gifts of leadership, with the result that he was an exceptionally good officer and much loved by his men. It was characteristic of him that, on one occasion in the Pacific when his outfit was having difficulty locating a Japanese battery, Archie, a fifty-year-old lieutenant colonel at the time, resorted to the brave but unhealthy expedient of standing up until he drew the Japs' fire. Equally characteristic was the hilarious

[43]

delight with which he told about his communications sergeant who was relaying a conversation between Archie and the general under whose command Archie's battalion was operating. From the General came a question to Archie as to whether his battalion was in a position to assault and capture a Japanese strongpoint a short distance away on the coast. To this Archie replied, after a survey, that they could probably take the outpost but that it might well cost half the battalion or more. The sergeant relayed this and then reported to Archie:

"The General says to go ahead and take the position. He doesn't care *what* it will cost."

Then, putting his hand over the phone, the sergeant interpolated to Archie: "Generous old son-of-a-bitch, isn't he?"

ELEANOR ROOSEVELT
Who united the Oyster Bay and Hyde Park Roosevelts

CHAPTER SIX

T. R. AND THE 1912
CAMPAIGN

M Y FATHER'S CLOSE friendship for T. R. made it natural that politics should be of continuing interest in my own branch of the Roosevelt family. A letter from my father to T. R. in 1886 is pertinent because it stressed a phase of T. R.'s career—the astonishing early public recognition of his capabilities—which has been overshadowed by his later accomplishments. "Dear old Ted," the letter reads, "I want to tell you how much pleased I am at your nomination [for mayor of New York City]. Whatever may be the result of the election, I feel that you have cause to be proud of yourself and that the family have cause to be proud of you. For a man 28 years old to be nominated for mayor of New York is itself surprising, for such a man to be nominated as you have been, as a representative of all that is best in city government is a high honor."

In the three-cornered struggle for mayor of New York, T. R. never had a chance, yet that he was nominated for that office at such a young age testifies to the impression he had made while serving in the state legislature from 1882 to 1884. This bumptious and inexperienced youth was being praised or damned in the press in his first year at Albany. By the end of his second year he was a candidate for speaker of the Assembly. Within another year his somewhat belated announcement that he would support James G. Blaine for president was deemed of enough national interest for the *Boston Globe* to publish a special edition featuring his decision. Unquestionably he had remarkable qualities. Equally

[45]

certain was the fact that people recognized and welcomed his leadership.

By 1912 I was already keenly and actively interested in political campaigning. My first reaction to T. R.'s announcement in February of that year that he would be a candidate at the Republican convention was one of disappointment. But as the campaign progressed, I saw him frequently, and enthusiasm replaced my regret. It was characteristic of T. R. that he had the patience to answer the countless questions which the young cousins asked him about the campaign. He explained how the delegates to the Republican convention in most states were chosen at party conventions dominated by the party leaders, and how these leaders, many of them officeholders, felt bound by self-interest and sometimes by threats of dismissal to serve the administration in office. He told us how in this campaign, for the first time, the new primary system would be tried in a number of states. On the basis of reports from almost every election district he estimated that, if the primary system were in force throughout the country instead of only in a few states, he would have from two-thirds to four-fifths of the delegates at the national convention. This was borne out by the returns from such key states as Illinois and Pennsylvania. Wherever the people had a chance to express themselves they were overwhelmingly for him. But we also saw the Taft forces garnering Southern delegates. As June approached, it was clear the Taft leaders would stop at nothing to deny T. R. the nomination. They were determined to obtain enough delegates from the nonprimary states to assure T. R.'s defeat, even if he were to win the delegates in the primary states. As early as June 6, I noted in my diary that "the steamroller evidently has a good hot fire, and things have now assumed the turn of 'anything to defeat Roosevelt,'—even the destruction of the Republican party." Eight days later, I noted with genially mixed metaphors that "the steamroller has been working in a most disgraceful manner, stealing delegates and proving its infamy."

There has been much speculation as to why T. R. threw his hat in the ring in this campaign. Many have attributed his action to ambition, others to spite. As one who saw much of him at this time and in the following years, I believe that his mental processes were comparatively simple. To begin with, he felt that during his presidency he had purged the Republican party of reaction and had reestablished it as the party of progress. Repeatedly he had assured the country in 1908 and 1909 that Taft was the best man to guide the party along its new course. Yet on his return from Africa in 1910, he found the Republican party again in the hands of the reactionaries, and Taft supinely letting them have their way. To T. R. it looked as if Taft not only had betrayed T. R.'s confidence in him but was undermining the reforms which T. R. believed were essential for the welfare of the party and the nation. As the 1912 campaign approached, T. R. felt increasingly his own responsibility to those Republicans who believed in progressive policies. Reluctantly he concluded that the only chance of forwarding the progressive principles in which he believed was to enter the race himself. Repeatedly he told his friends and relatives that, even though he had greatly enjoyed the presidency and delighted in power and popularity, he was not eager to be president again because he knew well the burdens which the office would impose on him.

As a practical politician he had to weigh the chances of success. If he lost the nomination the control of the reactionaries over the Republican party would be more firmly riveted than ever. He knew that during the preconvention campaign the party machine would remain in the hands of President Taft and his reactionary followers. His only chance would come if the party leaders could be made to see that popular sentiment was in his favor. The bosses might then decide that he was the better bet. He waited, therefore, until he was satisfied that he would, in fact, be the more popular candidate, and then announced his candidacy. He believed that if nominated he would be elected, for his vote-getting ability was great.

No sooner had he announced that he would run than he was charged with seeking to rule or ruin. His enemies said that he was crazy for power and, in his grasping for it, was prepared to wreck the Republican party. It is true that he enjoyed power, but it is also true that he entered the campaign knowing that the odds were against his getting the Republican nomination and that, if he were to become the nominee of a third party, he would face certain defeat. This is hardly the attitude of a man lusting for power. As for the contention that he would be—and ultimately was—responsible for the ruin of the Republican party, he felt, not without reason, that responsibility for the fate of the party lay with its leaders and that, if they failed to heed the popular demand for him and were determined to make the party once more the organ of reaction, the responsibility would be theirs, not his. Also, when later it was charged that it was his refusal to abide by the decision of the Republican convention which split the party, he pointed out that the action of the Taft forces in depriving Roosevelt delegates of their seats in the convention left him no alternative but to withdraw from the party, and that, if the leaders had followed the demands of the party members, they would not have nominated Mr. Taft. It was the reactionary leaders at the convention who forced the split, he maintained, not the defection of the Roosevelt supporters.

In retrospect it seems more than likely that he underestimated the dislike of the party bosses for him, and that he did not give enough weight to the possibility that, even if he had been nominated, the resentment of the professional politicians would have been so great that they would have given him only perfunctory support. Certainly his election under the circumstances would have been largely a personal triumph, and the machine leaders doubtless realized that, if elected, he would naturally have favored the appointment to government and party posts of men who had supported his nomination, rather than of those who had opposed him at Chicago.

I was a member of T. R.'s party that left for the convention in Chicago on June 14. I had gone up to Sagamore for breakfast that morning to find out whether and when he was going. Cousin Theodore was unusually silent, and had not yet made up his mind about what he should do. But everything was got in readiness, and as he left for New York City by auto he called out to me, "Well, Nick, I guess we'll meet at a lot of philippics soon." And then he muttered: "But we may fly back here tonight. And, by gracious, I hope we do." A little earlier he had told me that he was taking a volume of Ferrero and of Herodotus with him "to amuse myself and get my mind off the business if I go to Chicago."

The public record of the convention meetings has long since passed into history—the unsuccessful attempt of the Roosevelt forces to obtain a fair hearing for the contested delegates; the proposal presented by Governor Hadley, as leader of the Roosevelt forces, that only the uncontested delegates should vote on the contested ones; the election of Root as chairman; this gentleman's highhanded conduct of that office; Senator Jim Watson's automatic motions to table every proposal brought up by the Roosevelt forces; and the final nomination of Taft by Warren Gamaliel Harding, of Ohio. It was an edifying example of American machine politics at its worst. Seeing it from the inside was an initiation into American public life which was to be helpful in my subsequent writing about the political scene.

At the time it was one of the great shows in American political life. The celebrated Mr. Dooley had correctly predicted that the convention would be a "combynation iv th' Chicago fire, Saint Bartholomew's massacree, the battle iv th' Boyne, the life iv Jessie James, an' th' night iv th' big wind." It was all this and more, for it demonstrated how closely intertwined in the American way of life are deep purpose and good humor. The men and women there were intensely earnest—the Roosevelt supporters because of their profound faith in him, and the Taft forces because of their determination to preserve the Republican machine under their control. Feeling ran high. Old friendships were broken. Bitter things were said. The rift between the conservatives and progressives proved unbridgeable. And yet the thousands in the convention hall derived amusement and relief from such antics as the "choo-choo-chooing" with which the Roosevelt delegates greeted spokesmen for the other side so realistically that you could almost see the steamroller bearing down the hall. On one occasion, when Chairman Root had been particularly highhanded, a delegate rose and called out that he wished to make a point of order. Root banged and banged with his gavel to silence the hall, and when all was quiet he asked the delegate what he had to say. "Mr. Chairman," the man replied, "I wish to make a point of order. The steamroller is exceeding its speed limit." Everyone howled delightedly, and Mr. Root had the sense of humor to admit that the point was well taken.

I kept a very full diary of the convention, which was used among other documents as source material both by William Roscoe Thayer and William Draper Lewis in their volumes about T. R. It is a partisan account of the things seen and heard by an observant but prejudiced youngster who had access to the open and private meetings of the Roosevelt forces. I was not, of course, present at more than an occasional important personal conference of T. R.'s. But I was close enough to those who were to have a clear picture of what went on. Rereading my notes, I am struck with T. R.'s extraordinary hold on the popular imagination and his unfailing good nature. Where others raged he kept his head. No matter how tired or perplexed he might be he was cheerful and appreciative of what his various leaders and supporters were doing.

From the moment of our arrival in Chicago we lived in an atmosphere of excitement and turmoil. Even at the station the crowds had broken through the police lines and were packed on the platform, yelling and cheering. T. R. was finally wedged into a waiting auto, and we into another, and we started for the Congress Hotel through streets so crowded that the cars could hardly move. People filled the windows and lined the roofs and the elevated tracks. Cries of "Teddy" filled the air. At the street crossings, as far as we could see to either side or back or forwards, people were packed in like pins. Ahead rode T. R., waving his hat as he stood on the seat of the car, while the crowd roared its welcome.

At the hotel, T. R. at once went into conference with his leaders. These were, as might have been expected, a varied lot, including such outstanding men as Governors Hiram Johnson, of California; Herbert S. Hadley, of Missouri; Stubbs, of Kansas; and Henry Allen, who later was also to be governor of Kansas— all of them able and experienced politicians; and William Flynn, of Pittsburgh, and Ormsby McHarg—professionals of a different stamp; and amateurs like Alexander P. Moore (who married Lillian Russell and subsequently was ambassador to Spain) and Elon Huntington Hooker. The devoted James R. Garfield and Gifford Pinchot were also there.

One of my first assignments was to go to what had been heralded as the "big" Taft rally at the Taft headquarters. Messengers were wandering through the hotel lobbies urging everyone to attend this rally. My diary says that, after each such plea by the Taft spokesmen, a group of Roosevelt followers would cry out, "All postmasters attend!" At the Taft headquarters I found only a few people present, sitting quietly. By the time the star speaker of the evening, William Barnes, Jr., of Albany, boss of the Republican party in New York State, arrived the room was half-full. Mr. Barnes talked about the need of saving the country and the Constitution from the danger of monarchy. My notes indicate that the audience was listless, sedate, and polite, and that an ancient Negro gentleman stood back of Barnes, and, whenever Barnes paused, would point to the crowd and feebly begin clapping his hands, which was apparently the signal for dull applause. The references to subsequent Taft rallies that I attended indicate that other Taft supporters followed, more or less, the same line—that the country had to be saved from the menace of T. R. My notes also indicate that it was so quiet at the Taft headquarters that Roosevelt men went there to rest when they wanted to get away from the noise and hubbub of their own headquarters.

The enthusiasm for T. R. which the crowds had demonstrated was also in evidence among the Roosevelt delegates. On the night of the Auditorium speech, when T. R. wound up with the oft-quoted phrase, "We stand at Armageddon and we battle for the Lord," I attended one of the closed meetings of Roosevelt delegates at eleven o'clock. Under the chairmanship of Colonel Frank Knox, who in World War II was to be secretary of the navy, a resolution was read to the effect that the one thousand uncontested delegates should vote on the cases of the eighty disputed ones (as T. R. had proposed earlier at the Auditorium). While this was being discussed Governor Hiram Johnson, of California, appeared, and Colonel Knox interrupted to give him

[51]

the floor, announcing that Johnson had something important to say. In a speech that was brief, tense with emotion, and delivered with the sincerity and force for which the Governor was justly famous, Johnson said that he had just come from a conference with T. R. and that he was prepared to follow him to the end, bolt or no bolt, and would the gentlemen agree? The delegates rose and cheered and shouted their assent. Johnson then urged them to stand back of Roosevelt through thick and thin, to refuse to abide by theft. Senator Borah then took the floor and advocated caution, advising a bolt only as a last resort. He exhorted the delegates to use every fair means to win and to bolt only if nothing else could be done. Despite his oft-professed Progressive principles, he later supported Taft.

T. R., who well knew the effect of his own personality, attended a number of these delegates' meetings and invariably was met with great enthusiasm. Of his sincerity in the belief that he was being victimized by the bosses and deprived of the nomination, there can be no doubt. He was scathing in his contempt for the cynicism of the Taft leaders who, after settling enough of the contests over delegates in their own behalf to be able to control the convention, allowed a few contested delegates to be decided in T. R.'s favor. "They stole all the delegates that they thought they needed," he said at a meeting of the Roosevelt forces which I attended on the night of June 21, "But if a man steals a pair of horses from you, do you expect to be satisfied if he brings you back one and says he has no use for it?"

That was the evening before the closing day, when Taft was nominated and the bulk of the Roosevelt forces declined to vote. The Roosevelt delegates met after the Republican convention adjourned and declared their intention of nominating T. R. as the candidate of the new Progressive party. I reached this meeting just as T. R. addressed it. He accepted the nomination on two conditions, he said: first, that the delegates go home and find out the sentiment of the people; and, second, that they should feel entirely free to substitute any man in his place if they deemed it better for the movement, and that in such a case he would give that man his heartiest support. The next morning there was an-

T. R. SPEAKING

He never pulled his punches or pussyfooted when he spoke

other meeting, presided over by Governor Johnson, at which Jim Garfield moved that Johnson be empowered to select seven men, who should confer with him (Johnson) and with T. R., to organize and plan every party move. This was voted, Governor Johnson made a brief talk, and Judge Ben Lindsey moved that the birth of the new party be sealed by a prayer. Six weeks later the Progressive party held its formal convention and nominated Roosevelt and Johnson. The rest is history.

I did not attend the Progressive party convention in Chicago in August, but I helped out from time to time at the Progressive headquarters in New York and, when college reopened, at the headquarters in Boston. Throughout the summer and autumn I saw T. R. frequently; to Archie and myself had been assigned the job of keeping him exercised, which meant tennis every day and occasional hikes and wood chopping expeditions. As a tennis player T. R. was little better than any of us—and we were distinctly mediocre. This is perhaps just as well, for his tennis matches were usually interlarded with conversation on all manner of things and interrupted by political or journalistic visitors.

These visitors were a varied lot, for the Progressive party naturally drew to itself dreamers and theoreticians, as well as men of more practical minds. One evening at Sagamore, when George Roosevelt and I were sitting on the porch discussing the campaign with T. R., George remarked that before 1912 T. R. had been the progressive leader of the conservatives, whereas now he had become the conservative leader of the progressives. "Yes, yes," T. R. muttered, as he rocked back and forth in his favorite rocking chair, "that's it. I have to hold them in check all the time. I have to restrain them."

In my diary covering this campaign the most interesting entries have to do with the attempt on his life at Milwaukee. At the time I was campaigning in western Massachusetts with Charles Sumner Bird, the Progressive candidate for governor of Massachusetts, but a couple of weeks later, when T. R. was out of the hospital and back at Oyster Bay, he told us about it. Archie was helping him on with his overcoat, as his right arm was still stiff, and asked if it hurt. T. R. laughed and said there was no pain, but that the muscles were still black and blue all around the spot.

"He says it was only like the kick of a mule," Archie explained to me.

"That's all it was," said T. R.

"Well, I know what that's like," said Archie, laughing. "I've been kicked by a mule, and I never want to be again."

"But didn't it knock you over?" I asked.

"Yes," said Cousin Theodore, "it knocked me on my back, but I got right up." And he proceeded to show us just what happened.

My mother, who had just joined us, was standing next to me, and T. R. backed us off about three feet and then said: "I was standing like this, not well braced, and had my hat raised like this" (and he raised his arm a little, to show just how it happened). "There were two men standing there where you two are. Schrank [the would-be assassin] put his gun between them, so that no one could see, and fired."

The force, as he had previously explained, knocked him down, but he said that, curiously enough, the attack did not go to his head at all. When he got up he thought the bullet had merely hit him and glanced off, although he felt a burning sensation. What followed happened quickly. Colonel Cecil Lyon (head of the Progressive forces in Texas) tried to clear the crowd so that he could shoot the man, but he couldn't get a clear space. In the meantime, another member of the party, a man named Martin, who had apparently seen the man's gun before he fired, jumped and caught the assassin and brought him to T. R.

In various letters of the time T. R. told how he interceded to protect Schrank and went on to the Auditorium to deliver his speech, and there he found that the bullet had penetrated the copy of his speech, which he had in his breast pocket, and had been stopped by a steel spectacle case, which he later showed us. He realized that he was not badly injured, but when the speech was finished he was glad to be able to rest, and he resented, with justifiable bitterness, those persons who, even though they knew he had been shot, insisted on trying to shake hands with him before he was taken to the hospital.

[54]

My mother happened to be at the theater in New York with Cousin Edith on the night of the shooting. She later told me that they had seats on the aisle. Cousin Edith was on the inside, with two spare seats beside her. Just beyond sat George Roosevelt. My brother, Oliver, who also was working at the Progressive headquarters in New York, was to have been one of the party, but was detained at the office, and Mother, consequently, was delighted when, in the midst of the performance, he slipped into the seat next to Cousin Edith. As he went by her, Cousin Edith didn't look up, and it was not until he was seated that she noticed who it was. Then she leaned over and put her hand on his knee. She found him shaking violently. At that instant, she said, she realized that something had happened and gripped his hand firmly. Although he was trembling, his voice was perfectly steady as he told her that Cousin Theodore had been shot at, but not hurt. Mother said that Cousin Edith merely gasped and then quietly said: "You say he wasn't hurt, Oliver?" and asked him to go back to make sure. He reappeared soon and reported that Cousin Theodore had been scratched but had kept on with his speech. This reassured them, and, though Mother wanted to leave, Cousin Edith insisted on staying, saying that he couldn't be hurt if he went on with his speech, and that if they went to headquarters they would only worry terribly.

When the performance was over, reporters were already on hand, and George kept them away while Mother and Cousin Edith went out a side entrance and took an auto for headquarters. There they learned that he had actually been wounded, and Cousin Edith debated about going out to Chicago immediately or waiting till the *Twentieth Century* the next day, which she finally decided to do. Throughout that evening and the next day Cousin Edith, who stayed with Mother in town, was absolutely calm and self-possessed.

Neither this attack on him, nor the realization that most of the people in public life for whom he had once had respect were against him, nor the fact that, due to the inexperience of his associates, he had to pay constant attention to details of campaign management, dimmed his ardor or his good spirits. To the end he fought just as hard as he knew how. Only once did I note in my diary that he foresaw anything other than certain defeat, and even that once he insisted that, if he had a chance, it was only very small.

Most people have forgotten the intense hatred felt for T. R. by the conservatives. By 1912, when he had obviously become the leader of advanced progressivism, some of the bitterest abuse came from men and women who had once been proud of calling him their friend. In my diary for 1912 is an entry in which I resented a remark made to me by one of the leading socialites of Boston to the effect that Theodore's brother was "crazy" (which was not true), that he had had to be put in an institution, "and that Theodore is even worse." Henry Adams wrote to his brother Brooks, in 1912 that T. R.'s "mind has gone to pieces . . . till it has become quite incoherent and spasmodic. . . . He is, as Taft justly said, a neurotic, and his neurosis may end . . . in nervous collapse, or a stroke, or acute mania." The conservative press attacked him ferociously, as did many of his political opponents. Rarely in the past century has any leader, with the exception of F. D. R., been so violently and constantly reviled as T. R.

Fortunately T. R. was not vindictive, nor did he nurse resentment against those who had criticized him. In the heat of a campaign, of course, he fought back vigorously. He was outraged when false charges were made against him, particularly when he was sure that the person making them knew them to be false. But he was enough of a practical politician to know that things are said in campaigns which are not to be taken too literally, and that a politician may have to work tomorrow with a man whom yesterday he was bitterly attacking. Thus, in time, T. R. even resumed his friendship with Taft and Root, although it is doubtful whether there could have been the same warmth in 1917 and 1918 as there had been prior to 1909.

T. R.'s attitude about the first world war helped mend the breach. Where most Americans required two years or more to appreciate the nature of the upheaval which began in 1914, it took T. R. a little more than a month. By October of that year he began to preach that we should have protested against the violation of Belgian neutrality by Germany's invading army. From this it was but a step to the policy which shaped his thinking and speaking for the next four years—that what Germany had done to Belgium she would do to any other nation that stood in her way, and that it was only a matter of time before the United States would be near the top of her list of enemy nations. From this he reasoned that we could not avoid fighting Germany. This led him logically to the need for preparedness, and to the realization that only if we became a truly formidable fighting power would the Germans respect us. He also realized that, if we would have to join the Allies ultimately, the sooner we did so the better for all. T. R.'s vigorous enunciation of these ideas was soon being echoed throughout the land. As he phrased with bluntness and courage the feelings of right-minded men and women, they turned to him once more for leadership.

In a small way I was instrumental in the clarification of his attitude. When I was on my way to France, in October, 1914, to be an attaché in the American embassy, I met in London a war correspondent of the *Providence Journal*, G. Edward Buxton, who had just come out from behind the German lines in occupied Belgium. He so impressed me with his conviction that the Germans were immensely strong and that it was just a matter of time before they forced war on us that I gave him a letter of introduction to T. R., and I wrote Cousin Theodore asking him to be sure and hear what Buxton had to say. This he did, and from T. R.'s subsequent writings it is apparent that he was as much impressed by Buxton's convictions as I had been.

As T. R.'s emphasis on the need of adequate preparedness grew in force, the Wilson administration was reluctant to take effective steps to prepare the country for war. This was partly due to the clash of irreconcilable personalities. Wilson and T. R. were basically—one might say chemically—incompatible. T. R. was quick, sure, open, and unafraid. Wilson was vacillating, timid, devious, and loath to take action. T. R. was practical, gregarious vigorous, eager for action. Wilson was theoretical, cloistered, eager to avoid the unpleasant. T. R. was merciless as a critic. Wilson was implacable against anyone who dared criticize him. T. R.

[57]

believed that a president should lead the people in time of crises. Wilson believed that it was the duty of a president to follow public opinion. Undoubtedly he felt that T. R. was trying to push him into hasty action. And clearly T. R. felt that Wilson's failure to act with greater vigor and strength was doing the country and the Allied cause a great wrong. Wilson was often hypnotized by his own eloquence into believing that firmly expressed and well-phrased sentiments were as effective as physical force or strong diplomatic action against the world's greatest exponent of the theory of the glorification of brute force. T. R. correctly saw that Wilson's speeches and notes were lulling the American people into a false sense of security and were arousing the contempt, not the respect, of the German government, and that this made greater the dangers which the nation would face when the inevitable shooting war began. Thus T. R. found himself in the forefront of the opposition to the administration, the leading critic of Woodrow Wilson. His enemies saw in this either political ambition or a form of insane jealousy. It was, in fact, something simpler and nobler—a deep sense of moral obligation to do what he could to awaken the country to the great world crisis and to arouse a popular demand for adequate military and naval preparedness which the administration was so slow in pushing.

In retrospect the rightness of T. R.'s position seems indisputable. His fundamental premise—that our participation in the war was inevitable unless Germany had reason to fear our military strength—was correct. We ultimately entered the war woefully unprepared—which was what he had warned us for two years would happen unless the Wilson administration took more active steps to arm. It is clear now that, had it not been for T. R.'s voice, the administration would have been even more unready than it was. No wonder that Wilson had a cold, implacable hatred for T. R., and no wonder that T. R.'s contempt for Wilson increased as our participation was first delayed and then bungled. Himself experienced in foreign affairs, T. R. saw the futility and weakness of Wilson's long-continued note-writing to Germany. As an expert in the shaping of public opinion he realized the disastrous effects of some of Wilson's phrases such as "too proud to fight." Even Wilson's ambassador to England, Walter Hines Page, was shocked and grieved by Wilson's dilatoriness and weakness in handling the *Lusitania* matter—an attitude which resulted in Page's earning Wilson's resentment. "When Mr. Wilson," Page's biographer, Burton J. Hendrick, wrote about this affair, "found that one of his former confidants had turned out to be a critic, that man instantly passed out of his life."

Mr. Wilson's "too proud to fight" speech was followed by five months of lethargic note-writing to Germany and by the resignation of William J. Bryan as secretary of state. When only two of these five months had passed, T. R. wrote scathingly to his close friend Owen Wister: "If," he said, "after the firing on Sumter, Lincoln had made a speech in which he said that the North was 'too proud to fight,' and if he had then spent sixty days in writing polished epistles to Jefferson Davis, and if Seward had resigned because these utterly futile epistles were not even more futile, why, by July the whole heart would have been out of the Union party and most people of the North would have been following Horace Greeley in saying that the erring sisters should be permitted to depart in peace." The record is plain—Wilson failed to keep the country out of war, and at the same time was remiss in not preparing the country for the inevitable. If, as some of his defenders have maintained, he knew in the autumn of 1916 that the break was soon to come, then his failure to prepare the country stands out as an even greater dereliction of duty, and his willingness to have the campaign of 1916 waged on the slogan "he kept us out of war" shows a strange moral obtuseness. T. R. may have been severe as a critic of Wilson, but there is plenty in the record to show that much of his criticism was deserved.

There has been speculation as to what T. R. would have done had he been president in 1914. He himself has told us that he would have protested the invasion of Belgium as a violation of the Hague agreements. He wrote that, when the advertisement warning passengers not to sail on the *Lusitania* was published, he would have sent for the German ambassador and obliged him to sail on the same boat himself. When the Germans refused to heed our protests against the sinking of unarmed passenger vessels, he

[59]

would, he wrote, have seized German vessels in this country and would have held them, pending satisfactory action by the German government. These were, of course, the opinions of a man not in power. Responsibility might have changed his ideas. But his acts in the Venezuela case, in 1902, show that he had no illusions about the true nature of the German government, and that he was not afraid to back his warnings with force. In the Venezuela incident, it will be recalled, Germany seemed on the point of seizing Venezuelan territory, ostensibly to force the settlement of claims made by German citizens for personal damage. T. R. sent for the German ambassador, von Holleben, and told him that he could not acquiesce in the seizure of Venezuelan territory by Germany, and that he, T. R., requested that Germany submit the question to arbitration. When von Holleben said that his government would not agree to arbitrate, T. R. asked him to inform his government that if no decision to arbitrate came within a certain specified number of days he would order Admiral Dewey to take the American fleet to the Venezuelan coast to see that the German forces did not take possession of any territory. A few days later T. R. saw the German ambassador again and asked if there had been any answer from the German government. When told "No," T. R. informed the Ambassador that in such event it was useless to wait as long as he had intended; Dewey would be ordered to sail twenty-four hours in advance of the hour he had set. Within a very short time the President was informed by the German ambassador that the Kaiser had expressed a desire to submit the matter to arbitration. It is pertinent to note that T. R. at once praised the Kaiser publicly and warmly for his willingness to arbitrate. Not until years later did he say or write a word to suggest that the idea was not the Kaiser's, or that arbitration had been accepted by Germany only under duress. It is more than likely that this action was one of the reasons why the Kaiser had for T. R. not only great admiration but a large measure of respect. Certainly the incident in no way diminished the Kaiser's eagerness to see T. R., or the warmth of his welcome when, on coming out of Africa, T. R. was the Kaiser's guest.

Another illustration of T. R.'s effectiveness as a diplomat occurred early in the war when one of the German propagandists in this country, Professor Hugo Münsterberg, of Harvard, went to see T. R. to urge him to be friendly to the German cause. Failing to impress T. R. by his various political arguments, Professor Münsterberg turned his appeal to personal grounds, and said to the Colonel, as his final and supposedly clinching argument: "But you seem to forget, Mr. Roosevelt, that you were the Kaiser's guest." At once T. R. replied: "That is right. But *you* seem to forget, Professor Münsterberg, that I was *also* the guest of the King of the Belgians." The professor finally saw the point and abandoned his attempt to influence the former President.

T. R.'s quickness of speech and mind seemed to many people an indication of superficiality. Woodrow Wilson said of him in 1907 that T. R. "no sooner thinks than he talks," which, the Princeton professor smugly added, "is a miracle not wholly in accord with the educational theory of forming an opinion." In contrast John Hay, who knew T. R. much better than did Wilson, said of him: "Roosevelt . . . takes infinite pains to get at the facts before he acts. In all the crises in which he has been accused of undue haste, his action has been the result of long meditation and well-reasoned conviction. If he thinks rapidly, that is no fault, he thinks thoroughly, and that is the essential." Due to his photographic memory he could recall at the right moment some pertinent analogy derived from a book which he might not even have looked at for a quarter-century. What other American in public life would have thought of characterizing Wilson's elocution as that of a "Byzantine logothete," or would have described Elihu Root, rounding up contested delegates at the Republican convention in 1912, as a modern Autolycus—"a snapper-up of unconsidered trifles"?

Certainly, to those of us who knew him, his intellectual equipment was outstanding. As I look back on the men and women I have met, only Clemenceau and Winston Churchill stand out as his intellectual equals. Yet I doubt if either of these two men had the encyclopedic background that T. R. had. Neither had his extraordinary range of interests, which included ornithology, history, the Icelandic sagas, military lore, the German minnesingers, modern poetry, the Greek classics, and many other subjects. He was in no sense a great or an original thinker. He was not even a good writer. But his was an eager and vigorous mind, able to penetrate quickly to the essentials, with truly remarkable powers of concentration and an unusually large store of common sense.

The dynamic qualities of T. R.'s mind made those with colder intellectual machines distrustful or even hostile. The desiccated and dyspeptic Henry Adams, who viewed with distaste all occupants of the White House after his grandfather, John Quincy Adams, and who was an intimate of John Hay, Cabot Lodge, and others close to Roosevelt, looked upon T. R. as a bore when he did not consider him actually or potentially insane. Much of this probably stemmed from Adams's resentment of T. R.'s ebullience and energy and, in particular, his tendency to monopolize the conversation, which Adams regarded as his own personal and inviolable prerogative. Adams, himself eager for esteem and adulation, surely must have found this habit of T. R.'s deplorable.

More important as a critic of T. R., because a man of sounder judgment, is Oliver Wendell Holmes. "He was very likeable," Holmes said of T. R. in a letter to Pollard in 1921, "a big figure, a rather ordinary intellect, with extraordinary gifts, a shrewd, and I think pretty unscrupulous politician. He played all his cards—if not more." In this same letter Holmes expressed the opinion that T. R. "could never forgive anyone who stood in his way." It would perhaps be more accurate to say that he did not forgive those who had let him down—and there is a great difference between political opponents who fight in the open and those who play a man false.

It has been said of T. R., with intent to disparage, that he was the most astute politician to occupy the White House. The desired inference is that he was the most skilled in the practice of the unsavory wiles of machine politicians. Politically astute he unquestionably was, particularly in his flair for anticipating the popular and dramatizing it to his own advantage. Politically able he also was in obtaining the co-operation of those politicians whose support was essential for the achievement of his ends. As a skilled showman he was likewise most successful in the use of picturesque phrases. His important moves were almost always timed for their effectiveness, and he drove home his points with the emphasis of a great actor. But the grosser wiles of the politician—the readiness to promise anything to anyone, the cynical back-scratching which calls for the open or tacit support of an unworthy measure in exchange for its proponent's aid, the glib endorsement of bad projects solely because they may prove popular, the overall application of the standard of mere vote-getting regardless of the soundness of a measure or of the imperative needs of the country—these were alien to his nature and repugnant to his strong sense of right and wrong.

Looking back on the man's career, it is his courage which stands out above all else. Many men have shown bravery in the face of danger, but only a few have been brave enough to fight for what they believe to be the right, and to continue fighting when they are convinced that defeat and disaster are inevitable. Particularly is this true of public men in countries where popular support or opposition plays a large part in politics. John Quincy Adams had true moral courage. So had Clemenceau and Winston Churchill. It was characteristic of T. R. that when, in the 1900 campaign, he was scheduled to speak in a Colorado silver-mining town and was warned by the local political leaders that he must not criticize free silver lest some of the audience who favored free silver assault him, he marched on to the platform and began his address by saying: "I was warned that if I said anything against free silver here tonight I might be risking violence. I want you to know that I am against free silver, have always been against it, and always shall be." The audience, while largely disagreeing with him, cheered his courage and frankness. A few years later he spoke at a meeting in Little Rock at which the Governor of Arkansas, in introducing him, made what many interpreted as a defense of lynching. T. R. in this southern stronghold at once took exception to what the Governor had implied, and pointed out that it was incumbent on the governor of a state as on the President of the United States to do everything possible to put an end to lynch law. Here again his moral courage won him prompt applause.

[63]

Besides being fearless he was a persistent and wholehearted champion of right, justice, and fair play. To his more cynical critics this was either distasteful or laughable. They made fun of him for having rediscovered the Ten Commandments. But he

N. Y. Herald Tribune Syndicate

THE LONG, LONG TRAIL
Jay ("Ding") Darling's famous cartoon on the death of T. R., 1919

[64]

knew that the fight for right is unending and that most men not only need to be reminded of the old principles but in their hearts enjoy hearing them preached. His belief in the need of applying the homely virtues in public life was deep seated. Of course he made mistakes. To a critic he once remarked: "For every mistake of mine which you know about I have made at least ten others." But he would not surrender his convictions, nor would he abandon them in order to curry favor.

This was one of the reasons for his popularity. People sensed his integrity and derived confidence from his obvious strength of character. As some one well said in the 1912 campaign, it was the men who harbored crooked or dishonest schemes who most feared and hated T. R. while he was in the White House. The abuse that was heaped upon him came largely from those to whom reform was personally unprofitable. These people feared and hated him not because of his words but because they knew that he would, when he could, follow them up with deeds.

His family and friends well knew his quick indignation against deceit, unfairness, or evil. His standards of conduct were high and he applied them to himself even more strictly than to others. He hated misleading phrases—the "weasel words" of Woodrow Wilson, the promises of politicians made with no intent to keep them. His scorn for such was deep and stemmed from his keen moral sense.

This is why, when he died, we felt that the nation had lost a valiant fighter as well as a great-hearted leader. His gaiety, his buoyancy, his humor, his love for all manner of persons were his most endearing traits. His quick mind was a constant stimulus. But it was as an aggressive champion of right against wrong, of decency against evil, of justice against crookedness, of democracy against privilege that he contributed most to his age. He brought to public life the fervor of a revivalist preacher, the pugnacity of a pugilist, the dramatic sense of a great actor, and the capacity for achievement of a hardheaded politician. No wonder visitors to the United States regarded him as a phenomenon equalled only by Niagara Falls, and that his fellow countrymen were fascinated by him even when most critical of what he said or did.

CHAPTER SEVEN

PARIS IN WORLD WAR I

L IKE MILLIONS of Americans who read, on June 29, 1914, about the murder of the Austrian Archduke Franz Ferdinand at Sarajevo on the previous day, I had no conception of its probable repercussions. Not even when it was followed by the outbreak of World War I did it enter my head that, as a result, I should be in Europe within three months in the midst of the war, and that the world of peace, security, and order into which I had been born had become a thing of the past.

Early in October, 1914, when I was working for a master's degree at Harvard and serving as assistant to Professor Edward Channing in American history, a classmate asked me if I would like to go to Bordeaux as secretary to the American envoy there (the French government had recently left Paris for Bordeaux). As commitments to the university might present obstacles, I went directly to President A. Lawrence Lowell for advice. He said that what I could get out of working in the embassy in France during the war would be worth much more than anything I could get at Harvard and suggested consulting Professor Archibald Cary Coolidge, the wise and knowing head of the European history department. Coolidge also urged me to go.

Within two weeks I was in London. England had not yet felt the brunt of the war. Except that the volunteer system was draining off the best young men of the upper classes, social life continued much as it had in the Victorian era. The night clubs were full, the restaurants were patronized by immaculately dressed people, there were no shortages, the shops were thriving, and

London's unbelievable, toy-like tall taxis continued to jam the streets and delay the crowded busses.

Among other young Americans in London was my classmate Sumner Welles, who had not yet started his diplomatic career. He was "doing" London in style, with a chauffeur and car of his own, earnestly tasting the freedom offered a rich young Harvard graduate in London without family ties. He invited me to some of his parties, where the best of everything was sumptuously served, and, always the courteous and thoughtful host, he himself delivered me at the door of my hotel in the small hours of the morning. Except for the cosmopolitanism which became him naturally, and the fact that he combined studiousness with worldliness, there was nothing to suggest that within two decades he would dominate a whole phase of our foreign relations. Least of all did it occur to any of us that he would just miss being secretary of state due to the fact that his cold politeness repelled senators and congressmen, who felt that Sumner was snubbing them. The youthful Welles was as diligent in the pursuit of pleasure as the older Welles was to be in the conduct of foreign affairs. An urge to master problems, together with a deep ambition, drove him ahead fast when he entered the foreign service in 1915, but not even a comfortable fortune which he spent with good taste and generosity offset the handicap of his reserve. Many admired Sumner. Few were ever close to him.

The most interesting man whom I met in London, because he was the soundest in his foresight, was Ned Buxton, of the *Providence Journal*, to whom I have already referred in connection with T. R.'s attitude towards the war. Buxton had seen the German war machine in operation in Belgium and had interviewed leading Germans. He told me about asking the counselor of the German Foreign Office why Germany had not invaded France through the northern part of Switzerland instead of through Belgium. The German's reply was that, coincidental with Germany's order of mobilization, the Swiss deployed 150,000 troops on their northern border and another 150,000 in the interior, whereas Belgium had scarcely 70,000 soldiers in all. Furthermore, he said, the German general staff respected the Swiss Army, whereas it had contempt for the Belgian Army as poorly equipped and trained and without reserves. The implication of this was obvious and led Buxton, on his return to the United States, to do what he could to help T. R. and others waken the American people to the need for military preparedness. He felt deeply that we must begin at once to strengthen our military and naval establishment. This would enhance our prestige in German eyes and lessen the likelihood that Germany would force us into war.

Buxton's report about Germany helped clarify my own thinking about the war. Where others whom I met were primarily interested in how the war affected the British or the French or the future of Europe, he was thinking about its effect on the United States. His theory was simple: Germany would stop at nothing and was convinced that might would triumph. If an impotent America stood in her way, America would be brushed aside. Why should Germany fear or even respect such a "soft" nation which was unarmed, untrained for war, and unwilling to drop outmoded concepts about rights, jurisprudence, and ethics?

As a twenty-one-year-old neophyte in the diplomatic world I did not, of course, call on any of the important British officials, although I lunched and dined several times at the embassy. The Ambassador, Walter Hines Page, was helpful and interesting. He was a large, gangling man with a big nose, a pleasant voice, a simple and amiable manner, and an obviously first-rate intelligence. Both he and Mrs. Page were as frank with the British as they were with Americans, and happily free from the snobbish tendency to ape the English which some of their predecessors and successors displayed.

The only "notable" whom I met in London was the author Henry James, who dined with the Pages when I was there. With the candor and disrespect of youth, I described him in my diary as short, stout, and much given to rubbing his pudgy hands. When I was introduced to him he asked me to identify myself. Knowing that he was a friend of my brother-in-law's, Langdon Warner, I mentioned this relationship, which seemed to satisfy him and he moved on to meet another guest. At dinner, during a pause, he leaned across the table and asked me whether my sister, who had accompanied Langdon on a recent expedition on horseback in Mongolia, was much bettered by her journey. Somewhat puzzled by his question, I replied that she had enjoyed it and had seen so many new and interesting things that she seemed a new person.

"But wasn't she bettered?" he repeated.

"Yes, she liked it a lot," said I, still confused.

"But wasn't she bettered, wasn't she bruised?" he insisted tartly, which brought from me in a relieved but apparently reproving tone:

"Oh—battered. You mean battered."

"Yes. Bettered. That's what I said," and he turned to Mrs. Page.

That evening I noted in my diary: "Frankly I wasn't much impressed with H. J. He had a most interesting face—a wonderful face. But the mannerisms and pompousness were trying. In comparison to the Ambassador he was much the least interesting of the two."

From London to Bordeaux the trip was uneventful. There we went to the house which John Garrett had rented as the embassy headquarters, and were at once put to work. Mr. Garrett's task was to take up with the French Foreign Office matters which in Paris would have required personal representation. Most of his contacts were through two undersecretaries, de Margerie and Herbette, but on important occasions he saw Delcassé, then as ten years earlier, minister for foreign affairs. To Mr. Garrett's other assistant, John Gilman d'Arcy Paul, and myself fell the task of relieving him of as much routine as possible, and, under his direction and supervision, preparing official correspondence. We found him patient, reasonable, considerate, and able. As I saw more of him I admired the thoroughness of his knowledge of diplomacy and international affairs and the adroitness with which he handled people. Always courteous and gentle, he yet had strength and courage. Wishful thinking played no part in his mental processes, and he was not easily deceived. Of our career diplomats of the last half-century he and Norman Armour, in my opinion, were the ablest.

Among those who had moved to Bordeaux when the French

government left Paris was Georges Clemenceau. He was in the opposition at the time—as he had been throughout most of his tempestuous career. At the outbreak of the war his personal news-paper, *L'Homme Libre*, had been suppressed by the government, so he at once issued a new one, called *L'Homme Enchaîné*—in it-self characteristic of his mordant use of words. He criticized the members of the Poincaré government in terms which galled and exasperated them in direct proportion to the truth of what he wrote.

A friend in Paris had given me a letter of introduction to Clemenceau, and a few days after my arrival in Bordeaux I pre-sented it. He was living in a tiny flat on the second floor of a small house in the Cours St. Jean. I was ushered into a very hot, cell-like room, and found a chunky, thick-set old man with a drooping, bushy white moustache, deep-set mongoloid eyes, and ferocious black eyebrows. He wore grey gloves and was done up in an overcoat and a cap, as he had caught cold and was afraid, as he explained, that he might "*attraper du mal.*" He offered me a chair and, calling for more wood, drew up as close as he could to the small fire in the grate, and, after asking my relation to T. R. and making some laudatory remarks about him, began questioning me: "What did they think of the war in America? What was the attitude of the newspapers? How long would we tolerate von Bernstorff's activities? How strong was the anti-German feeling in America? How did I find the spirit in England?"

When, to this last question, I replied that I did not think that England yet was fully awake, he said: "Ah! You also noticed that?" and launched into a torrent about the war and how for forty years he had warned that it was inevitable and had opposed all measures that might weaken France's ability to resist. He had been mayor of Paris during the Franco-Prussian War, and ever since then had been sure that another war was inevitable. I was interested to hear him say that the contrast between the spirit of the French people in 1914 and in 1870 was striking. In those days the country was badly divided and was unready for war. Now the unity and determination of the people was magnificent and the military leadership under Joffre was excellent. As for the

British, he feared that they were relying too much on their fleet and that they would not grasp the seriousness of the task ahead until they had a severe setback. For the Poincaré government he could say little, except to deplore its eagerness to muzzle the press —meaning, presumably, himself.

It is amusing in retrospect to find in my diary an indignant entry a few days later to the effect that Clemenceau had "committed a gross breach of etiquette" in quoting me in *L'Homme Enchaîné* about the American attitude towards the war. A week- or more thereafter I took Arthur Ruhl, roving correspondent for *Collier's*, to see the old Tiger, and I later noted in my diary that "I told C. what I thought of his publishing a private conversation." But we were soon friends again and spent another hour that passed quickly. After some generalities about the war, Ruhl said he had a personal question to ask—whether Clemenceau wrote or dictated his articles. Clemenceau arose and going to a table picked up some loose sheets written in a fine hand. "*Le voilà!*" said he, "This is it, I've only started tomorrow's article. And tomorrow morning at three or three thirty I'll finish it."

"At three o'clock in the morning?" I said. "But don't you sleep?"

"Yes. I go to bed at nine and get up at three. [This all in French.] It's nothing at all."

"Then you are like Napoleon!" said I. He laughed.

"No, it's not a tour de force," said he, returning to the writing. "I have so much to say that I can't help writing it. For the last fifty years I have done nothing but think and study politics and history. If after all that time I haven't enough to say—well, that would be just too bad for the country." And he proceeded to tell us in simple but vivid French how he divided mankind into "those who talk" and "those who act." All his life he had spent fighting the talkers. For sixteen years he had edited a newspaper, and during that time never wrote an article. Not till he was fifty-three did he take to writing—and he had written ever since. We marveled at his clearness and force. It was, he said, merely because he had something to say. And that was the secret of his career. He had never feared to express himself. He had fought against the

[71]

French having colonies, because they did not have children to colonize them. He had fought against their conquering territory, for they would spend much money and many lives, and then when Germany attacked, they would not be ready. He had fought against the first ministry because it was maladministering. He knocked it down, and as quickly as he had knocked it down, another sprang up, just as bad. He knocked that down, and a third. He told us that the proudest moment of his journalistic career had occurred when France went into Tunis. He opposed and criticized this action on the ground that it was better for France not to have colonies, that the occupation might well offend and even alienate Italy, and that the expense would be unduly great. He wrote a three-inch article to this effect in his paper. A few weeks later Bismark said to the *London Times* correspondent, showing him that three-inch article, "Who is this man Clemenceau?" and added, "He will bear watching."

His vigor was such that it was hard to believe that he was seventy-three years old. But three years were still to pass before, at last, he took over the government of France and harnessed his driving energy, clear intelligence, and ripe knowledge to the task of uniting the discordant and disheartened Allies in the final drive for victory in World War I. Like Winston Churchill in World War II, Clemenceau poured his own overflowing faith into his people. Like Churchill he had a record of clear foresight and a fighting spirit that could not be downed. Like Churchill he had a feeling for reality that made him distrustful of theorists and idea-mongers. And more, even, than Churchill, he had a detached and scathing wit which delighted his admirers and outraged his opponents. The famous remark attributed to him on first hearing of Wilson's Fourteen Points—"*Tiens! Le bon Dieu n'avait que dix!*" ("The Good Lord had only ten")—was very probably one of the causes for Wilson's icy dislike of Clemenceau. When Winston Churchill, then first lord of the admiralty, called on Clemenceau wearing the uniform of a group known as the Elder Brethren of Trinity House and the Frenchman expressed interest in the uniform and asked what it was, Churchill explained in painful, anglicized French: "*Moi, je suis le frère aîné de la Trinité.*" To

[72]

which Clemenceau replied: *"Ah, ça! Nous n'avons pas ça en France!"*

A few days after Christmas the French government moved back to Paris, dutifully followed by our outpost of the American embassy. On New Year's Day the entire staff of the embassy attended the diplomatic reception given by Poincaré in the Élysée Palace. Wearing the traditional garb of headwaiters, we were shown into an anteroom where we were to be joined by Ambassador Sharp. While waiting for him, Mr. Garrett and I went through a large drawing room that was dimly lighted, and from the door we watched the crowd in the reception room. It was a brilliant show, as all the foreign representatives save our own were in full dress. The members of the British embassy wore dark uniforms with silver and gold braid, with swords. The Ambassador, Sir Francis Bertie, looked a little less ferocious than in his regular clothes. Iswolsky and the Russians were the most resplendent, in silver-braided uniforms with white trousers striped with gold. Next in conspicuousness was the Dutch chancellor, who wore a bright red coat on the back of which was a blue ribbon with a gold key hung over it.

We were then formally grouped in a horseshoe, the British (Bertie was dean of the corps) at the extreme left of the door. Next to them were the Russians. Then the Japanese, the Spaniards, ourselves, the Swiss, Dutch, Swedes, and so on around through the Balkan states, China, and the South American republics. Soon the chattering ceased and an official announced, *"Messieurs—le Président de la République!"* Everyone bowed, and Poincaré, wearing a dress suit with the red ribbon of the Legion of Honor on his breast, stepped in briskly. Then Bertie in clear but anglicised French expressed the greetings of the diplomatic corps. Poincaré replied that France had not desired war. His voice was clear and full of indignation as he spoke of the violation of the rights of civilization by the Germans. He shook hands with Bertie and started on his rounds, followed in single-file by his Cabinet. First came Viviani, tall and unpleasant-looking, then Briand, looking partly fierce and partly bored, then little Delcassé, as beaver-like as ever—and so on down the line, including Ribot (the oldest-appearing of the lot), Millerand, the ugly Thompson, and all the rest. As soon as the last Central American republic had been reached, everyone hurried out again, and we went home.

In Paris the Ambassador, the Garretts, the Robert Woods Blisses, and other older members of the embassy constantly invited the young attachés to meals and cocktail parties, with the result that we soon came to know other diplomats and also the little group of Paris Americans who for years had been intimate with the diplomatic set. We saw often the icy Edith Wharton, always shadowed by the cynical and aloof Walter Berry, and watched her appraise new acquaintances, catalogue them, and lay them aside in her mind for future literary use, much as a prudent housewife might pick up choice items for her deep-freeze. As time passed I came to know well Mrs. Don Cameron, the widow of Pennsylvania's famous senator and Republican boss after the Civil War, and daughter of Judge John Sherman, brother of William Tecumseh Sherman. She was a *grande dame*, truly a citizen of the world, charming, brilliant, and even in her old age still vivacious and beautiful. A close friend of Henry Adams' and John Hay's, she had been an outstanding leader in the social life of Washington since the days when her husband was secretary of war in President Grant's cabinet. She had the warmth, sympathy, and tolerance that Edith Wharton so signally lacked, and a broad knowledge of world affairs.

Throughout most of my stay in Paris the second secretary of the embassy, Arthur Orr, and the military attaché, Colonel James A. Logan, and I lunched together regularly several times a week. Logan spoke with authority about the military and Orr about international affairs. I served as audience and heckler. It was an education more valuable than any that I had at Harvard, and only equaled by my later long sessions with Professor Roger Bigelow Merriman, of the history department of Harvard, who arrived in Paris at this time as exchange professor. There was a gusto and humor about Roger which was lacking in both Orr and Logan, and, of course, he had a more detailed and scholarly background than either. He was an avid observer with boy-like curiosity but mature powers of evaluation and had an excellent memory for anecdotes and *bons mots* and a gift for setting current events in the perspective of earlier happenings. His particular interest was speculating about the changes which the war would bring about in the world. To him the invasion of Belgium in 1914 was surprising only because it had not been accompanied by the invasion of Holland, as the possession of the Low Countries was essential to any enemy of England contemplating the destruction of that country. He elaborated his theory that the true purpose of the Spanish Armada had been to furnish protection for an invading force to cross the channel.

Roger Merriman was staying at the hotel where I lived, and he and I looked upon the Zeppelin raids—mild precursors of the "blitz" of World War II—as sources of excitement and adventure. I slept through the first one, but in subsequent raids we would sally forth into the darkened streets, hoping to glimpse a Zep caught by one of the searchlights used by the French to spot them. We knew that the danger from bombs was negligible. The hazard was greater from the occasional taxis driving without lights and from possible gangsters using the blackout to cover assaults on persons in the streets. The general reaction of the Parisians was one of curiosity. The few bombs that exploded in Paris aroused bitterness and disgust—not fear.

Wilson's famous personal agent, Colonel Edward M. House, was in Paris during one of the raids, and the Garretts arranged for him to drive over to that part of Paris where the bombs had fallen. I went with them and found Colonel House torn between his interest in seeing the damage done by bombs—craters several yards wide in the streets—and uneasiness lest his inspection become public knowledge and be twisted by the Allies or the Germans for propaganda purposes. But the Texas Colonel's capacity for being noncommittal, when not completely silent, afforded no opportunity for even the most skilled inventor of misleading propaganda to make anything out of this visit or out of his reaction to the bombing.

My relations with Colonel House were scant, but with his understudy, Hugh Campbell Wallace, who later succeeded Sharp as ambassador to France, I was brought into close contact. Wallace had been chosen by Wilson and House to visit European countries unobtrusively and to maintain close contact with House, so that, in the event that anything happened to House, Wallace could carry on in his place. He was a large-boned, friendly Westerner with a drooping moustache—the type which we have come to associate with Western sheriffs in the movies. He knew no French and little or nothing about France. His knowledge of European diplomacy was sketchy. But he was shrewd and hardheaded, and had a diligent though slow mind and an eagerness to see and to learn. I accompanied him on a trip to the front—one of those well-staged, perfectly safe tours which the French government used for the purpose of impressing distinguished foreign visitors and winning their sympathy. Wallace's obvious thrill when a German sniper hit the trench above the peephole through which we had just been looking had a spontaneity that was engaging. So also was his curiosity about the smallest details of life in the front-line trenches.

I also accompanied him on his visits to various officials in the French Foreign Office and elsewhere. Just before we both returned to the United States, two of these men in the Foreign Office, Ponsot and Leger (better known as the poet St. Jean Perse), invited Wallace and myself to a lunch to meet various members of their staffs, and I was amused to realize in the course of the lunch that they had invited Wallace as a man likely to have much influence with Wilson (he shortly became ambassador). Then they prudently decided that, in the event T. R. became active once more in American politics, it might be useful if the French had some good unofficial contact with him, and hence they included me in the party.

Our work at the embassy had early crystallized into looking after the interests of German and Austro-Hungarian prisoners of war and civilian internees. This involved inspecting the prison and internment camps throughout France. It was part of the general procedure for us, after visiting a camp, to invite the local officials to a meal or a drink, and as they became enthusiastic about their favorite theme of *"La France—l'Amérique"* and drank toasts to both countries, they usually included a toast to T. R. On one oc-

casion, when a banquet was given in our honor by the local digni-
taries and the time for toasts came, they dispensed with references
to *l'Amérique* and simplified the procedure by drinking to *"La
France—la famille Roosevelt!"* Even in remote parts of Corsica,
where we visited camps on two separate occasions, curiosity
about T. R. was intense, and special marks of friendship and
hospitality were showered on me because I bore his name.

Fortunately Mr. Garrett believed in encouraging his assistants
to get out and about, and early in May of 1915 he suggested that
I run over to London for a week. This I did, accompanied by
Arthur Orr, and throughout our stay we saw many English and
American friends. It is amusing, in the light of subsequent history,
to read in my diary that many of these were "hot agin the government, and particularly Churchill, whom they consider to be
a very efficient man but a poor head of the navy in a war. They
complain that he takes no council and that he and the rest of the
cabinet are given more to retaining their places than to effort in
prosecution of the war." When I went to a session of Parliament,
I noted that Lloyd George made an excellent impression, but that
I "felt a strong dislike to Churchill the moment I heard and saw
him." In later years my admiration for him was unbounded.

Roger Merriman had given me a letter to James Viscount
Bryce, author of *The American Commonwealth* and former ambassador to the United States. Even though Lord Bryce was already almost eighty, I knew that he had maintained his keen interest in America and world affairs, and I hoped that a talk with
him would be enlightening. I found a small, white-bearded old
man with keen but rheumy eyes which kept blinking continuously. After the exchange of amenities he began plying me with
questions with so much persistence that I never had a chance to
do anything other than answer him. What did the French feel
about the progress of the war? What did they think about the
use of poison gas? When did they think the war would be over?
Did I notice any difference between the spirit in Paris and that in
London? What details did I know of the Chicago mayoralty election? What had I heard recently from T. R.? Here and there he
interjected a comment, such as, for example, that he had never

thought we would permit foreign influences in our local politics. But instead of pumping the old gentleman, as I had hoped and planned to do, he reversed the procedure and, when he had extracted as much as he could out of me, brought the interview to a close with the skill and charm of a veteran. If I came away with few additions to my store of knowledge, I at least had seen how a keen mind keeps alert and how an elderly gentleman can remain youthful in spirit and outlook.

Not even my realization that Germany would stop at nothing to win the war had prepared me for the shock when, the day after my interview with Lord Bryce, I saw large posters on the billboards which the newspaper vendors carried, reading: "LUSI-TANIA SUNK!" The horror of the thing was bad enough—in those days we were not hardened to the mass murder of neutrals and noncombatants. But its implication—war between us and Germany—was staggering. I went directly to the Cunard office. A small bulletin in the window merely stated that the vessel had been torpedoed. The crowd in the street was patient in the face of no definite information about how many had been lost and who had been rescued. Several times that evening I returned there. By the next morning some details were available, and the Cunard Company had begun to post lists of passengers and of known survivors. It was apparent that many hundreds had drowned. It was equally apparent that America's entry into the war was unavoidable. The only real question, thenceforth, was when this would take place.

Several months after the sinking of the *Lusitania* I went to Compiègne to visit the hospital and laboratory supported by the Rockefeller Foundation there under the direction of Dr. Alexis Carrel. His establishment was only a few miles from the front. We were surprised to find the town itself as quiet and peaceful as the Riviera, with the streets full of civilians, women and children, even though the guns at the front could be clearly heard. Dr. Carrel was a charming man with a serene and spiritual face notable for its squareness and for its twinkling eyes and finely carved features. He combined American frankness with French courtesy and spoke with unusual clarity, precision, and humor.

In fact, few men whom I have met were more interesting and at the same time more appealing. He talked at length about the experimental work in surgery and chemistry which he and his associates were carrying on, despite the fact that they were subjected to German air raids and occasional strafing by artillery. From his work the talk shifted to the ease with which human beings adapt themselves to changed conditions. He cited examples of French peasants returning to their fields in the front-line area, ploughing and planting with an artillery barrage going on over their heads. By a natural transition he passed on to his belief in the effectiveness of psychic powers and in the unplumbed possibilities of psychotherapy—a field which in later years was to be the subject of much speculation on his part.

After lunch Dr. Carrel took us through the laboratory, and there we met Dr. H. D. Dakin, who was developing the antiseptic solution for the treatment of wounds that later was to bear his name. I was struck with the combination of faith, confidence, and selflessness with which he went about his work. In a world in which human ingenuity was being directed almost exclusively to destruction, these two doctors, Dakin and Carrel, were concentrating on the healing and health-giving processes. Of few men at the time could it as truly be said that they were dedicating their lives to the betterment of mankind.

Military leaders, diplomats, policy-makers, writers, teachers, scientists—these were our constant contacts. But Alice Garrett, the galvanic wife of our "chief," was not content to see us restricted to such limited circles. So she injected into her entertainments a procession of authors, musicians, and artists, and for a short time even tried to force the young secretaries to attend a class in gymnastics held in her rooms at the Ritz each Sunday morning. Accustomed to having her plans carried out efficiently and promptly, only her sense of humor averted the mutiny that would surely have occurred had she continued to insist that our one morning of freedom must be devoted to the pursuit of physical well-being through the teachings of a middle-aged ex-dancer who had evolved a cult of acquiring physical perfection through balancing in awkward poses and alternately flexing and relaxing

[79]

previously unsuspected muscles. Subsequently, Mrs. Garrett also tried to impose diet fads on the secretariat, but she found that, while she could control what we were offered at her own table, she could not restrain our appetites when we were beyond the reach of her observing eye and correcting voice. By way of asserting our independence we would regale her with details of the forbidden dishes which we had enjoyed without her presence—and I suspect that in this struggle for mastery she was secretly glad to lose.

One of the particularly engaging individuals whom she collected as antidotes to diplomats was the Spanish painter Ignacio Zuloaga. He was a tall, dark man, full of vitality and fun, differing from the traditional artists depicted in such operas as *Bohème* or *Louise* only in that his talents were great and he was completely natural and unaffected. At his studio, we found him happily unaware that a world war was in progress. The picture of the moment, the book of criticisms he was reading, the recollection of a beloved spot in his native Spain, the warm enjoyment of having an appreciative visitor—these things completely absorbed him, and he overwhelmed guests with the intensity of his reactions. The opportunity to do a portrait of the many-sided Mrs. Garrett was a challenge to him because of the obvious difficulty of catching more than one of her kaleidoscopic moods. As she, at the moment, was interested in exploring her potentialities as a pseudo-ballerina, he picked a black Spanish dress and mantilla and, if I remember rightly, balanced her on the tips of her toes.

The portrait was more interesting as a specimen of Zuloaga's work than as a likeness of Alice Garrett. When I remarked to Edith Wharton that it made Mrs. Garrett look like the devil's wife, she said in her characteristically highhanded and imperious manner: "What more could you expect? It's horribly vulgar, but any portrait done by such a man would be. Everybody knows that Zuloaga is nothing but a charlatan. He can't paint, anyway. He never learned how." Which is one way for a great novelist to write off a great painter.

This was in February of 1916. The war was in an apparent stalemate. I had been in France nearly sixteen months and was getting homesick and disgruntled about the Wilson policy of watchful waiting. So, as I knew I could not afford to take up the foreign service as a career, it seemed best to resign. This I did in March of that year, and in June and July I attended the reserve officers' military training camp at Plattsburg. If my conviction that it was only a question of time before we would be forced into the war was sound, it was logical to get what military training I could in order to be the better able to take my part when we went in. Unlike my Theodore Roosevelt relatives, I was not cut out to be a soldier, but like them, in time, I went overseas in the Army, and, with the signing of the Armistice, found myself once more thrust into diplomatic affairs.

CHAPTER EIGHT

SPANISH INTERLUDE

BEFORE GOING overseas with the Eighty-first Division in 1918, I was to have another short trip abroad—this time to neutral Spain, where I spent the winter of 1916–17 as secretary to Major James F. Case, representing the American International Corporation. The A. I. C., as it came to be known, was just beginning its briefly hopeful career, encouraging American investments and engineering enterprises abroad, so as to create a steadily increasing demand for American goods. Willard Straight and the group of businessmen and bankers who backed the A. I. C. hoped it would not only stimulate current business in the United States but would also serve as a safety valve for American production after the war.

This mission was to place me as an observer in a series of negotiations which smacked of an E. Phillips Oppenheim novel of international intrigue. Court favorites, shady financiers, wily politicians, princes of the church, and even the King himself passed under my youthful eye. Spain was unmodernized, with a group of wealthy titled families at the top and a mass of uneducated, impoverished peasants and workers at the bottom. Church, Court, and King dominated Spanish life as they had for centuries, despite the fact that, constitutionally, the government was vested in a cabinet responsible to the legislature. The church was powerful in politics and controlled much of the nation's wealth.

Alfonso XIII, then at the height of his popularity, liked to boast that if Spain were to become a republic he would have a good chance of being elected its first president. He was more forward-looking in his social concepts than most of his contemporaries on the thrones of Europe, but he never faced the impact of modern industrialism on Spanish feudalism. Had he done so, he might have forestalled the revolution that led to his exile. But such enlightenment was more than could be expected from the heir of the Bourbons and Hapsburgs. Alfonso enjoyed being king too much to work hard. Good-hearted, kindly, and well-meaning, he lacked force.

The American ambassador to Spain, Joseph E. Willard, was the father of Belle Willard, who had married my cousin Kermit. Thanks to this, the Willards treated me virtually as a member of their own family. Hence I saw much of diplomatic life in Madrid. Because of the war, the representatives of the Allies and of the Central Powers were never invited to the same functions (except by the King or the Minister of Foreign Affairs on formal occasions) and the cleavage separated Madrid society into distinct groups. As the United States was still neutral during most of my stay in Madrid, the American embassy had relations with both. Through friends there and through letters which I had to the Dutch minister, I also saw both sides. As a youngster of twenty-three, I found the social life entertaining and realized only dimly how incredibly narrow it was. Most of the time, conversation turned on polite amenities, with gossip of who was doing what in the diplomatic corps. I remember a lunch at the Dutch legation where special interest was expressed about a dachshund presented to Lady Hardinge, the wife of the British ambassador, by the Princess Frederick of Hanover, which annoyed the Russian ambassador, who thought that it was not right to have a German dog if one was the wife of the British ambassador. With full seriousness he protested that the dog barked like a German. On another occasion, also at the Dutch legation, I met the three daughters and a sister of the German ambassador and several other high-ranking Germans, and I noted in my diary that "a commoner looking lot I have rarely seen." By way of contrast, I later described a dinner at the American embassy, where, when the meal was over, the guests adjourned to the conservatory. "To enter it, one goes down a step," the diary reads, "We were just getting settled when, as I

[83]

happened to glance towards the door, there appeared a tall, strik-ing-looking woman with grey hair and dressed in grey, with a high diamond collar around her neck. It was Mme de Geoffray, wife of the French ambassador. She paused for fully three-quart-ers of a minute, looking about the room, with her head held high, and then stepped down, and with an air of graciousness that in anyone else would have seemed condescension, she made the round of the company." Hers were the style and manners of the old French aristocracy—the antithesis of the heavy, flat-footed, dowdy German princesses I had seen at the Dutch legation.

Our ambassador, Mr. Willard, was helpful not only in advice but by bringing us into contact with Spaniards who could be of influence. But as the chief project on which the A. I. C. was con-cerned was one in which several rival groups were at odds, Mr. Willard suggested that the best course would be to go direct to headquarters and have an audience with the King. This he ar-ranged for March 14. The following extracts from an account of the interview, which I wrote immediately after we left the Royal Palace, are interesting primarily because of the picture which they give of a way of life that seems gone forever.

"We joined Mr. Willard at the embassy and drove to the palace. The Ambassador marched past the saluting guards and opened a door which led to a carpeted stone staircase. Up this we went, and out into a gallery, where a guard in uniform with a big halberd gave a thump on the floor, and an individual who looked like an undertaker stepped forward, saying in good English: 'This way please.'

"This man, who had a red nose, was unshaven, and wore an old black frock coat with black tie and black gloves and a broad black band round his tall black hat, turned out to be one of the high-ranking grandees of Spain. His official function was that of sec-ond introducer of ambassadors. He led us on around the gallery, and at the corner another guard thumped his halberd on the floor, and so passed the royal stairway, where two more guards thumped at the announcement of 'The American Ambassador.' One stepped out to stop Major Case and myself but was waved aside by our guide. We were then led into a a palatial coatroom where our duque curtly remarked: 'Hats and gloves, please. No canes.' So putting on the left grey glove, and balancing the topper in the hand, we went through into the King's antechamber. This is a big room, with a high ceiling, heavily gilded, with tapestries and red velvet hangings, and a fine portrait of the Queen Mother. In the center hung an enormous gilt chandelier, which, if it fell, would go through a stone floor. There were numerous officers in dress uniform and quite a number of persons in long coats, some more funereal looking than others.

"After about ten minutes, the duque, who had left us, returned and whispered, 'Now come, please,' and led us to a small door at the side of which stood a jovial, fat, bearded officer who shook hands warmly with us and made some remarks in Spanish to Mr. Willard which he answered in English. I noticed Mr. Willard trying to hitch his hat in a formal position in his left hand, and in a second I saw Major Case trying to put his in the same position—the left arm crooked, the hat resting a few inches in front of the heart. So that we should all three appear similarly arrayed, I hitched mine into the same position. As I did so, the signal was given, and we passed through the door into a little room. I heard a clicking of heels and had an impression of a blue form bowing first to Mr. Willard, then to Major Case. When Mr. Willard introduced me, the King said, 'Yes. You have been here, I know. You are a son . . .' which brought forth a chorus of the word 'cousin.' He then pointed to a sofa and two chairs, saying 'Won't you please sit down." He placed the Ambassador in a corner of the sofa nearest him, and Major Case next to Mr. Willard. He himself took the chair next to Mr. Willard, and I took the chair opposite him, next to Major Case.

"The office was small, hardly 12 by 14 feet. The only furniture besides a fine yellow rug was the sofa and two chairs, which we occupied, at the nearer end of the room, and an Empire desk at the opposite end. There were many papers on the desk and what I took for diplomas piled up in a corner of the room back of it. On the walls were some maps and a portrait—apparently of Alfonso XII. On the desk rested a spiked helmet.

"The King wore the blue uniform of captain general of the

Spanish Army, with a red collar and with high boots and spurs. Across his breast was a broad, light-blue ribbon. A line of medals was pinned over his heart. Under these medals were embroidered the stars of four military orders, and from between the second and third button of his jacket a red ribbon protruded on which hung the Order of the Golden Fleece. I should say he is about six feet tall, rather broad of shoulder and straight, though by no means thick chested. He has a distinctly refined face, with a smooth somewhat tanned skin, a high forehead, and a long thin nose. His eyes are brown, and well set, though they are not his best feature. The lower part of his face is disfigured by the Hapsburg lower lip, which is not as exaggerated as in Philip IV's portraits but is nonetheless a notable defect. His hands are large, with tapering fingers, and on his left wrist he wore a gold bracelet.

"No sooner had we sat down than Mr. Willard produced a brand of cigarettes which he knew the King liked. Alfonso took one, as did Major Case and I, and before we had time to look for matches, the King whipped out a little gold lighter and lit first the Ambassador's and then Major Case's cigarettes. He then put it out, relighted it, and lit mine and then his. I was interested to note the superstition. When later more cigarettes were produced, he again put his lighter out after lighting two, and then lit it again.

"When we had touched on various business propositions and Mr. Willard was about to leave, the King said: 'One more thing. What do you think about the war? Are you going in?' [This, be it noted, was on March 14, 1917, three weeks before America entered the war.]

" 'You know as much as I do,' said Mr. Willard. 'You know we are arming our merchant vessels.'

" 'They aren't being armed against Spain or South America,' said I. 'Or even England,' added Major Case.

" 'No,' said the King, smiling. 'Obviously not. But what will they do?'

" 'Well, if one of our ships is sunk, that means war,' the Ambassador replied.

"The King: 'I will be very frank with you. I do not like these what you call half-measures—this between war and peace. You

[86]

are in a false position. If I were doing it, it would be either one or the other. But this business of waiting—if you want to know my personal opinion, you have done too much waiting. How long is it going to continue?'

"Here Mr. Willard interrupted. 'Yes sir. It may be true we have hesitated, but you mustn't forget that by this very hesitation, the President has got the whole country back of him.'

"The King: 'Yes, but . . .'

"Mr. Willard: 'I know how Your Majesty feels. But you must remember that the people of our country did not want war. One of the reasons Wilson was re-elected was because he kept us out of war. Now those very same people who supported him because he kept us out of war will support him all the more now that he goes into it, because they feel that he has done everything possible to keep out of it.'

"The King: 'Yes, they tell me all parties are back of him now, the war people and the pacifists.'

"Mr. Willard: 'Your Majesty, when do you look for the end?'

"The King: 'October.'

"Mr. Willard: 'How will it end?'

"The King: 'It is my opinion that it will have to end then unless they are all crazy. By that time three million will be killed, and they will not want to face another winter. If it goes on longer the rulers will not be able to hold their countries. Their people will say, "Why did you not stop sooner, when we might have preserved something? Why have we kept on and yet had no victory?" They will be ruined. It will be very much as things are at present. On the west front there can be no change. There may be a few miles advance each way. But it is a draw.'

"Mr. Willard: 'Who is going to bring about peace? The Germans?'

"The King: 'I don't think so. Honestly or not, they asked for peace in December. I do not think they can ask again. It must come from the Allies. Every time England says she is ready to carry the war out to the end, the more unified the German people become. And I have bad news of Russia.'

[87]

"Mr. Willard: 'What is that?'

"The King: 'They have no more bread in St. Petersburg—Petrograd, you say?'

"Mr. Willard: (interrupting) 'Petrograd, yes.'

"The King: 'They have been firing on the mob in the streets. Several companies have gone over to the people and either killed their officers or the officers have given in. Troops are to be brought up from the front.'

"Mr. Willard: 'That sounds bad. But it will be in hand soon won't it?'

"The King: 'What I have given you is the best of it.'

"Mr. Willard: 'Your sources are good?'

"The King: 'Yes. My ambassador. But an ambassador isn't worth much. When he hears a machine gun going off in the street outside his house, he stays at home and is quite ready to believe the worst of the tales brought him.' "

This, as we later learned, was the very start of the bolshevist revolution in Russia.

After touching on other subjects, the King finally rose. We had been with him for an hour and a quarter. He clicked his heels together and, bowing, shook hands with us. We marched out, got our coats, and walked down the long corridor, where the halberdiers thumped again, and so down to the auto and back to the Ritz.

As the King indicated, the imminent entry of the United States into the war created new problems. Shortly after the declaration of war, the A. I. C.'s Spanish interests were dropped, and the Cases and I returned to the United States.

The next time I saw Alfonso was in 1932, at the Coronation Church in Budapest, during the funeral services of his aunt, the Archduchess Isabella. The church was small and crowded. The area directly next to the catafalque had been set aside for the diplomatic corps. As America headed the alphabetic list of the corps, I, as American minister, was in the front row, with my knees almost touching the platform on which the bier rested. On my right was the Austrian minister. On my left was the Cardinal of Hungary. We were crowded together on small collapsible chairs.

As the Cardinal took part in the service he was frequently rising and sitting down. Being unusually broad, he several times landed on only part of his chair, with a substantial portion of his anatomy balanced on my left knee until I managed to edge him off.

At the end of the ceremony, as the guards came to carry out the catafalque, the King of Spain, who was one of the chief mourners, had to push his way between those of us in the front row and the platform on which the coffin had rested. In the process he trod on my right toe. I never batted an eye. He never said a word. That was my last contact with the last king of Spain.

CHAPTER NINE

THE BREAKUP OF AN EMPIRE

SHORTLY AFTER the armistice of 1918 I was detailed as one of ten aides to President Wilson when he came to Paris. He never spoke to us or required any duties of us, so, although I was present when he arrived and for a number of days thereafter went to the functions which he attended, I had no dealings with him.

Wilson, in December of 1918, was at the height of his fame. A messianic quality in his speeches had aroused hopes among the peoples of Europe that he would usher in a new era—hopes soon spoiled when the advocates of conflicting interests read contradictory interpretations into his words. But on that fourteenth day of December no European—with the possible exception of the cynical old Tiger, Clemenceau—was yet disillusioned. The reception of Mr. Wilson was cordial, friendly, and enthusiastic.

"Pa" Watson, later a major general and friend and aide of F. D. R., was at the time a colonel in charge of the group of presidential aides. I went with him to the Gare du Bois de Boulogne, on the morning of December 14, where the President was to detrain. We arrived about an hour before he was due. French functionaries were rolling out red carpets. Officials appeared, the important ones in frock coats and high hats. A detachment of the Garde Républicaine was there, and the band of that organization was assigned a place on the platform to play "The Star Spangled Banner" when Mr. Wilson stepped off the train. A few minutes before ten there was cheering as Clemenceau came down the stairs, vigorous, stocky, and tough-looking, wearing a high hat and his inevitable grey gloves. As he was being "shot" by the movies, President and Madame Poincaré were announced. At ten on the dot, President Wilson's train pulled in. The band sounded flourishes and played the national anthems as the Wilsons were greeted by the Poincarés. Rarely have I seen a man grin with more satisfaction than did Wilson. As soon as the presidents started up to the street, the crowd of "notables" broke like a mob, and Clemenceau, General Pershing, Ambassador Sharp, and the rest were pushed up the stairs in the rush of the reception committee to see the presidents leave. Guns boomed. Crowds cheered. The accolade of the Parisians came from the heart.

The aides had not been assigned places in the presidential cortege. As I left the station to find a taxi, I passed General Pershing's car, the four stars showing in all their glory. On the back seat was a large, stout, jovial-looking Negro woman, and beside her sat a big, portly, round-faced Negro man, both smiling happily. They were Mrs. Wilson's maid and the President's valet. Next to the driver sat one of our group of officers detailed as aides to the President—a Harvard graduate and member of the Knickerbocker Club and the inner circle of old New York society.

Life in Paris as an inactive aide of an invisible President soon palled. When, therefore, Professor Coolidge of the history department of Harvard asked me if I would join his mission to Vienna for the American Commission to Negotiate Peace, I hailed the opportunity. The collapse of the Austro-Hungarian Empire meant a complete reorientation in central and eastern Europe. Vienna would be the best place to see history in the making. To a would-be historian this was the chance of a lifetime. To be there under Coolidge would be particularly interesting as he had a scholarly knowledge of Europe and was wise and shrewd in appraising conflicting claims, statements, and influences.

Our echelon of the Coolidge mission was held up a few days at Berne by passport formalities. At the Austrian border two of the Emperor's private cars were attached to the through train to Vienna for our comfort. Everywhere we saw, either in the open or freshly covered with paper, the well-known initials "K. und K."—*Kaiserlicher* and *Koeniglicher* (Imperial and Royal)—which under the reign of Emperor Franz Josef had become inseparably identified with the Hapsburg monarchy. They were symbols of unity in a region which for generations had been divided by racial, religious, social, political, and economic conflicts—a unity originally imposed by force but fused through the industry and skill of Franz Josef. The old Emperor, who had ascended the throne in 1848, had been dead only two years when we entered this remnant of his former empire, but despite the great impress of his personality, the way of life that he had fostered and the ingenious political structure that he had built had gone with the storm. The houses in the sunny Salzkammergut were still trim and clean, looking as if they belonged in a picture book. The passengers on our train still read their favorite Viennese journals. But, as we were soon to learn in cold, drab, starving Vienna, the storm had been a hurricane which had demolished the frame of the empire.

In its place seven racial groups divided the Hapsburg heritage, each nation taking as much as it could grab. Italy seized parts of the Tyrol, the Trieste area, and Dalmatia. Serbia incorporated Croatia, Slovenia, the rest of Dalmatia, and other regions into what became Yugoslavia. Romania helped herself to Transylvania. Galicia became part of the new Republic of Poland. Bohemia and Slovakia joined to form the Czechoslovak Republic. This left Vienna and a truncated Tyrol under the so-called Austrian Republic, and the central plains of Hungary under the provisional presidency of a left-wing Hungarian magnate.

The breakup had occurred in the two months between the Armistice and our arrival in Vienna. The change was so complete that the inhabitants of the former empire were in a daze. The citizens of the new nations were dazzled by the ease and completeness of their release from their obligations to the Hapsburg monarchy. The Austrians and Hungarians were paralyzed to find themselves stripped of their wealth, influence, and accustomed ways of life. The new nations were fired with exaggerated nationalism; the Austrians could think only of recreating in some new form the old ties of empire; and the Hungarians were bent on winning back the territories they had lost to their new neighbors. The points of view were irreconcilable.

We soon learned that the Viennese were crushed—not alone by the dissolution of the world that they had known and loved but by the insoluble problems of mere survival. Only shelter remained to them with reasonable security, thanks to decrees which prohibited landlords from ousting tenants. But shelter did not imply heat—Vienna's coal had come from sources now cut off—nor light, which was rationed to a dark minimum, and Vienna's winters are long, cold, and gloomy. As for food, the Viennese had become accustomed, after 1916, to an increasingly deficient diet, but with the dismemberment of the empire the bare essentials for survival were often unobtainable, even at a great price. As the winter dragged on, the greenish-yellow lines of malnutrition around pinched mouths and reddish noses became accentuated.

The Viennese despaired not only of the present but of the future. The middle classes and the élite—including artists, musicians, actors, professors, engineers, lawyers, and doctors who had helped to maintain the best in a great and gay cosmopolitan civilization—faced not only spiritual but also physical extinction through financial attrition. Many of these people came from families which had prided themselves for generations on passing on to their children the cultural heritage of old Vienna. They had done this by frugal living, saving every groschen, so that the next generation might better obtain the high education and thorough technical training which they so greatly cherished. They foresaw few openings for musicians or other artists in the new Austria. Already Vienna was so saturated with doctors, engineers, and professors living in genteel starvation that it would be as cruel as it would be futile to prepare children for a lifework in these professions. The lower classes lived in even more abject poverty than before the dissolution of the empire. Unemployment was widespread.

The decay of the city was not solely human. The new poverty made it impossible to maintain private and public housing at survival levels. The physical disintegration of the city had begun—leaking roofs, broken windows, collapsing walls, which could not be repaired. Public and private palaces housed the homeless, speeding up the processes of deterioration. Vienna was repeating the experience of Rome in its period of decline, when public buildings which the heirs to the Cæsars could not—or would not—maintain in repair, had been used to house the proletariat and to stable goats and donkeys. Through the centuries the accumulation of rubbish, filth, and the dust of the ages had completed the decay that had begun with disrepair. In Vienna a similar process had started.

As I spoke German, Mr. Coolidge not only used me to talk with many who came to our mission but also charged me with reading the Austrian newspapers and meeting their editors. Among the latter, one of the great figures of continental journalism of the nineteenth century was still alive—Dr. Moritz Benedikt, the owner and editor of the *Neue Freie Presse*—vigorous, pugnacious, highly intelligent. It used to be said that, next to Dr. Benedikt, the old Emperor Franz Josef was the most powerful man in Austria. Wickham Steed, who spent ten years in Vienna as correspondent for the *London Times* before he became editor of that great paper, described the *Neue Freie Presse* as having an influence probably unsurpassed by that of any journal of equal circulation in the world, and he characterized Dr. Benedikt as "a journalist of genius—a tyrannical, vindictive genius, under whom his staff and many of his readers groan, but a genius nevertheless."

His detailed knowledge of people and conditions in central Europe in the past half-century was of help to me in understanding the fundamentals of the Danubian problem. As clear as he was voluble, he was patient in his efforts to enlighten me about the commonplaces as well as the complexities of central Europe. He explained that Austria's immediate objective must be to live through the crisis caused by the breakup of the empire. German-speaking Austria was so dependent on the territories which had made up the former empire that it could not survive economically unless pressure was brought to bear from the outside on its neighbors to resume their commercial intercourse with Austria. He pointed out that within the boundaries of the new Austria the necessary raw materials were not to be found. In later talks he

[94]

repeatedly insisted that in his opinion the only solution was a tariff union among Austria, Czechoslovakia, Hungary, and Yugoslavia. He added that such a union could not be political, as Magyars and Czechs alike were too intolerant and aggressive. Before the war their coexistence under a single government had been possible only because of the personal prestige of the Emperor. Dr. Benedikt took it for granted that German Austria would unite with Germany, but did not feel that this would occur soon. Above all, he said, the Austrian Republic must be able to get the necessary foods and raw materials in order to pull through until the next harvest. The alternative was starvation and economic ruin, with the consequent danger of the spread of communism.

Although every conversation in Vienna and Budapest sooner or later centered on the problems of Austria, Hungary, or the neighboring nations, we had occasional reprieves from this routine. Some of these we owed to an ebullient and charming Hungarian nobleman who had been engaged by some Albanians to indoctrinate us about their country, but whose passion for dinosaurs so greatly exceeded his interest in Albania that, whenever we met, he lectured us at length on the difference in tooth structure between herbivorous and carnivorous dinosaurs or on their diets and modes of life. Another variation came through an introduction to the gentle Franz Lehar, of musical-comedy fame, and his dynamic brother, formerly a colonel in the Hussars. Lehar lived in a large apartment house which, he told me with pride, the "Merry Widows" had built for him. He was a short, stocky, square-headed man with a kindly twinkle in his eye, as indifferent to political and economic questions as his brother, the colonel, was obsessed by them. Franz was hypnotized by the dream of a Vienna that was no more—and probably never, in reality, had existed. "The world was so happy before the war," he said to me, when I complimented him on the beautiful music he had written. "Life was so pleasant. When one lived in such a wonderful place how could one help writing beautiful music?"

On the occasion of my first visit to Lehar, his brother suggested that Franz play some excerpts from the operetta he was composing at the time, called *Die Blaue Masur*. His touch was

[95]

heavy and his technique only fair. He played from memory and sang the words from a typed manuscript, but his zest and rhythm carried him through with spirit. When he tired of this he showed me his collection of photographs, garlands, ribbons, and medals to commemorate the *Merry Widow*. I was amused to find that the item which pleased him most was the original drawing by John T. McCutcheon of a cartoon in the *Chicago Tribune* captioned: "I'd like to kill the man who wrote the Merry Widow Waltz."

His brother, taller and leaner, was interesting as a type that was found only in the Hapsburg Empire—an officer who, instead of the usual strong sense of nationalism, had an overwhelming loyalty to a dynasty. He was typical of other central European military men in that he took for granted such dogmas as "might makes right," "right rests with the victor," and "the victor can do what he wishes." But, where most others whom I met were passionate Austrians or Hungarians, Colonel Lehar cared only for the Hapsburgs. In spirit he remained the subject of the Emperor, and two years later he risked his life in a futile attempt to replace Charles on the throne of Hungary, of which more anon.

After a while Franz Lehar turned from music to politics and asked me what Americans really thought about the origins of World War I. When I told him that we were convinced that Germany had started it, Franz interjected: "But don't the Americans know that King Edward spent years running around Europe trying to bottle up Germany?"

The Colonel, his brother, interrupted. "Come now, Franz," he said. "There's no point in talking like that. We all know that Germany started it because the moment was convenient for her. Other circumstances had prepared the way, but Germany started the shooting."

Among Mr. Wilson's famous Fourteen Points was one which called for "self-determination"—that is, that the people of Europe should have the right to determine for themselves their own sovereignty. To the Austrians this doctrine meant the right to rule over non-Austrian groups within the former territories of the empire. To the Yugoslavs it meant the right to annex Croatia and Dalmatia to the former Kingdom of Serbia. The Hungarians construed it to justify their retention of Transylvania, and the Romanians based their claim to that area almost exclusively on this point. Frequent appeals were made to our mission for an authoritative definition of what the term meant. But since neither Mr. Wilson nor the State Department ever furnished such a definition, we had to be discreetly noncommital.

The extent to which the doctrine inspired minority groups may be judged from a petition which was brought to me one day during the absence from Vienna of Professor Coolidge. The delegation which presented it consisted of a half-dozen distinguished-looking, elderly gentlemen wearing frock coats and high hats. Most of them had long white beards. All were blue eyed, with fine features. Their spokesman said that they were citizens of the town of Gottschee, in Slovenia—a town, they told me, which had been founded seven hundred years ago by a group of Germans. It had remained a German-speaking community throughout these seven centuries, a German ethnic island in a sea of Slavs. Because the Slavic population extended for miles in all directions, the entire area, including Gottschee, had been incorporated into Yugoslavia. This fact, the spokesman said, troubled the citizens of Gottschee, for they realized that if they were to remain permanently under the rule of what they had always regarded as an inferior race they would lose their cultural identity, of which they were justly proud. The town had a population of about sixty thousand people—all of German descent. After lengthy discussions among many groups of the citizens of Gottschee, they had decided that, in the name of Mr. Wilson's Fourteen Points, especially of that one setting forth the principle of self-determination, the town of Gottschee wished to be annexed to the United States. Nearly every family in Gottschee, the delegation explained, had relatives who had been—or were then—in America, and they therefore petitioned the Peace Conference and the American government to authorize this union. They then handed me a petition with many signatures.

I told them that I knew that the American peace delegation would be as touched by this expression of confidence in the United States as I was and promised to forward their petition to Paris, but I pointed out that there were aspects of their proposal which would require special consideration and that practical difficulties might make it hard to carry out their wishes. Then, very solemnly, the elderly gentlemen filed out of my office, and I led them to the elevator and again thanked them profusely. The petition went to Paris—and never again was heard of.

A few weeks later a little war—one of several that went on almost unnoticed during that first winter after the Armistice—was started between the Austrians and the Yugoslavs, each side insisting that its actions were justified by the principle of self-determination. The fighting took place on the southern border of Carinthia, near the town of Klagenfurt. The crest of the Karawanken Mountains lay a few miles south of the Klagenfurt Basin and formed the frontier line. The area between the basin and the mountaintops had for generations been peopled by Slovenes who had pushed across the mountains from neighboring Slovenia. Because of the steepness of the mountains, these Slavs were cut off from their kinsfolk on the other side of the border. Their economic and social ties had long been with the German-Austrian elements in the Austrian province of Carinthia. Because they were of Slovene blood, however, the Yugoslavs insisted that their territory be incorporated in Yugoslavia and, early in 1919, sent in troops to occupy the Klagenfurt Basin. The Austrians took several sample polls in the district, and, when they discovered that a majority of the people polled wished to remain under Austrian rule, the government in Vienna resisted the advance of Yugoslav guerillas and served notice that they were doing so in the name of self-determination. The war was not very bloody, but as its continuation might embarrass the Peace Conference, in Paris, the Coolidge mission in Vienna was instructed to report on its progress. Mr. Coolidge wanted to send me to Klagenfurt but was denied permission by the American delegation in Paris. So, instead, he charged me with ferreting out as much information about this "war" as I could gather in Vienna and, in particular, to keep in touch with the Italian mission in Vienna, which was deeply concerned about what the Yugoslavs planned to do with the territories which they had taken from Hungary and Austria.

The Italian mission was headed by an able, intelligent, and amusing Italian general by the name of Segre, a stocky, rollicking man, who was at heart kindly and friendly towards the Austrians yet rather enjoyed playing the role of the stern conqueror of the great empire which had long been the traditional enemy of Italy. Segre and I met almost daily for weeks. Usually we spent the first half of each meeting exchanging formalities and compliments. Then, without asking me directly, he would try to find out if I had any news which he did not have, while I tried to find out what, if anything, he knew which I had not yet heard. I think that he, like myself, recognized that there was something farcical about this middle-aged Italian major general and this youthful American captain fencing about a border incident which neither the American nor the Italian governments would admit existed.

Another little war occurred at about this same time between the Czechs and the Poles, and, although our mission had no direct contact with it, we had reports and were interested because of its possible repercussions. The first news of it was brought by the celebrated American pianist and conductor, Ernest Schelling, who, thanks to his friendship for the pianist Paderewski (at the time president of Poland), had been sent to Warsaw as American military attaché. He stopped off in Vienna on his way to see President Wilson, in Paris, and insisted that the Americans had turned against the Poles and that Paderewski was near a nervous breakdown in consequence. When we pressed him for details we learned that the Czechs had moved their troops into the coal district of Teschen, which the Poles had occupied in the name of self-determination, since much of the population of the area was Polish. An official Czech communiqué stated that the Czech seizure of Teschen had the approval of the Entente. Placards authorizing the action had been put up in the neighborhood, signed, among others, by an American officer whose father, of Czech origin, had been left in Prague by George Creel, chairman of Mr. Wilson's Committee on Public Information. Later, from one of the most levelheaded professionals in the American diplomatic service who had been stationed in Warsaw, we heard that the decision of the Czech government to advance into Teschen had been influenced

[99]

by Creel's own remarks while in Prague. Creel, according to our informant, had told the Czechs that they were the favorite sons of the Allies, and that the United States, in particular, would support them through thick and thin. At the time, this closely reflected American public opinion. But the Czech officials, trained in the European school of indirection, accepted these remarks from a man represented as an influential friend of President Wilson as indicating that they need fear no opposition, either from the other allies or from new nations such as Poland.

In retrospect it is obvious that Creel had not intended to give the impression that anything which the Czechs did would have our support. Certainly the young officer who signed the placards had acted completely without authorization and should have been court-martialed. But the incident was an illustration of the troubles that arise when well-meaning Americans give unsolicited advice about political problems of which they know little. This incident, fortunately, soon was settled, and Paderewski's nervous breakdown was averted.

CHAPTER TEN

HUNGARY GOES RED

Early in March Mr. Coolidge asked me to take charge of our mission in Budapest. When I demurred he remarked that it would not be often that I could have a front row seat at a revolution. Neither of us realized how soon his forecast would come true. I arrived in Budapest on March 17, 1919. Four days later the revolution occurred. I left on the second day following, bound for Paris to report about it to the American members of the peace commission.

It was a red revolution, though not particularly bloody, and brought in a Communist dictatorship to replace the provisional republic of which Count Mihály Károlyi had been the head. It called for an alliance of Hungary with Soviet Russia against the imperialist Western nations which, according to the Communists, were brazenly dismembering Hungary. From the very start, the appeal of the Communists was to Hungarian nationalism, despite the fact that the Communist leaders then as now worked towards a form of imperialism in which the interests of Soviet Russia governed at the expense of all other nations. The implication was that the Communists would prevent the dismemberment of Hungary —a thing which they were neither inclined nor able to do.

Except to students of Hungarian history, the details of this revolution are of little concern. But the fact that, while the Allies were still discussing a general peace settlement in Paris, Soviet agents, acting under directions from Moscow, infiltrated the government of Hungary and managed to take it over was of international importance. Inasmuch as they directly challenged the victorious nations, the example, if successful, might well be followed by Germany. The prospect was one of chaos, if not a renewal of the war.

Hungary, it will be remembered, had long been jealous of its independence and had broken away from the collapsing Hapsburg Empire in the last few weeks of the war. It signed a separate armistice with the French commander of the Allied forces in eastern Europe several days before the German Armistice was concluded. Count Károlyi, who negotiated the armistice for Hungary as acting prime minister, told me that by throwing himself upon the mercy of the French at this early stage he expected France to champion Hungary at the Peace Conference.

His hopes were unfounded. For this mistake of judgment he was bitterly attacked, his critics ignoring the fact that no other policy—or man—could have won for Hungary the leniency that its leaders sought. Neither a stronger nor a more devious leader than Károlyi could have nullified the forces of nationalism in the neighbor nations which made the dismemberment of Hungary inevitable. Why should the victorious Allies have denied to the Yugoslavs, Romanians, and Czechs territories formerly incorporated in Hungary where the Magyars were only one of several racial groups?

I had numerous long talks with Károlyi, not only during this particular crisis, but during a previous visit to Hungary. A member of one of the most powerful noble families of Hungary, he was also related to the leading "magnates," as the great landholding aristocrats were known. Large of frame but somewhat gangling, he had a harelip, a cleft palate, and was walleyed. So completely had he dominated these handicaps that after the initial meeting one was never conscious of them. He was an armchair liberal, lacking political experience and unfortified either with strong convictions or a forceful personality. His enemies said that he was a tool of the radicals, who gladly used a count belonging to one of the most famous families in eastern Europe to spearhead the revolution which they planned and of which he was only dimly perceptive. Just as the members of his own class had no confidence in him, so the radicals distrusted him, fearing that his relatives and other fellow magnates would influence him to check the innovations which the revolutionists intended to impose. Károlyi was thus, in fact, the unsupported head of a disjointed nation, tolerated by reactionaries and radicals only because both thought that he could influence the Allies against the final dismemberment of Hungary at the Peace Conference.

From one of the leading conservatives, Count Mikes (pronounced Mee' kesh), I received, two days after my arrival in Budapest, a forecast which was remarkable for its accuracy. The trend of the Károlyi cabinet, he warned, was constantly to the left, and Károlyi was rapidly losing his power. It was only a question of days before the Communists in Károlyi's own government would get complete control, and the country would thus be turned over to the Soviets from within. The three Communist leaders in the Károlyi government already virtually dominated the situation. Count Mikes said that the police and the militia had been won over to the Communists, and that only by using loyal troops as a police force to back up a counterrevolutionary government was there any possibility of saving Hungary. He asked for military occupation by the Entente and for a new government to operate under the direction of an Entente commission. This commission was to have certain "true" men (including, of course, himself) to advise it.

Mikes's warning against Károlyi's weakness was impressive, but his emphasis on a counterrevolution inclined me to discredit his forecasts. Most of the analyses given me by persons of his class in Vienna had been based on fear and self-interest rather than on fact. Two days later, however, he proved to have been correct, almost in every detail.

The crisis which gave the Communists the chance to take over the government from Károlyi occurred, as I have already indicated, as a result of the presentation of a virtual ultimatum to the Hungarians by the French chief of the so-called armistice commission. This demand called for the military occupation of a large part of Hungary. Due in part to my inexperience and in part to lack of instructions, I was present, along with a British and an

Italian representative, when Colonel Vix, the French head of the armistice commission, delivered his ultimatum to President Károlyi. The United States had no member in this commission, but my predecessors of the Coolidge mission in Hungary had kept in close touch with Colonel Vix. Accordingly, when Vix asked me to attend a meeting at his office with the British and Italian representative, and when he explained that he was directed to present to President Károlyi a decision of the Peace Conference in Paris, I accepted his statement in good faith. When he said he wished the Hungarian government to have ocular proof through the presence of representatives of the French, British, and Italian governments that this decision had been taken by the Allied Powers in Paris, I tried to get into telephonic communication with Professor Coolidge in Vienna for instructions. As I could not get through to Coolidge in time, and as the British and Italian representatives expressed the view that it would not look well if the United States was not represented, I went with them. Had I realized then what I learned within a few weeks—that France had taken upon itself the role of guiding and shaping the policies of the Eastern European nations in the exclusive interest of French military needs—my suspicions would have been aroused.

We were received by Károlyi in the Royal Palace. Vix handed him a memorandum. When Károlyi had read about half of it, he said that before going further he wished to send for his minister of war. Vix suggested that he also send for the prime minister. Both were summoned. When they had read the memorandum and discussed it in Hungarian, Károlyi said that the proposal was impossible—that it clearly showed that Hungary was to be dismembered and that no government which signed such a document could survive a day. "You might as well make Hungary a French colony, or a Romanian colony, or a Czech colony," he said in English to the British representative.

After further embittered remarks from the Hungarians, Vix terminated the interview by insisting that he be given an answer by 6:00 P.M. the next day, March 21. We then left.

It was not until a year later that I learned how this astonishing decision had been put across. My informant was Professor Charles

Seymour, who later became president of Yale University. He and Professor Day, of Cornell, had been the American members of the subcommittee of the Paris Peace Conference concerned with the detailed study of Romanian affairs. The proposal to change the armistice line in Transylvania was first put before this committee by the French. Professor Day and he looked it over and saw that it was a matter of great importance which concerned the Allied Supreme Council rather than their committee and insisted that it be referred to the Supreme Council.

A few days later General Bliss, the American representative on the Supreme Council, sent for Seymour and Day and asked them to brief him about the proposal. This they did, pointing out the danger of revolution in Hungary if the decision were presented to the Hungarian government and urging General Bliss to oppose its adoption. They heard nothing further about it until news came from Budapest that the decision had been presented to the Károlyi government and a revolution had taken place.

As soon as this news was published General Bliss sent for them. He was much annoyed and wanted to know how this decision had been reached and who was responsible for it. Day and Seymour pointed out to Bliss that it had been passed by the Supreme Council and that they (Day and Seymour) had given General Bliss all the information about it before the session and had urged him to oppose it. At first Bliss denied this and said he had no recollection of it. They sent for the records of the meeting, and there it stood, in black and white, with his signature to it. Bliss had signed the minutes unaware that in so doing he was, in effect, sanctioning this action which he opposed.

Following the presentation of Vix's note the Károlyi government apparently decided that it was healthier for the newspaper printers to go on strike. Thus, rumors came thick and fast: Károlyi had resigned; a Bolshevik government had been set up; Károlyi had not resigned; Béla Kun (the Communist leader) had been made president; Károlyi had appealed to the proletariat of the world; Károlyi would remain in power; the Allied missions must leave at once; the French had been arrested; the Allied missions would not be allowed to leave; Colonel Vix had been killed by the mob; the Russians had crossed the Carpathians; Colonel Vix was well and free; the Russians were not across the Carpathians.

So it went throughout that hectic day and on into the night. As Freeman, one of the members of the British mission, and I returned to our rooms in the Ritz after dinner, we heard a volley of shots, and then some more, and soon Weiss, one of our staff, came in and said that the Reds had fired at the Allied flags above the entrance to the Ritz until they were taken down.

In the meantime I had sent the two army stenographers attached to our staff, Berryman and Snyder, down to a British gunboat which was moored in the Danube outside the Ritz, to leave our files, so that they would not fall into the hands of the Communists. When after half an hour they had not returned—it was a five-minute trip—I was much worried. Later I learned that they had reached the boat safely but, hearing shooting near the hotel, thought the climate more salubrious on board ship. During a lull in the shooting Berryman returned to the hotel for some blankets, and they then settled down for the night on the gunboat. As they were dropping off to sleep the Red guards seized the ship. Berryman and Snyder were arrested along with the British crew but were promptly released. The Communists removed all arms and ammunition from the gunboat and dismantled the engine, taking the intake pipe with them. As far as I know, this was the first time in British naval history that a vessel of the British Navy was thus unceremoniously captured at its moorings by a small detachment of landsmen.

Early on the morning of the twenty-first we could see from our window the Red guards still pacing up and down in front of the British gunboat, and, except for an occasional passing truck, all was quiet. We breakfasted as if nothing had happened. Then the newspaper arrived. It published the proclamation in full. A soviet government, alliance with Russia, and an appeal to the Germans to break with Paris, etc. As on the previous day, more wild rumors were brought to us, including "assurances" that the foreign missions would be arrested and shot. Acting on the advice of a Hungarian-American on our mission, we did not attempt to leave our hotel. At lunch we noticed that the Ritz had little red signs on the windows saying that it was under the protection of the Red guards.

The afternoon passed like the morning—with frequent new rumors and increasing uncertainty. Toward 6:00 P.M., Freeman, of the British naval mission, was sitting in our room writing when a member of our mission who was standing by the window looking out on the Danube said: "There comes a British gunboat!" Freeman cried, "My God!" and rushed out to get his hat. A minute later I saw him strolling down to the quay, his hands in his pockets, and gazing at the stars, while the little boat came in, colors flying, perky and businesslike, as if she were pulling up to a regatta landing at Cowes.

As we stood watching the new gunboat moor alongside the old one, a taxi raced to the quay, red flag flying, and four Red soldiers jumped out and ran to the moored gunboat. They had with them the spare parts which they had removed the previous day. When Freeman got back, he told me that the newly arrived gunboat had been accompanied by two monitors which had anchored below the town. Doubtless, word of this had reached the Reds and they had decided not to antagonize the British Navy by attempting to hold the captured gunboat a prisoner.

CHAPTER ELEVEN

REVOLUTION AND
REACTION

IT WAS MY good fortune that Professor Coolidge had asked one
of his associates, Philip Marshall Brown, a professor of international law, who had been long in the foreign service, to spend the
week end in Budapest to help me get started as head of the mission
there. He arrived in the afternoon of the day on which Colonel
Vix had presented the ultimatum to Count Károlyi. Brown was
a wise and experienced observer, broad-minded and liberal in his
approach.

As communications between Budapest and the outside world
were cut off, Professor Brown and I decided that one of us should
go to Vienna to report to Mr. Coolidge. Obviously Brown was
the one to stay on in Budapest. Accordingly, I joined the representative of the Hoover food mission, Lieutenant Haynes, who
had obtained a special train from the Communists to take the members of his mission out of Hungary on the night of March 22. He
had also talked the Hungarian Communists into giving him a million francs in cash to pay for a trainload of fat which Mr. Hoover
had dispatched from Triest, but which had been held up at the
Yugoslav-Hungarian border.

It was a measure of the insecurity of the Communists' control
that, instead of sending us from the main railway depot, they took
us to a station in the outskirts of Budapest. The train—a locomo-
tive and a private car—did not even stop for us, but merely slowed
down enough for us and our effects—including two silver strong-
boxes containing the million francs in cash—to be dragged aboard
the moving train. Our party included several members of the

food mission and two of the field clerks attached to the Coolidge mission. No sooner had we got under way than we put the strong-boxes on the table in the compartment and began to count the cash, which was in French francs, English pounds, and American dollars. For an hour or more we sorted, stacked, and listed these bank notes, never knowing when they might be snatched from us by the Red guards, and uncertain whether we were being taken to the border or to a prison camp.

When we had checked the million francs we found that we had a couple of hours before we would normally be due to reach the Yugoslav border town of Koprivnica. As most young Americans under similar circumstances would have done, we organized a game of poker. Through the black night our train with its Red guards chugged along slowly, while we, under the dim gaslight, concentrated on improving the hands we drew, in order the better to keep our minds off the uncertainty which we felt about our fate. Round after round we dealt the hands, discarded, drew, and placed our bets. One o'clock in the morning passed, then two. If we were actually being taken to the Yugoslav frontier, we were now overdue. But the engine puffed on steadily, and we continued our game.

Suddenly the train slowed and stopped. On a dimly lighted station platform we saw some officers in the drab brown of the Serbian Army. One of them came on board, saluted, and welcomed us to Yugoslavia. He told us that we must change trains, so taking the million francs in hand, we walked out of revolutionary Hungary into peaceful Yugoslavia—out of uncertainty back to security. I still remember vividly hearing a cock crow—several hours before dawn—as we waited at this little border station.

A Yugoslav train took us to Laibach, where the food mission representatives got in touch with their colleagues in Belgrade, and where I telephoned Professor Coolidge in Vienna. He told me to go to Paris as quickly as possible and said that he would meet me there.

Two days later I reached Paris and reported to the American delegation in their headquarters at the Hotel Crillon. There I joined Mr. Coolidge, who had just arrived. We talked with Allen W. Dulles, then one of the secretariat, who informed us that at 2:30 P.M. we were to appear before the "Commissioners." These were Secretary of State Robert Lansing, General Tasker H. Bliss, and Mr. Henry White, formerly ambassador to France and Italy. Neither Mr. Wilson nor Colonel House—the other two members of the American delegation—took part in routine meetings such as this.

Ten minutes before the hour we were in the antechamber waiting. William Bullitt, fresh from Russia, entered the Commissioners' room just as we arrived.

"He has the President's ear," someone whispered in an awed tone. "He's just back from Lenin."

In a few minutes he came out—an unimpressive figure, who was soon to earn the disapprobation of all of us connected with the Peace Conference.

At precisely 2:30 the recording secretary, Christian A. Herter (who, thirty-three years later was to be elected governor of Massachusetts), said to us:

"The Commissioners will see you now."

We were ushered into a small room in the Crillon, where the Secretary of State was slumped in a chair behind a desk. He was flanked by two tired old men with long and rather disheveled white moustaches, Messrs. Bliss and White. Herter asked the Secretary if he wished to deal first with Austria or with Hungary. Mr. Lansing passed the question on to Professor Coolidge, who suggested that we start with Hungary. Lansing then said to me: "All right. Captain Roosevelt, will you tell us about Hungary." I summarized what had happened. Mr. Lansing and General Bliss threw in an occasional question. Then the Secretary asked me what my solution was. As a twenty-six-year-old army officer it struck me as incongruous to be asked to give a solution for dealing with such a serious international crisis. I replied that I felt it was up to Paris to offer a solution, and added that the British and Italian representatives in Budapest had suggested military intervention. Both Bliss and Lansing rejected this as impractical.

"Isn't there any other way out?" Mr. Lansing asked. My reply was that delay might induce the Germans to profit by the example of Hungary and defy the conference. Both White and Bliss concurred in this, and Bliss, looking at his watch, said he would try to get to Mr. Wilson before the President took up this question with the French at three o'clock. We talked a little more

N. Y. Herald Tribune Syndicate

REPUBLICAN ISOLATIONISTS VS. WOODROW WILSON, BY "DING"
They rejected Wilson's plea to help Europe after World War I

while Herter tried unsuccessfully to get Mr. Wilson on the telephone, and as our allotted ten minutes were then up, Mr. Lansing announced that he had to leave.

At that time the Commissioners seemed ineffective. In retrospect this same impression persists, but it is clearer now than it was then that this was due not so much to their personalities as to the fact that Wilson was the principal spokesman for the United States and by nature played a lone hand. His distaste for criticism led him not only to shun those whose opinions differed from his but also to keep advisers at arm's length. Already he was dissociating himself from Colonel House, one of his few intimates—a man who had sought to make up for his own (and Wilson's) lack of knowledge of Europe by mobilizing experts as advisers for the American peace delegates. One of the by-products of Mr. Wilson's lone-wolf technique was that the other American commissioners were confined to dealing with the mass of secondary problems which inevitably come up at international conferences. This is an important wheel-horse function, but as none of the three Commissioners was a man of outstanding ability or force, they had little, if any, influence on the shaping of policy. General Bliss had been a meticulous professional soldier. He was long past his prime. Mr. White's horizon was limited by a snobbish overconcern with high society. Mr. Lansing, who had been a good solicitor of the State Department and whose specialty was international law, rather than international politics, was, to quote a phrase which Henry Adams used to describe him to me, a "first-rate clerk." Whatever initiative these men had was stymied by Mr. Wilson's individualistic method of work. Furthermore, they, like all other members of the delegations to the Peace Conference, were held in leash by the fact that an international gathering such as that at Paris in 1919 can neither impose settlements nor mete out justice. Its function must be to make compromises and adjustments between conflicting claims. Horse-trading was thus unavoidable. As national interests were in constant and often irreconcilable conflict, points were yielded only reluctantly, and then only in exchange for concessions which could be profitably paraded by the beneficiary. The resulting treaties were thus foredoomed to be unsatisfactory. Like other treaties before and since Versailles, they would be modified in the process of enforcement or by the tacit lapse of clauses impractical to enforce.

The contrast between the gentlemen at the Peace Conference and Herbert Hoover, who was in Paris as head of the American Food Administration, was striking. Colonel Logan, Mr. Hoover's chief of staff, took me to see him the same day I went before the Commissioners. Mr. Hoover said that he would sum up the situation in Hungary as he understood it, and asked me to correct him if in any details he was misinformed. He then asked me what his representatives in Hungary thought should be done about the trainloads of fats. I told him that they felt that, as these shipments had been agreed to in advance of the revolution and paid for in cash, they should be delivered. Mr. Hoover asked if I agreed. He then rang for a stenographer and dictated two cables. One was to his representatives in Yugoslavia, where the shipments were being held up, directing that the trains be sent forward forthwith. The other was to the Yugoslav government stating that if further obstacles were placed in the way of these shipments he would hold up shipments to Yugoslavia. When, later, he learned that the French were trying to force the Yugoslavs to delay the shipments, he obliged the French authorities to cease interfering. We discussed the possibility that the Communists in Hungary would make political capital out of the shipments of fats, but agreed that the essential thing was to get the trains into Hungary so that the fats could be distributed to the people who needed them, regardless of politics.

Mr. Hoover was fortunate in not having to bother with political or diplomatic compromises. As the food czar of the world, he could dispose of the supplies which he controlled without asking anyone's O. K. Because he was free to act—and acted without delay—we marveled and applauded. Because the Commissioners could not act even if they so desired, we judged them harshly, which was as unkind as it was unfair to them.

Early in April we were back in Vienna and found that the French and British representatives there had begun very quietly to flirt with Hungarian counterrevolutionists in the hope of using them to overthrow the Communist government in Hungary headed by Béla Kun. The British leaned towards the re-establishment of a monarchy. The French objective was more immediate —to oust the Communists by any means.

The French delegate, who had arrived there shortly after the Hungarian revolution, was one of the better second-string Foreign Office men, Allizé by name. He had been French minister to Bavaria and was at the moment minister to Holland. He looked like a caricature of a Frenchman of the boulevards in the gay nineties. With a wavy moustache and long hair, his daily costume included a high, broad collar, a flowing four-in-hand of bright colors, a brown derby (model 1901), and a narrow-waisted coat, resembling a cutaway but made of rough cloth. His trousers were ballooned and were of a checkerboard pattern. The shoes were long in the toe and flat, and his spats harmonized with the rest of his costume. Under this comical exterior he was a man of wit, discernment, and Gallic clarity of thought. He and I were in the same car on the *Orient Express* to Vienna when I returned from Paris. Thereafter I talked with him often and enjoyed the combination of sympathy and skepticism with which he viewed eastern Europe—sympathy for the people, and skepticism about the solutions put forward in their behalf. Openly he favored union between Austria and Bavaria, which meant, of course, the dismemberment of Germany and the creation of an all-powerful Catholic South German state to counter the weight of Protestant Prussia. I presume that this plan was approved by the Vatican, although it must have been viewed with reservations by those policy-makers in the church who, while never abandoning their dream of increasing the Vatican's influence in Mid-Europe, must have known of the practical difficulties in the way of maintaining Germany as two separate entities. Everything in Allizé's past—his origins, his education, his Catholicism, his culture—made him a bitter opponent of bolshevism. As a trained diplomat, he was aware of the possibly adverse reactions from military intervention against the Béla Kun régime. The alternative was to back any Hungarians who might be able to drive out the Communist government.

[114]

Great Britain's representative in Vienna was as nearly a caricature of the nineteenth-century English civil servant as Allizé was of the Parisian dandy. Stoop-shouldered, monocled, tongue-tied, tall, awkward, and angular, Colonel Cunningham was a resourceful, courageous, and effective British agent. His mannerisms were calculated to mislead people into underestimating his intelligence.

For a month or more, he and Allizé extended their contacts with potential Hungarian counterrevolutionists. They never told us their plans, but from Hungarian informants we gathered that money and arms—the latter only in small quantities—were being made available, and that a definite coup was being projected. In Hungary the Communist leader, Béla Kun, was finding it difficult to run the country without outside aid. Although Russia was free with advice, it was unable to give him the kind of support which a generation later it gave to another Communist government in Hungary.

In May, almost simultaneously in Austria, Hungary, and eastern Europe, came one of those psychological *détentes* in European diplomatic developments whose causes cannot be determined. Fear of the extension of communism faded. In South Germany and in Austria, socialist governments which had hesitated to repress Communist activities, after the outbreak in Hungary, began to take action. Austria even went so far as to arrest the Hungarian minister and his mission. The Viennese newspapers printed stories that an anti-Communist coup in Hungary was in process of formation, and the incredible Allizé even gave an interview stating that the Béla Kun government would fall any minute. Relief was widespread not only in eastern Europe but in the countries of the West, for it was generally believed that if communism were crushed in Hungary it would not spread elsewhere.

In the midst of all this—it was on the afternoon of May 4— Mr. Coolidge asked me to go for a walk with him in the Prater. We talked of many things at first.

"What," said A. C. C., "do you think could be done to strengthen the government of Béla Kun more than anything else in the world? I mean something which more than anything else would give it a new lease of life."

"I can't imagine," said I.

"What would you say if I told you that Paris wants Béla Kun to send delegates to the Peace Conference?"

"That they were crazy!"

"Well, they do. Cunningham told me this morning that Allizé had received instructions from his government to invite the Hungarian government to send delegates."

"But they're insane!" was all I could say. The fire engines had got the blaze under control and would soon extinguish it. Only oil could make it burn again. And Paris had sent the oil.

"Can't they protest?" I asked.

"The instructions are definite."

"But Cunningham is a man of ingenuity," I insisted.

"Yes, but the decision comes from above."

It was a bad moment for the Western world. If Béla Kun received the invitation, his prestige would be so enhanced that bolshevism would be revived in strength through eastern Europe. We were helpless as we waited and watched.

Fortunately Allizé hesitated, even though his instructions were categorical, reading that the invitation was to go to the Hungarian government, "*tel qu'il soit*" (whatever its composition). He realized the disaster which would probably result from carrying out his instructions and believed that they should be rescinded, but he did not feel that he alone could take the responsibility of refusing to carry them out.

At this juncture, Colonel Cunningham came to the rescue, persuading Allizé to hold up the invitation and to protest to the French foreign office. At the same time, Cunningham, using the channels of influence which in England are still open to wearers of the old school tie, saw to it that the British representatives in Paris brought pressure on the French government to rescind this order. My recollection is that Arthur Balfour—next to Lloyd George the most influential member of the British delegation—was an old friend of Cunningham's, and that it was to him that the Colonel telephoned.

With canny caution, Cunningham told Allizé that, as one of his staff was about to leave for Budapest, it would be well for this officer, Major Borrow, to take the message to Béla Kun with him under orders not to present it until Monday noon and to keep in touch by telephone with headquarters in Vienna. Allizé agreed. Borrow left for Budapest on Saturday night. He remained there Sunday and Monday. Toward eleven o'clock Monday morning, just an hour before the time limit expired for presenting the invitation, Cunningham telephoned him to return to Vienna without delivering it. The decision had been rescinded. Béla Kun was left out of the Conference.

The only plausible explanation of France's original decision is that Allizé had been overconfident in his reports to the Foreign Office in Paris about his negotiations with Béla Kun and had prematurely anticipated Kun's capitulation and acceptance of the French terms. Presumably the Foreign Office, thinking a Hungarian *coup d'état* had already been accomplished, at once invited the new government, *"tel qu'il soit"*—that is, whether conservative, coalition, liberal, or radical—to send delegates to the Peace Conference in order thus to give it the prestige of official recognition by the Entente.

The incident was enlightening as an example of the part played by the personal element in the conduct of international relations. Had the highly intelligent Allizé not been initially so overconfident and, later, had he not been stiffened by his apparently simple-minded British colleague to resist the orders of the French government, communism would have had a new lease of life in 1919.

The last time I saw Colonel Cunningham he gave me a message for A. C. C. laconically, brokenly, in short jabs of words, with a completely bland and vacuous expression on his face. Without further ado he left. Suddenly he reopened my door and said: "How's the Professor? Still writing letters to Santa Claus?" and withdrew before I could even laugh.

In those few words he aptly summed up Mr. Coolidge's principal occupation during the preceding months. True, Professor Coolidge had sent on to Paris much useful information. But he might as well have addressed his communications to Santa.

CHAPTER TWELVE

A HAPSBURG POSTLUDE

EARLY IN MAY, 1919, a telegram to Mr. Coolidge, signed "Lansing, Secstate," directed that forthwith he wind up his affairs in eastern Europe, disband the personnel of the mission, and report to the American Commission to Negotiate Peace at the Hotel Crillon in Paris. With jubilation we younger members hailed this first step in our return to America. The older and wiser A. C. C. hoped, and was permitted, to resume his original assignment of 1918—participation in the drafting of the peace treaties with Austria and Hungary. To this work, during the ensuing summer he brought his familiarity with current eastern European problems. He was able to influence his British, French, and Italian colleagues in favor of peace terms which should be at the same time just and reasonable. But the cards of history were stacked against Austria and Hungary, and the people of those countries were destined to pay heavily for the mistakes and blind spots of the Hapsburgs.

Glad as I was to get home and to turn my back on the problems of eastern Europe which we had watched so futilely, my interest in the area persisted, and in the succeeding years I welcomed the occasional contacts with friends from Austria and Hungary. One of these meetings was with Count Paul Teleki in the summer of 1921, during the first session of the Institute of Politics at Williamstown. He had just resigned as prime minister in the government which had been formed in Hungary by the counterrevolutionists under Admiral Horthy. One evening, when we were talking about Hungarian affairs, the conversation turned to the attempt of the former Austro-Hungarian Emperor, Charles, to regain the throne of Hungary only a few months before. It had been reported in the American newspapers at the time that Count Teleki had had advance notice of the Emperor's plans, and I asked him if this was so.

He answered: "Most assuredly not," and added that he had since found out that no person of responsibility or importance in Hungary knew anything about it.

A summary which I wrote immediately after our conversation gave his story as follows:

The Emperor's arrival in Hungary in March of 1921 not only had been unexpected by the government, but had obviously occurred ahead of the plans made by his own followers. Teleki based this latter assumption on the fact that the palace of Bishop Mikes at Szombathely, where Charles made his headquarters, was being renovated when the Emperor arrived, as if to prepare for his coming the following month. Besides this, a large number of the troops under the Emperor's followers in West Hungary were on leave at the time, and Colonel Lehar (my friend of Vienna, brother of the *Merry Widow* man), who was in command, had hardly 150 men on duty. Had the Emperor been expected, a larger force would have been in readiness. Teleki added that one of his ministers who saw a lot of Bishop Mikes, the Emperor's host, told him that he was satisfied that Mikes had expected Charles on April 25 instead of March 25.

Disguised as a Spaniard, with a Spanish passport, Charles left Switzerland for Strasbourg and there met a Frenchman, also with a Spanish passport. They bore letters from the British Red Cross and went through Germany to Vienna. There some of the Hungarians had arranged for the Emperor's passage to Szombathely, across the Hungarian border, which was made by changing from autos to wagons to autos, to avoid capture by the frontier guards.

As Teleki was prime minister at the time, I was naturally curious to learn how and when he got the news. He explained that he was staying at Count Tony Sigray's country estate with Grant Smith (the American commissioner) on the first holiday that he had had in eleven months. Teleki had left word in Budapest that he was not to be disturbed about anything short of a matter of gravest concern. On his third day at the Sigrays' he received this urgent message from Szombathely: "Come at once. Something terrible has happened!" He and Count Sigray immediately motored to Szombathely. Fortunately the news of the Emperor's arrival at Bishop Mike's palace had not yet spread, but the problem remained how to prevent the situation from getting out of hand with the almost certain result of civil war.

When Teleki presented himself to the Emperor he found him determined to push on to Budapest—if necessary, with troops. Charles was convinced that he had only to show himself in the capital and the people would rise to greet him. Teleki explained to him that to advance on Budapest with troops would certainly mean civil war. In view of the gravity of the emergency, Teleki took it upon himself as chief of state to detain the Emperor at Szombathely until the problem could be settled. Teleki's first act was to have himself named commander in chief of the Army. He then sent for Colonel Lehar and asked him the direct question: "If I give you an order, and the Emperor gives you another, what will you do?"

"I should resign," said Lehar.

So Teleki sent for one of the strongest Hungarian generals and held him in reserve ready to replace Lehar in case the latter resigned. At the same time, Teleki assured himself of the support of two of Lehar's principle officers. They convinced him that in case of a showdown they and most of the troops would side with Teleki. To make assurance doubly sure, however, Teleki had some extra battalions stationed near by to be called in case Lehar and the others changed their minds.

Then started the negotiations, during which Teleki told me he sent four *miles* of telegrams to Budapest—they totaled sixty-five hundred meters. It was obvious to everyone except Charles that the proposed plan of an immediate restoration was impossible. The Emperor would not listen to reason and insisted on going to Budapest. Finally Teleki decided that the Emperor would be safer in Budapest and agreed to let him go.

"I will go at once," said the Emperor.

"No. You will go in three hours," said Teleki, "and it is I who will go at once."

But the Emperor was impatient and left in a high-powered car twenty minutes after Teleki, reaching Budapest before him. There, instead of the warm reception which he expected, the Emperor found everyone surprised and displeased. Of the scene with the Regent, Admiral Horthy, I know nothing except that Teleki said Horthy told Charles just what Teleki had told him—that restoration was impossible and that the Emperor must leave at once.

Accordingly they sent him back to Szombathely, but Charles was still unconvinced and refused to believe that, between himself, the lawful king of Hungary, and the government of Horthy and Teleki, the Hungarian people and Parliament would choose the latter. Teleki therefore decided that, if he could get a vote of Parliament showing complete confidence in himself as prime minister, the Emperor would see that the Teleki government had the backing of the whole country. When Parliament met, Teleki consulted with the heads of the parties and urged them to pass any kind of a resolution, even if it was only about the weather, so long as it was unanimous. This they did, and then, at last, Charles began to realize that his cause was futile.

Before the Emperor finally left Hungary, Teleki asked him why he had thought that the time had come to try such a coup.

"It was my own idea," said Charles.

"But you must have had advice from someone," Teleki insisted. "You must have received word that the time was ripe."

"Yes, but I cannot tell from whom."

Teleki continued to press him to no avail. Finally he said to him: "But, your Majesty, it is not as Paul Teleki that I ask this. It is as prime minister of Hungary, and I must *insist*."

"Well," said the Emperor finally, "it was Briand!" (at the time prime minister of France).

Here Teleki turned to me and said: "You can imagine how I felt. It simply bowled me over," and he added that later the Emperor told him of his own accord that Prince Sixtus, his brother-in-law, had acted as go-between with Briand and that apparently the plan had been hatched at a lunch at which Sixtus, Briand, the Princess Murat, and several other French reactionaries were present. Teleki gathered that Briand's idea was: "Go ahead, and if you succeed, we will talk about negotiations. If you fail, there will be nothing lost."

The incident is enlightening not only as a sample of the complete cynicism of French foreign policy but also as showing how handicapped are kings and princes through the isolation in which they live. Later in Hungary I saw more evidence of this when I came to know other members of the Hapsburg family. Well-bred, courteous, well-educated, most of the Hapsburgs had few contacts with any but their own relatives and with sycophants and court toadies. Hence they lacked experience in sensing the true course of events. Charles, who was a devout and upright man, had been told repeatedly by his family and close associates that the throne of Hungary was his by divine sanction as well as by legal right. Thus wishful thinking, reinforced by religious faith and the promptings of his family, led him to believe that he had only to reach out his hand to take back what was lawfully his.

It would be unkind to blame Charles for his anticipatory gesture in this instance. There can be no doubt about the genuineness of the Emperor's disbelief when Teleki told him that his return to Hungary at the time was impossible. From other sources I later heard that many of the Hapsburgs—presumably including the Emperor—looked upon Horthy's and Teleki's resistance to the restoration in 1921 as "disloyal" and blamed it on Horthy's selfish desire to continue as "His Serene Highness the Regent of Hungary." Yet no dispassionate observer of conditions in Hungary and the neighboring states at the time can doubt that Teleki and Horthy were right or that, if they had yielded to the Emperor's insistence, there would have been not only the civil war against which Teleki warned the Emperor but also a new invasion of Hungary by the neighbor nations, led, in all probability, by the Czechs.

That Briand must have been aware of these probable consequences is axiomatic. He was far too wise about the affairs of Europe to have been blind to them. The presumption, therefore, is either that, out of courtesy to Prince Sixtus, he hesitated to say flatly that France would oppose a successful *coup d'état* by the former Emperor, or that, if the coup succeeded, he thought it might be helpful to him to have in Hungary a king by the grace of Briand who could be used as a counterweight to the Czechs, Rumanians, and Yugoslavs when they sought to do anything of which France disapproved .The only other possible explanation is that Briand, foreseeing the sure failure of this attempt at restoration, encouraged it in order to eliminate Charles permanently from the scene. This, too, implied complete cynicism—a quality which, while widespread among Frenchmen, the world had not regarded as a characteristic of Briand, whose pose had always been that of a man of candor, reasonableness, and good faith.

CHAPTER THIRTEEN

A GENERAL SEEKS THE PRESIDENCY

IN THE WINTER of 1919–20 I joined the group working for the nomination of General Leonard Wood for president in the Republican convention to be held in June, 1920. I had seen the General frequently when I returned from Europe in the spring of 1916 and was much impressed with his ruggedness, his earnestness, and his modesty. Close association in the next few years enhanced my admiration for him. He had courage, common sense, tolerance, fairness, and gentleness. In 1916 he had seemed the ideal man for the presidency. I said so on one occasion to T. R. and found him sympathetic to the idea. When I told the General of T. R.'s reaction, he was, of course, pleased, and encouraged me to sound him out further. This I did, and T. R. asked me to tell the General that he was favorably inclined towards his nomination but was not in a position to come out for him openly, and that, even if he were, he doubted if such an endorsement would help the General more than it would hurt him, in view of T. R.'s own relation to the Republican leaders and the fact that the difference between the Progressive party and the Republicans still remained to be adjusted. A few months later, when the Republican convention met, T. R. was asked by the convention leaders if he regarded the selection of Root, Knox, or Fairbanks for presidential candidate as suitable. He replied in the negative, and suggested, instead, Leonard Wood or Henry Cabot Lodge. As the intermediary between the Republican convention leaders and T. R. was Nicholas Murray Butler, who hated Wood, Butler told T. R. that Wood was "impossible" but that he would consult about Lodge. Ultimately the nomination went to Charles Evans Hughes.

In March of 1920, General Wood asked me to accompany him as secretary and aide, which I did through the preconvention campaign, going everywhere that he went. As a political experience it was illuminating and disillusioning—illuminating because for the first time I had the chance to tour the country and meet political leaders of all kinds in small as well as large centers; and disillusioning because it showed clearly that it takes more than ruggedness, earnestness, sincerity, patent honesty, and force of character to make a successful presidential candidate. General Wood's lack of political experience made it difficult for him to distinguish the sheep from the goats. He welcomed the support of any political group, regardless of machine politics. Furthermore, he made the mistake of shifting the management of his campaign, putting it, first, in the hands of John T. King, an able, practical politician from Connecticut, then turning it over to William Cooper Proctor, a soap manufacturer who was as inexperienced in politics as was the General, and finally associating with Proctor former Postmaster-General Frank H. Hitchcock, who had managed the Taft campaign in 1908 and the Hughes campaign in 1916.

King was already out of the picture when I joined the General. I found Colonel Proctor not only ignorant of politics but blind to his own ignorance. High-minded, upright, zealous, his plan for obtaining the nomination for General Wood was to use in a presidential campaign the advertising methods that had proved successful in selling soap. If you spent enough on ballyhoo, enough people would buy your soap. The basis of ballyhoo was publicity, and the basis of commercial publicity in those pre-radio days was the press and billboards. Therefore, to win a presidential nomination all you needed was to turn over enough money to a large staff of publicity men who would placard the merits of your candidate from ocean to ocean. As a concession to political custom, the candidate should be exhibited to the voters, but there was to be no restricting him to a few speeches in strategic centers. Instead he was to be booked from one end of a doubtful state to the other, speaking a dozen or more times a day, traveling by night and sleeping and eating on the run. Soap-makers knew that the right kind of publicity could sell even the wrong kind of soap. Surely, therefore, publicity could "sell" a presidential candidate who had so many admirable qualities as Leonard Wood. If enough people became convinced that they wanted Wood, the convention would have to nominate him, regardless of how the political leaders in the different states felt about him.

Such tactics could be—and were—successful in winning delegates in many states where primary elections were held. General Wood was a national hero, well known and much admired. But the super-salesman technique ignored the fact that a national political convention is made up of men who are playing for position and power, and that to these men the art of compromise is the essence of politics. Conflicting aspirations and jealousies must be adjusted. A candidate's vote-getting capacities are, of course, important, but his probable relations with the party leaders must also be carefully considered. Politicians live on patronage. Hence it means much whether a candidate is likely to "play the game" with the boys or to by-pass them and fill political offices without regard to organization needs. A man of strong and independent character aspiring to the presidency goes before a national convention with two strikes against him, regardless of the number of delegates he may control. If, in addition, he has obtained delegates by horning in on local situations in defiance of the wishes of the local bosses, he has even more handicaps to overcome. It takes skillful handling by an astute campaign manager to effect the necessary combinations through which alone enough additional votes can be garnered in a convention to obtain the nomination for such a candidate.

The General accepted the importance of this side of his campaign to the extent of bringing in the professional and experienced Frank Hitchcock. But the General, ever appreciative of favors done him, and awed by the amount of money which Colonel Proctor had poured into the Wood campaign fund, was unwilling to offend Proctor by putting Frank Hitchcock in full charge. Tactful, shrewd, and eminently practical, Mr. Hitchcock did his best to avoid ruffling Colonel Proctor's vanity and yet to overcome the bad effects of the Colonel's inexperience. But he was up against a man who was unable to see merit in other people's suggestions. The Wood organization thus was run by two men working along different lines and often almost in open conflict. To make matters worse, the General was reluctant to grapple with the resulting situation and bring the men together. This angered both. General Wood failed to realize that, if Hitchcock resigned (as several times seemed likely), the effect on Republican leaders throughout the country would be disastrous. "What's the matter with this man Wood?" they would say. "First he took on an expert political leader, John T. King, and dropped him. Now he has dropped another expert, Frank Hitchcock." The inevitable deduction would have been that here was a man with whom professional politicians could not get along. Hitchcock's resignation would have further steeled the professional politicians to prevent Wood's nomination in Chicago.

One of my tasks, ably abetted by Mrs. Wood, was to get the General to establish close relations with Hitchcock without alienating Proctor. Another was to induce Proctor to organize his part of the campaign, which included arranging General Wood's speaking itinerary, in such a way as to leave the General enough time to think and to confer with important people. In looking back over letters which I wrote home at the time, it seems incredible that the General should have put up with Proctor's plans. "Let me give you a sample day," I wrote on March 29, 1920, from Houghton, Michigan. "It was day before yesterday. We got up at 5 (having gone to bed after 11 and having made six speeches that day) and had breakfast in a cafeteria. Then a two hour ride in a day coach, and arrived at a town called St. Louis, Michigan, at 8:30. Made a speech in the street, much against his will, without even being allowed time to go to the hotel. Interrupted in the middle of his speech to be taken twenty miles by auto to a place called Ithaca. Five minutes in the hotel and then off to speak at 10 A.M. Taken away before the speech was finished to go twenty miles by auto to Alma. Had ten minutes leeway per schedule. The managers proposed to take him early to the meeting. I stepped in and said it was out of the question, and told them I would take him to Senator Roberts' house and if they would come back in twenty minutes I would let them have him. So he went upstairs and washed, and in the meantime I had Mrs. Roberts make him some tea, and when he came down, he sat in the library for a full five minutes and drank tea. Then he was rushed over to a factory and spoke standing up in the auto for twenty minutes. From there to a banquet, arriving late, and having to speak in time to catch a train. Driven away at the last minute before finishing speech, and at station found train was twenty minutes late, and so we drove him off about a hundred yards from the station to wait sitting in the sun. But the people soon spotted him and he had a crowd around him. Then we had a four-and-one-half-hour trip on a day coach. Everyone knows him, and it is impossible to keep people from coming to speak to him. At our destination we boarded a trolley full of a local committee and rode for an hour and three quarters, arriving late for a banquet. From the banquet where he spoke, he was taken to the Armory to address a big crowd, and then two hours by trolley back to Grand Rapids, arriving at 11:30 to take a train to Chicago. The train was three hours late, and the local committee had bought our tickets on a through car instead of on a local car starting from there, so that we had to change the reservations in order to be able to get him to bed a little after midnight."

The General was of no help to us in this struggle to save him from his friends, not only because he felt strongly his obligation to spend himself to the utmost to justify their loyalty to him but also because he was completely tireless and was as proud of his endurance as a young athlete. He was the only man I ever met who was more energetic than T. R. He had trained himself in the Apache campaign, in Arizona, to snatch a few minutes of sleep at any time of day or night, whether sitting or lying down, and carried this gift profitably into later life.

General Wood went into the Republican convention with more delegates than any other candidate. None better epitomized the antithesis to Woodrow Wilson, and the country was thoroughly tired of the Wilson leadership. But so tired was it, in fact, that the Republican leaders realized that they could win with a nonentity. This proved to be the final undoing of General Wood, as it was of the unquestionably able Governor Lowden of Illinois and the battling Hiram Johnson of California. Five months before the convention assembled, the controversial Harry Daugherty, shortly to discredit Harding's administration as attorney-general, had summed it up neatly when he remarked that "at the proper time after the Republican National Convention meets, some fifteen men, bleary eyed with loss of sleep and perspiring profusely with the excessive heat, will sit down in seclusion around a big table. I will be with them and will present the name of Senator Harding to them, and before we get through they will put him over." Daugherty was right, and neither the techniques of selling soap nor the political manipulations of an astute former postmaster-general in behalf of General Wood nor the strenuous campaigns of Governor Lowden and Hiram Johnson were of any avail. The rank and file of professional politicians realized that not since the days of Chester Arthur had there been such an opportunity to get power back into their hands. Harding would be thoroughly "safe." He was, in fact, the politician's presidential candidate *par excellence*, handsome, kindly, amenable, and, above all, one of the boys.

General Wood in defeat was outwardly serene and cheerful. If he felt any bitterness he hid it even from his intimates—and it is hard to believe that a strong, ambitious, able man like Leonard Wood, who came so near to being nominated for the presidency, could have seen the prize filched from him and handed to a mediocre political hack like Harding without at least tasting the dregs. I was with him when the final news came. He sat in silence for several minutes, looking grim and worn. But General Wood had had blow after blow in the course of his struggle to waken the country to the need for military preparedness and to obtain the right himself to take an active part in the war, and he had learned the hard way that when an adverse decision is irrevocable there is nothing to do but take it chin up. This he did.

Not so, however, with a lesser contender for the nomination who, in his own mind, had always seemed the one man above all others best qualified to be president of the United States—Nicholas

Murray Butler. On his way home from the Chicago convention the president of Columbia University, who had been New York's favorite son, issued a statement to the press describing General Wood's supporters as "a motley group of stock gamblers, oil and mining promoters, munition makers and other like persons" and charged them with seeking to buy the nomination for Wood. They represented, he said, "all that is worst in American business and American political life." Then, apparently in order to ingratiate himself with the Harding forces, he pictured himself as the valiant leader who had saved the Republican party from this sinister group by bringing about the nomination of Harding.

To General Wood this attack on his devoted followers, including such persons as Henry L. Stimson, Mrs. Douglas Robinson, Governor Allen, of Kansas and many other honorable and distinguished individuals, furnished a fitting opportunity to release his pent-up emotions. In a brief message which was printed from one end of the country to the other he attacked Dr. Butler's characterization of the Wood supporters as a "vicious and malicious falsehood" and as a "self-seeking, cowardly attack, made under the cloak of an alleged public service which was never intended or rendered." He concluded that he regretted to make such a statement, but that it was necessary "in this instance to brand a faker and denounce a lie." The *New York Tribune* published an open letter to Dr. Butler, addressed by Langdon P. Marvin, J. Lloyd Derby, A. L. Boyce, Paul Hammond, Monroe Douglas Robinson, Kermit Roosevelt, and George Emlen Roosevelt, pointing out that General Wood had been far ahead as the popular candidate in the *Literary Digest* poll, and that foremost among his supporters were men who, under the General's leadership, had attended military training camps at Plattsburg and elsewhere and who "gave time, work and money without any thought of self. . . . There never was a more unselfish, patriotic following," they said, "for any man, at any time, for any political office." They then contrasted General Wood's activities from 1914 onwards with those of President Butler in a manner which must have brought a blush of humiliation to the puffed-up cheeks of that perennially self-satisfied trumpet-blower. Dr. Butler, incidentally, is the only man of my acquaintance who listed in *Who's Who in America* the small number of votes he received as an unsuccessful contender for the Republican nomination for the presidency— 69½ out of 1,028 possible votes. The only time he came nearer the presidency was when the electoral college made him the residuary legatee of James S. Sherman, who died while candidate for vice-president on the Taft ticket in 1912. Dr. Butler thus received the eight electoral votes of Utah and Vermont for the vice-presidency, which left him still a considerable distance from the White House.

CHAPTER FOURTEEN

THE WASHINGTON CONFERENCE

EARLY IN 1921, Alan Dawson, chief editorial writer of the *New York Tribune*, asked me if I would like to try writing editorials for that paper. My only previous newspaper experience, besides a three-column letter to the *Tribune* from the officers' training camp which that paper had published as an editorial in 1918, was in the form of occasional articles which I sent to the *Neue Freie Presse* in Vienna and regular correspondence for *Le Temps* of Paris which began in 1919. Dawson regarded my experience in Europe and in American politics as a good substitute for reportorial training, but had I known then what I now know about newspaper work I should have insisted on starting as a reporter in the city news department. Even in the writing of editorials the reporter's training in ferreting out the essential and in phrasing it concisely and readably is of value. After a quarter-century of editorial work for the two greatest newspapers in this country, I realize that the skeptical approach which the experienced news gatherer develops is a healthy corrective for the editorial writer's tendency to allow his prejudices to color his interpretations.

As the summer of 1921 steamed on and Dawson patiently rewrote the editorials I wrote for him, it became apparent that the Harding administration was going to call an international conference, and that limitation of armaments would be one of the principal problems to be discussed. Accordingly, I began to study this subject with its cognate field, the adjustment of conflicting claims in eastern Asia and the Pacific. In September, two pages of a Sunday editorial section of the *New York Tribune* were devoted to a signed article of mine analyzing and summarizing the problems to be considered in Washington. The timing coincided with the publication of the formal invitations to the conference, with the result that forthwith I was hailed as an "expert," whereas, in fact, my familiarity with Far Eastern problems was scant.

Largely because of this article the *Tribune* decided that I could be useful in helping to cover the Washington Conference. Shortly after my arrival in Washington I was asked by the *Haagsche Post*, then the leading Dutch weekly, to send a weekly cable to Holland about the conference. This gave me a valuable connection with the Dutch delegation, which included a number of exceptionally well-informed persons. Other friends put me in touch with the Belgians, who, like the Dutch, had a special interest in Far Eastern affairs. As correspondent for *Le Temps* of Paris I had a good approach to the French delegation. As for the British—they were so skilled in using American newspapermen that they made even the least experienced cub reporter feel that the success of the conference depended largely on the way he maintained his detachment and refused to allow himself to be influenced by any partiality for Britain's point of view. Britain's case, they insisted, must rest on its own merits. At the same time they added that, if any American correspondent wanted information—especially off-the-record background in order better to understand a subject which the conference might discuss—he must not hesitate to call on the British delegation for help. American newspapermen found the British particularly co-operative whenever the State Department was reluctant to elucidate the American position about a disputed problem. Thus, the British, under the genial guidance of the astute Lord Riddell, staged one of the most effective propaganda shows in the history of modern journalism.

A few personalities at the conference stand out vividly. The most distinguished in intellect and appearance was Arthur Balfour. His prestige was great as an elder statesman, an astute politician, and a philosopher. The British used him as their spokesman at conference sessions, but as he felt awkward under the American custom of direct questioning by the press, he was exposed to contact with newspapermen only on rare occasions, and then only after having been coached on how to evade questions which he did not wish to discuss. When Mr. Balfour received us, we correspondents were made to sense that we were being given the privilege of viewing a rare old master who was to be seen with reverence and heard with awe.

In my notes from day to day, I sketched his first meeting with the press. It was in his apartment on Connecticut Avenue. Reporters were crowded into the living room. Mr. Balfour was in the center of the room, gazing hard at the yellow carpet on which he stood, occasionally looking up, rubbing his hands together, then fingering the buttons of his coat, then placing his hands behind his back, then rubbing them again, then holding firmly to the lapels of his coat. Tall, loosely knit, with long white hair, a whitish moustache streaked with straw, fine features, thick large round spectacles, a collar four sizes too big and very low, a boiled shirt, a little black bow tie tucked under the edges of the collar, a long frock coat, trousers that hung down over his heels, squaretoed boots, and a general appearance of indifference to dress, Balfour slowly teetered from toes to heels, and for ten minutes discoursed about the weather. "When last I was here, you know, it was winter. Yes. The St. Lawrence was quite frozen. There was lots of ice. And by a strange coincidence, this time as I landed in Quebec there was snow everywhere. In fact the snow lay on the ground all the way down to Albany." Turning to his secretary, Petersen: "It was Albany, wasn't it?" Petersen nodded. "Yes, Albany. The snow lying on the ground. Everywhere. Snow. Quite charming. And here I find it is spring," etc. etc. etc., in a delightful way, and, I think, with a twinkle in his eye as he looked at the carpet. He said nothing of importance but gave an impression of a simple, kindly soul, without guile, animated by the highest principles and by a desire to see the world made a better place in which to live. Nothing so narrow, so selfish, so mundane as the placing of British interests above those of other nations could possibly enter the head of anyone as benevolent and disinterested as this gentle citizen of the world. It was a perfect act—so good that even the cynical among the reporters came away with a feeling of friendliness for this distinguished old gentleman who, under his modest and diffident pose of disinterestedness, was known to be one of the shrewdest and most effective agents of British interests in modern times.

In contrast to the secluded Mr. Balfour, Mr. Charles Evans Hughes, the American secretary of state, received the correspondents almost daily, and with incisive phrases gave out as little information as he thought desirable. An experienced officeholder, he knew the value of the press at the same time that he disliked most newspapermen. His geniality was a pose and his ready smile lacked warmth. But his mind was keen, his experience wide, and his record imposing. With most of the newspapermen he got along well. But the few who sought to bring out points which Mr. Hughes preferred not to discuss aroused his resentment. Part of the fun of these conferences was to watch Mr. Hughes as, day after day, towards the end of the meetings, the shrill, plaintive voice of Frank H. Simonds, at the time one of the outstanding American journalists, would call out with intensity mingled with cheerfulness and apparent diffidence: "Mr. Secretary." It was public knowledge that there had been a feud between these two which started when Mr. Hughes was governor of New York. So, when this exceptionally able student of international affairs questioned this exceptionally intelligent Secretary of State we lapsed into expectant silence. At the sound of the familiar, rasping voice, the Secretary would toss up his whiskered chin with defiance and assume a would-be patient and receptive smile. Then, slowly and with dart-like phrases, Mr. Simonds would ask a question which sounded as innocent as, in fact, it was subtle, usually designed to trap the Secretary into an expression of opinion on a subject about which he had been purposely uncommunicative. It took self-control on the part of Mr. Hughes to answer adequately and to conceal his anger.

Also famous as a figure was Aristide Briand, head of the French delegation. A great orator, M. Briand suffered from the disadvantage of all Frenchmen abroad—his oratory fell flat in translation. Furthermore he felt—and looked—like a trout attempting to make itself at home in a vegetable garden. Everything about

[135]

America was a trial to him—the climate, the food, the ice water, the noisy traffic, the barbers, the persistence of the people in talking English. To make him even more uncomfortable, the British and Italians twisted his honest and proper presentation of France's pride in being the leading military nation in Europe into something sinister which threatened the peace of the world. Briand, as a matter of fact, had been on the defensive even before he left France, for to him the limitation of armaments was a bit of Anglo-Saxon sophistry, designed by scheming Englishmen to strip France of her leadership in world affairs.

In public relations Briand was the perpetual butt of polite and unobtrusive—but nonetheless deadly—British ridicule, and being by nature a humorless man, he felt compelled to repudiate the British innuendos just "to keep the record straight." He nearly resigned in a rage and returned to France when, in reply to a question addressed to a British spokesman by an American journalist as to why the French were so insistent on retaining the right to build submarines, the British spokesman replied that he couldn't possibly figure it out, unless, perhaps, it was in order to catch sardines. M. Briand devoted an hour or more to explaining in detail to the press that the French Navy did not engage in the catching of sardines, and that, even if it did, it would not be so stupid as to use submarines for this work—all of which brought hilarious delight to the American and British correspondents.

Most of us were aware during this session, which began just twenty years before Pearl Harbor, that the real menace to peace in the Pacific was Japan. It was thus with special interest that we established relations with the Japanese delegation and correspondents, and sought to see behind the masks which the Japanese spokesmen assumed in their contacts with the Western world.

The active head of the Japanese delegation was a remarkable man, Admiral Baron Kato, later prime minister of Japan. He was one of the two prominent Japanese of that name at the conference. One had as a first name Tomasaburo. To the American newspapermen he, of course, became known as "Tom" Kato. The other, whose first name was less easily pronounceable, was forthwith nicknamed Krazy Kato—not because of his personal characteristics, but because, at the time, Herriman's cartoons of Krazy Kat were at the height of their popularity.

In my notes I described Admiral Baron Kato as a wiry little man with a high, narrow forehead, well rounded and baldish on top. He had delicate features, hollow cheeks, a hard mouth, and deep-set eyes which were motionless and inscrutable when he was silent, and which blinked just like those of a monkey when he talked. He spoke in a low voice, but with authority and perfect self-possession. The overall impression was one of refinement combined with cruelty—an aristocrat by breeding, but ruthless, merciless, and brutal by profession. After attending one of his press conferences I noted: "Again I had the vivid impression of this man ruling a country which he had conquered by arms." Of another meeting, in which he sat at a table with all the Japanese officials and newspapermen standing behind him, and all the American and European newspapermen in front of him, I wrote that there was something menacing about him, as if he were disposing of our fate—on one side of the table all the Japanese, determined, imperialistic, Prussian, efficient, and on the other side, we poor innocents of the West, arrogant but impotent, proud but not brave, ready to talk much but reluctant and slow to act.

Because of Admiral Kato's poker face and because none of us had seen even a trace of emotion ever change his expression, many of the American correspondents set themselves the task of trying to draw a laugh or a smile from him. For weeks we got nowhere. During much of this time there had been speculation as to whether the Japanese would agree to scrap their largest uncompleted battleship, the *Mutsu*. The Japanese Navy—obviously including Admiral Kato—was absolutely opposed to scrapping it. This was well known to all of us. In a lull during one of Kato's press conferences, an enterprising American reporter called out in a cheerful voice: "Is it true, Admiral, that you are *still* in favor of scrapping the *Mutsu?*"

Before the interpreter had even translated this twist to the Admiral, who posed as knowing no word of English but understood it perfectly, Baron Kato burst out laughing and everyone joined in. After sidestepping a few more questions, he held up his hand, and the interpreter said to us: "Baron Kato says, please don't ask him any more questions or his head will be entirely empty." Whereupon the little Admiral smiled, rose, and bowed—the usual signal that the press conference was at an end—and resumed his mask as we filed out.

The Washington Conference brought out clearly the interaction between European and Asiatic affairs. Yet most American observers—myself included—failed to see that America's vital interests in Asia, *ipso facto*, gave it vital interests in Europe. We were thinking regionally instead of globally. We knew that Japanese expansion could only be on the Asiatic mainland or in the Dutch East Indies and the Philippines. We realized that the likelihood of such aggression would increase in direct proportion to the reluctance—or inability—of the British to hold Japan in check. I, for one, began shortly after the Washington Conference to warn that when the war in Europe was resumed we would probably be forced into it through the back door, i.e., through Japan's deciding to push its imperialist aims while Europe was too deep in self-destruction to interfere. Yet I failed to follow this reasoning to its logical conclusion—that it was in our own interest to take active steps to prevent another European war. Although only a handful of Americans had understood this in the twenties and early thirties, there is no excuse for the blindness of those of us who had been closely following world affairs from 1914 onwards.

As early as 1923 it was clear that the Washington Conference had not checked Japan's ambitions. But many of us hoped that the limitation of naval armaments would make aggressive war as unprofitable for the Japanese as it would be for us. Unfortunately the limitations applied only to capital ships, and no restrictions were placed on the use as naval bases of the former German islands in the Pacific which Japan controlled under a mandate from the League of Nations. If the relative strength of the American, British, and Japanese navies had been fixed for all categories of vessels, and if the United States had then maintained its Navy at the permitted maximum, an attack by Japan would have been so unlikely to succeed that the Japanese naval leaders would not have risked it.

The Washington Conference was hailed by most Americans as inaugurating permanent peace in the Pacific. The Navy League and those few individuals who campaigned for a strong Navy were branded as warmongers, while the Harding, Coolidge, and Hoover administrations allowed our Navy to stagnate. My own friends alternated between ridicule and indignation when I insisted that neglect of our naval strength exposed us to the danger of a Japanese attack. People then, as later, resented being reminded that war had not been abolished. Those of us who warned against the warlike ambitions of a particular nation were denounced as anxious for war, whereas, in fact, our sole objective was to awaken the country to the danger which lay ahead, so that it would not again be forced into a war, unprepared. But the American people, traditionally uninterested in naval and military problems, gladly accepted in the twenties and thirties the doctrine that the best defense against war was to assure the world that the United States would not fight, and then smugly washed their hands of Asia as well as Europe. Encouraged by America's neglect of its armed forces, Japan and Germany pushed their plans for war, grateful to American pacifists and sentimentalists for lulling the American people into a false sense of security.

CHAPTER FIFTEEN

THE FAR EAST IN FERMENT

M Y INTEREST in the Orient received a fresh impetus in the winter of 1925–26 when I went to the Far East for the *New York Times*, to which I had transferred from the *Tribune* two years previously. Since the publisher of the *Times*, Mr. Adolph S. Ochs, had told me when I joined his staff in 1923 that he favored having editorial writers get out into the field, I took him at his word and proposed that my itinerary include the Dutch East Indies, the Philippines, China, and Manchuria.

Important new trends were apparent in the Far East. Russia was fomenting nationalism in China, the Dutch East Indies, and French Indo-China, not out of devotion to nationalism per se, but as a means of weakening the position of the European nations and of Japan in China and elsewhere in Asia, thus increasing the relative influence and strength of the Soviets, who, like their Czarist predecessors, were reaching out to dominate Asia. Japan was backing the northern Chinese war lords and preparing for the annexation of Manchuria by extending the standard-gauge railroad system of the Japanese-owned South Manchurian Railway. Japanese and Russians alike encouraged the Chinese campaign against the long-established special privileges of foreigners as manifested through the treaties guaranteeing extraterritoriality and the independence of such foreign concessions as Tientsin, Shanghai, and the British crown colony of Hongkong. The Russians seemed to feel that they had more to gain by the crippling of British influence in China than they had to lose in the event that the antiforeign movement boomeranged against Russians in China. The Japanese were so contemptuous of the Chinese that they were sure that Japan could easily reimpose by force, for the exclusive benefit of the Japanese, any of the privileges which other foreigners had for generations enjoyed in China and which the Chinese were being encouraged to abolish for all. Still further to complicate matters there was a split between American business and missionary leaders in China, the former advocating the retention of special privileges for foreigners, and the latter supporting the antiforeign campaign of the Chinese. In the meanwhile the independence movement in the Philippines was receiving new impetus from a prejudiced and embittered campaign directed by the *New York World* and abetted by other newspapers in the United States against the allegedly "hard-boiled" and "militaristic" administration of Leonard Wood who had been appointed governor general of the Philippines in 1921. The resultant problems were sure to be much in the news. It would be a great help to an editorial writer to have learned about them on the spot.

Mr. Ochs realized better than I that, while the prestige of the *New York Times* gave its representatives an entree anywhere, the family name, coupled with the fact that I had friends in government service in the Far East, would enable me in a comparatively short time to plumb the best sources of information and to meet most of the leading figures in that vast area. Accordingly he gave me a free hand in planning my itinerary and time. It was characteristic of him that, just before I sailed from New York, he told me that he did not want me to feel obliged to write a line while I was away, because, if I had to send dispatches, time would be taken up preparing them which would better be spent in seeing people. Furthermore, if I had to seek interviews for direct quotation, people would not talk to me so freely. In this, too, Mr. Ochs was wiser than would have been any other publisher of my acquaintance. Thanks to this injunction of his I met with a degree of responsiveness and frankness rarely accorded any journalist.

In order to save time I obtained advance information on key people in each place which I was to visit, and to one of these I sent a list of the persons to whom I had letters of introduction, together with the names of those whom it had been suggested that I might see, and asked him to make appointments with anyone whom he thought I should meet. Thanks to this prearranging, I lost no time in beginning my quest for information. It was strenuous, for in the notes and diaries of the period there are entries of "Up at 4:30 this morning" or "up at 6, and met so-and-so for breakfast at 6:45," followed by interviews all morning, afternoon, and evening, including lunches and dinners and rarely to bed before eleven. The steamer trips—sometimes lasting as much as a week—gave me my only rest, although these were in large part occupied with reading and with writing up and amplifying my notes.

This latter process was complicated by the realization that my papers would probably be examined by Japanese agents, even if locked up when I went out, and that, in consequence, it was incumbent on me not to put in recognizable form any reports of conversations which might be embarrassing to my informants if seen by prying eyes. Not only was this scanning of private papers common in the Far East at the time, but it was sure in my case because of a sequence of events which convinced the Japanese that I was merely masquerading as a newspaperman. It began in Java, when the Japanese consul general attended a dinner given by the Governor General of the Dutch East Indies at which I was a guest. I could see that the Japanese was skeptical when I told him that I had a roving commission for the *New York Times*. Newspapermen in Japanese eyes in those days were about on a social level with scavengers and panders. The Dutch also were known to view them with distaste. There was, thus, obviously something fishy about a newspaperman being invited to dine with the Dutch governor general and being accompanied there, and often elsewhere, by the American consul. A month later, when I reached Manila, General Wood asked me to stay with him throughout my visit. Shortly after my arrival he had as guest at lunch the Japanese consul general in Manila. This gentleman said that he had heard from his colleague in Batavia that I had been there, and when I explained that I had a roving commission for the *New York Times*, he accepted my statement politely but obviously with the mental reservation: "Why, if this man is merely a newspaperman, as he says he is, does the Governor General of the Philippines have him as his house guest?" Two months afterwards, when I reached Peking and stayed in the legation compound, the Japanese minister to China told me that he had heard from the Japanese consul general in Manila that I had been the guest of Governor General Wood and began plying me with questions which showed that he did not believe that I was a bona fide newspaperman. In Japanese eyes it was now obvious that I must be on some mission which was clearly secret and probably sinister. The very fact that I told each Japanese official whom I met that when I reached Japan I wanted above all else to see Japanese gardens was the final proof to them of my cunning and deviousness. Obviously I was inventing this diversion in order to camouflage my fell purposes. Hence from Peking on, the Japanese overwhelmed me with courtesies and hospitality and closely watched my every move. On my arrival in Japan I was presented —unasked—with a schedule carefully designed to keep me so busy that I could not possibly do what I wanted. That my interest in Japanese gardens was genuine never entered their heads.

My itinerary took me to the Far East through Europe. In Holland I talked with Hendrik Colijn, then and on several other occasions prime minister of the Netherlands. He was frankly worried about Japanese penetration southward towards the Dutch East Indies and said that the Dutch were disturbed by the possibility of American withdrawal from the Philippines. Such withdrawal, he said, would encourage nativism throughout Asia and would effect a fundamental change in the balance of power in the Pacific.

From The Hague I went to Paris by way of Brussels, and thence to Genoa, where I boarded a small boat of the Royal Dutch Mail for Batavia. As we sailed down the glassy Strait of Malacca to the tip of the Malay Peninsula I followed our course on the charts and was struck with the fact that directly opposite the entrance to Singapore harbor, and only a few miles away, were the nearest of the Dutch East Indies. Until I saw these Dutch-owned islands so close to Singapore I had not grasped how inevitable it would be that, if the Japanese decided to take the Dutch East

Indies, they would have to occupy Singapore, and if they wanted Singapore they would have to take the Indies. The understanding which this trip gave me of that all-important and obvious—but rarely mentioned and little understood—fact was in itself of enough value to justify the long journey. In the Far East the Dutch and British were indissolubly linked together. This was sure to affect their relations in Europe.

That the British military, naval, and colonial leaders realized the potential threat to Singapore from Japan was apparent from their plans to establish a naval base there, and from the provisions already made to insure a supply of water and oil to the city of Singapore by pipe lines buried under a heavy concrete causeway connecting the island with the mainland at Johore. I chartered a launch and sailed round the island on my return to Singapore from Java a month later and saw the location of the proposed base—with a popular Japanese tea house directly overlooking it.

In the week that I spent in Singapore, meeting colonial Britishers by day and marveling by night at the persistence and ferocity of the tropical insect life, I could sense the subtle forces wearing down the white men—too much heat, ever present tropical diseases, too many gin slings, too much servility on the part of the Orientals, the boredom and petty snobbishness of a small white man's community, with its cleavages between government and business, and underlying all, the never voiced but always present consciousness that the Orientals in their hearts despised the whites. Later I was to learn more about this from teachers, missionaries, and some of the more sensitive among the other whites in the Orient, and to realize how important to international relations in the Pacific was the depth of this dislike or contempt. It was one of the chief factors in the independence movement in the Dutch East Indies which only in the last few years has finally come to a head. It lent fuel to the Philippine campaign for independence in the twenties and thirties. It brought about the forcing out of the Europeans and Americans from most of China. It encouraged the Japanese war lords to attack Pearl Harbor. Today it is still a stumbling block to mutual understanding.

Some of it, of course, was due to the arrogance and ill manners of white men in the Orient and elsewhere. The epithet "barbarians," often applied to the early European and American traders by the Chinese, was well merited. But a good measure of the latent racial antagonism was, and is, due to the innate conviction of various Oriental races that they are superior to all others. The situation is further complicated by conflicts between levels of civilization—between medieval feudalism and modern industrial democracy, to name two of the most extreme contrasts. We of the West are so addicted to clock-watching and to governing our lives by timed routine that we cannot comprehend the reactions of people to whom time means little and punctuality nothing. We are obsessed with a speed mania. Most Orientals are never in a hurry. We work furiously just for the sake of keeping busy. Most Malays work only enough to earn the bare necessities of living. As an observant Hollander put it to me in French when endeavoring to explain this trait to me. "*Nous autres, nous épargnons l'argent; eux, ils épargnent le temps.*" The nearest English equivalent is: "We [of the West] seek to lay by money; they [of the East] lay by spare time."

Furthermore, most Orientals are free from our obsession with facts. To the Occidental a fact is compelling, definite, absolute. To the Oriental, a fact, if inconvenient, is something to be ignored. He regards lying as a legitimate weapon in the battle of life. It is reprehensible only when it fails of its purpose. To view this indifference to fact and to truth as a form of moral obloquy is to judge the Oriental by European, not Asiatic, standards. It has its counterpart in the scorn with which the Oriental regards the Occidental's blindness to deceit—his inability to detect even the more obvious untruths. To the Easterner this is proof of the Westerner's obtuseness and slowness of wit; in short, another demonstration of his inferiority. To many Europeans and Americans, the suavity and apparent humility of Orientals are marks of a servile, and therefore an inferior, nature. In contrast, the impatience and brusqueness of the Occidental are regarded by the Orientals as proofs of ill-breeding. Thus the differences in fundamental attitudes create unvoiced but deep discord and continue to play a dominant role in the relations between the East and the West.

CHAPTER SIXTEEN

THROUGH DUTCH EYES

M Y INTEREST in the Dutch East Indies was to see how the Dutch handled the Indonesians. In particular I wanted to know to what extent they sought to "dutchify" the Javanese. I knew that Dutch policy had been summarized in the slogan, "Keep their bellies full but their heads empty," and that the Dutch were widely charged with "exploiting" the natives. But the truth about the relations between the Dutch and the natives was not easily found in books or reports.

In my two weeks in Java I visited schools, hospitals, and agricultural stations, traveled by automobile through much of central Java, and talked with dozens of persons, including American officials and businessmen, Dutch administrators and teachers, Germans, Chinese, and a good many natives. Obviously in such a brief time I could only scratch the surface, but, by concentrating on the field of my particular interest and carefully checking on the sources of my information, I learned much that was useful.

My stay in Java left with me a vivid impression of a people forever on the move, carrying incredibly heavy burdens slung from poles across their shoulders—a people rejoicing in bright colors, the men with batik turbans and sarongs or brilliant shorts, the women wearing highly colored shirtwaists. Most of them seemed genial, smiling, and cheerful despite the weight of their burdens, the wet tropical heat, and the obviously overcrowded living conditions in the country as in the towns and cities. Even the streams and canals seemed crowded—men and women bathing or washing their laundry, usually so many of them together that one marveled that there was room for all. Every square yard of soil was cultivated, the roads lined with tiny garden-farms, each with its minute rice paddy and with its fighting cocks and its big carabao, or water buffalo. It was a teeming, verdant, fruitful land —but one in which the span of life was short.

The attitude of the Dutch towards the natives seemed to be one of benevolent paternalism. The Dutch felt that they had a duty to be helpful, patient, and kind in their dealings with the natives, who, in turn, were vaguely and reluctantly aware that the Dutch had brought them material benefits such as roads, and that Dutch technicians and even Dutch doctors could be useful. Most of them cared little about politics, having from time immemorial left that to overlords, who frequently were of alien origin. European culture was meaningless to them. European standards of justice were incomprehensible. As for the European passion for work—for getting things done—to most of them this was one of the white man's manias, and a not very pleasant one, at that. They did not object to toiling from dawn to dark, so long as they lacked any of the simple needs of life. But once these needs were met and they had enough to live for a few days without working, no contract, no threat of punishment, no persuasion could keep them at their appointed tasks.

I visited many agricultural stations in Java, and everywhere found highly trained Hollanders working to improve strains of animals and crops and devising controls for diseases and pests. The principal beneficiaries of these new techniques were the Dutch producers of the leading tropical crops—rubber, gutta-percha, quinine, camphor, tea, coffee, spices, sugar, etc.—but in actual practice the native farmers also gained from them. Had it not been for Dutch ingenuity and persistence, Java would never have been so extensively—and intensively—developed; standards of living would have been lower, health conditions worse, and the total population smaller than it actually was.

The contrast between modernized Java and the Java of old was most apparent in the *kratons* or private palatial establishments of the native sultans and princes. I visited three of these and in each case stepped back a few centuries into a civilization that was an offshoot of medieval India. One of these was the Sultan's palace at Jogjakarta, to which I was accompanied by the local Dutch official. We passed through an unimpressive outer gate into a large open courtyard, which separated the inner palace from the outside world, and thence were led into the inner court. In the center of this court, which was shaded by enormous banyan trees, was a pavilion which covered about two acres and had a white marble floor and tall teakwood columns supporting a high red tiled roof. From this pavilion came the muffled gong-like sound of the gamelang orchestra. In the shade we could see figures going through slow, rhythmic dancing. Squatting on the ground, in complete silence, were several hundred Javanese, wearing formal court dress. For the men this consisted of highly decorated sarongs of batik with broad, elaborate belts, the upper part of the body being naked. The women wore costumes resembling pictures of the court dress of native Indian princesses, with highly colored veils.

We were seated near the edge of the pavilion in the shade overlooking the dancers as we waited for the Sultan's brother, who was to receive us officially. The sounds of the gamelang made a continual accompaniment to the movements of the dancers. Every now and then a native violin would break into a plaintive air on three or four notes in a minor key. Occasionally an elderly gentleman, dressed in gorgeous silks, who seemed to be the director of the orchestra and of the dancing, would read in a monotonous but musical voice from a book in front of him. The dancers, all men, dressed in colored but sketchy clothes, slowly went through the postures which conventionalized the action of the drama that was being intoned by the old man.

After a while the Sultan's brother appeared—a slick, oily person with fishy eyes, wearing an unbuttoned shirt, a sarong, and no shoes. His teeth were black from chewing betel nut. As he spoke no Dutch, my guide addressed him in Malay. He led us to a small European house in the corner of the court, which was the Sultan's office, where we were ushered into a little anteroom. The Sultan came out and greeted us, inviting us into his suite. The moment he appeared, his brother and the few attendants present knelt on the ground and salaamed to him. The Sultan wore a turban, a colored shirt, and a sarong. He talked volubly in Malay and frequently laughed, showing a fine set of false teeth. For a sultan, and particularly for one of his line, he was still comparatively slender and young looking. On the walls of his office were photographs of his predecessors and forebears, and hardly a one weighed under three hundred pounds. The office itself was tawdry, showing, as is so common in the Orient, bad taste in the selection of European furnishings. On the Sultan's desk as an ash tray was a porcelain saucer made by the Appolinaris Water Company—the kind used as souvenirs on dining cars. The Sultan sat at this desk, and directly opposite him sat my Dutch companion. On the Sultan's left was his brother. I sat on the Sultan's right. I noticed that the brother seemed to regard the Sultan with condescension, although whenever addressed by the Sultan he raised his hands to his face in reverence and bowed. The conversation, which took place through the Hollander as interpreter, consisted of platitudes about Javanese and American dancers. The Sultan did not care for American jazz and thought that the training of the Javanese dancers was more strenuous than that which our athletes undergo in preparing for a football match.

After a while the Sultan showed me a photograph of General Wood and told me (what I later learned was not true) that the General had been decorated while at Jogjakarta. I had been warned that the Sultan wanted an American decoration and had said as much to various Americans. Apparently he thought that I might be able to further his ambition. For a while he gazed on the picture of the General and said nothing. I, too, maintained a discreet silence.

He then pressed a bell. Instantly the door between his office and the anteroom swung open, and a servant appeared, squatting cross-legged in the doorway. The Sultan spoke, the slave salaamed, the door closed, and in a minute a procession of slaves appeared, crouching as they entered the presence of the Sultan, each bearing a different bottle. As I realized that the Sultan, being a Mohammedan, was probably a dry, I asked for what the Dutch call "limonade," the least deadly of their nonalcoholic drinks. The slaves, carrying whiskey, gin, and other drinks, slunk away crouching, and two trays were brought in, each with two glasses of lemonade. The tray with the Sultan's and my glasses was of a finer silver, and the little silver holders for the glasses and the silver covers for them were of plainer but finer work than on those for the others. As soon as the Sultan took off the silver top of his glass, I removed mine and then raised my glass to him. Shortly thereafter the interview ended. It had lasted about an hour, and save for the chance to see what kind of man the Sultan was, and what the formalities of his court were, it had little value.

The brother then took us out of the Sultan's presence to see the family house, a drab mixture of modern European and Oriental styles, over-gaudy and shoddy. More interesting were my glimpses of the Sultan's attendants, who represented a civilization remote from our own. I was amused to see in the distance a gorgeously attired menial walking down the court bearing a gold platter and followed by a small boy holding a gold umbrella over the bearer's head. When I asked my Dutch companion what this was, he told me that it was food for the Sultan. I knew that in the old days the sultans themselves were always followed by slaves carrying gold umbrellas, but I did not realize that the benefit of the umbrella extended to the food destined for His Majesty's stomach.

Among the more thoughtful Dutch officials I found a curious contradiction when they endeavored to appraise the relative merits of their own and the Malay civilizations. Most of them believed that European culture was—or could be—a valuable corrective to Oriental mysticism. In particular they felt that the scientific approach—the emphasis on accuracy, verification, rationalization, precision—was important. They deplored the persistence of superstitions and the readiness of the natives to believe in supernatural forces, such as spells and magic, which we in Europe and America had long since discarded as false or nonexistent. And yet, even the most practical and unmystical of the Dutch treasured stories or actual experiences which belied their avowed skepticism. So, for example, the mayor of Samarang, Mr. de Jongh, one of the ablest Dutch civil service officers, himself a son and grandson of colonial officials, called my attention, as he was driving me through Samarang, to a house which was partly in ruins. In front of it was the stump of a great *Ficus religiosa*—the sacred banyan tree. The house, he told me, had been owned by a Dutch woman who lived there with her daughter. The tree in front of it had been a fine specimen of the banyan, but it shaded the house too much and she wanted it removed. When she ordered her gardener to cut it down, he refused, saying that to do so would bring bad luck. She persisted, but he made it plain that under no circumstances would he touch it. She thereupon hired two men to cut it down. They also warned her that evil would follow if the tree were removed, but she persuaded them to go ahead. Before the tree had been completely cut down the roof of the house fell in, killing the owner and severely injuring her daughter. Within two weeks the two men who had cut the tree had both died. De Jongh, who was a literal person, said that, of course, it was only a series of coincidences. But it is easy to see that such an incident can prey on the minds of people continually oppressed by the nerve-depleting tropical climate and living among a people to whom superstitions are as vital as belief.

On my return to Batavia, the Governor General, to whom I had talked before starting on my auto tour, invited me to dinner. At the palace we were met by an aide. "Some of the other guests," my diary notes, "had already arrived and in the course of the next five minutes the whole party was assembled, with the exception of the Governor General. It included the German consul, whose wife was a German princess and a cousin of the Kaiser. Like all German princesses whom I have seen she was tall, rawboned, and ugly, with large flat feet and a sour look. I was told that she was the subject of tongue-wagging in Dutch circles because she refused to curtsy to the Governor General, who is traditionally accorded royal honors. The German took the position that, as a cousin of the Kaiser, and herself a royal highness, she would not make obeisance to an official who had no royal blood. After I had seen her and talked with her for a few minutes I made up my mind that if I were governor general of the Netherlands East Indies I would see to it that she curtsied regularly.

"We all sat around informally until a few minutes before the dinner hour, when we were marshaled into the big reception room. The ladies were lined up according to the rank of their husbands, and, at right angles to them, the gentlemen. At precisely eight-thirty a gong was sounded in a neighboring room and the aide-de-camp, in a loud voice, announced: "His Excellency, the Governor General of the Netherlands East Indies." At the same instant His Excellency came in as if shot out of a cannon and hurried past the curtsying ladies. I was so astonished at the speed with which he moved that I did not have a chance to check on whether the German princess lived up to her reputation. He then galloped past the men, giving us a collective bow, and rushed for the leading lady, whom he grasped by the arm, and started with her at a fast walk towards the dining room. This entire performance could not have taken more than thirty seconds, and by the time I recovered my breath and trailed along behind the rest of the party he was already seated and the others were trying to find their places. The dining room was a fine, large hall, handsomely furnished in the French Louis XIV style, with a ceiling about twenty-five feet high. Behind each guest stood a native in elaborate uniform, and behind these servitors were native butlers and stewards. The meal was good but very quickly served, as apparently the Governor General did everything on the run.

"The moment His Excellency had finished eating, everybody rose and he led the procession in a rapid rush for the veranda. His aides then took the ladies, one by one, up to him and he talked with them for a few minutes alone, and standing. The gentlemen were then led up, also one by one, and were permitted to have an audience with him for a few minutes. When my turn came he had a few platitudinous remarks to make about his undying friendship for the American people and asked to be remembered to General Wood. When the last creature had had his few minutes with His Excellency, we left.

"All of this is supposed to be in accordance with the traditions of the Dutch court. If this is so, Dutch royalty steps on the gas more than the ordinary Dutchman does."

Nearly all the Dutch with whom I spoke in the Indies echoed

the fears expressed to me at The Hague by Prime Minister Colijn —that Japan would seize the Indies and that, if we gave the Filipinos their independence, the Indonesians would start to free themselves of Dutch control, and the Indians would break away from Britain. It was a quarter-century ago that they voiced these fears. All have since been realized. The Japanese attack was, of course, pure greed—to obtain control of the oil and other riches of the Indies. Our granting of independence to the Philippines was inevitable, whether or not it was premature. Undoubtedly it fired the Indonesians and the Indians to greater activities to throw off the alien yoke. Very probably their objective would have been more difficult to attain if the Dutch and British alike had not been so drained of strength by World War II. It is one of the ironies of history that the nation which most encouraged the Indonesians and the Indians to seek their independence—Soviet Russia—is the nation which has shown the greatest contempt for the independence of other nations and for the right of individuals to live their own lives as they wish. Perhaps the cynicism which is so characteristic of the Soviet leaders led them to believe that the forces of disunity in the Dutch East Indies as in India proper would, in time, fragment the newly independent people and thus make them easier prey for Communist imperialism than they were while under strong British and Dutch rule. But traditional European colonialism in Asia is near its end. This in itself is creating new world conditions, whether or not Soviet Russia extends its dictatorship over the long-suffering masses of Asia.

CHAPTER SEVENTEEN

AMERICANIZING MALAYS

IN GOING from the Dutch East Indies to the Philippines I was struck not only with the lack of cultural background of the Filipinos, compared with the Malays of Indonesia, but also by the intensity with which we were trying to Americanize the Filipinos. In the Indies two powerful cultural forces had for centuries influenced the Malays—a transplanted Hinduism from India, and a vigorous Mohammedanism, stemming originally from Arabia and North Africa. In contrast, the Filipinos had been, during the three centuries prior to the American occupation, the neglected wards of backward Spain. While, theoretically, they had been subjected to the cultural influence of Roman Catholicism, the Filipinos had accepted the Catholic forms of worship without being much influenced by Catholic cultural traditions.

The very backwardness of the Filipinos when they came under the American flag was a challenge to the American people. Ignorant of the cleavage between the Oriental and Western points of view, and lacking experience in dealing with other races, we believed that we could create overnight a colonial system which would be superior to that of the British in India, the Dutch in the East Indies, or the French in Indo-China by the simple expedient of picking up American institutions and attitudes bodily and setting them down in the Philippine Islands. We were happily blind to the fact that these institutions and attitudes were the products of centuries of evolution and adaptation to our own ways of life and to our own political and social traditions rather

[154]

than to theirs, and we never even stopped to consider whether the Filipinos either wanted them or could learn to absorb them.

Not only this, but we attempted to modernize the Filipinos in a single generation. Within less than two decades we gave a people who were largely illiterate, who knew nothing of modern democratic political systems, and who were living on a primitive economic level a form of government which was modeled closely on our own. A small group of politicians quickly twisted this system into one in which authority was gathered into their hands while responsibility remained in the hands of a powerless American executive. When, in 1921, General Wood was sent out as governor general with the express mission of restoring to the American executive the powers which the Filipino politicians had taken unto themselves, these politicians sought to undermine and discredit him by charging him with being highhanded, arbitrary, and "militaristic." They dramatized themselves to the world as Right striving for independence and General Wood as Evil in the guise of tyranny. What they really wanted was not independence, but full control of the machinery of government by Filipinos, while the Americans, with no authority over their acts, were to assume full responsibility for what the Filipino politicians did.

The fact that the organic law passed by the American Congress in 1916, establishing the form of government for the Philippines, made no provision for administrative assistants or expert advisers made recourse to the use of military aides inevitable. This was astutely played up by the Filipino politicians, who charged General Wood with "surrounding himself" with military men, and who failed to state that no other Americans were available to serve as assistants to the Governor General except the Vice-Governor and the Insular Auditor. As the General was, by nature, tactful, sympathetic, and understanding and never lost his temper or his patience, many of the Americans in the islands who had expected him to give the politicos the "shellacking" which the business community thought they deserved became critical of him. "He had them stretched over a barrel, bottom side up, waiting for him to paddle them," was the way one of the group expressed it to me, with rueful regret that the General had not forthwith applied the birch with vigor. A few businessmen were more understanding, but the resentment of the majority, because he refused to "get tough," created a coolness that isolated the Governor General at a time when he needed the support of all Americans.

During my stay in the Philippines I went with General Wood on inspection trips by automobile on the island of Luzon. Usually his arrival was unannounced. I was struck with the friendly reception accorded him and with the thoroughness with which he cross-questioned local officials. Always he checked on details of sanitation and public health, visited the hospitals, inspected the schools, and asked sympathetic and understanding questions. Even as bitter a critic as the Filipino speaker of the House, Manuel Roxas, wrote of these inspection tours that they had produced remarkable improvements in the government service. The people and the officials, he said, felt that General Wood had a personal interest in them and knew what they were doing. "His approval is eagerly sought," Roxas wrote in 1923, "and his disapproval is a thing to be avoided."

The Filipino political leaders whom I met were as cordial as they were frank. Most engaging was Manuel Quezon, most cultivated Sergio Osmeña, most unreliable Manuel Roxas, and wisest Juan Sumulong. Quezon was president of the Senate, Roxas speaker of the House, Osmeña in opposition, and Sumulong on the Supreme Court. Quezon and Roxas were part Spanish, Osmeña and Sumulong part Chinese. Both mixtures were good, the injection of foreign blood into the Malay strain apparently producing people of greater energy and staying power than the pure-blooded Malays. These men developed the same theme—the need of giving the Filipinos their independence. Only Judge Sumulong had reservations, and these were not about ultimate independence but about the disadvantage of premature withdrawal of the Americans.

General Wood, like all Americans, had a special friendliness for, and interest in, the Moros, the cantankerous Mohammedan individualists who live on the island of Mindanao and in the Sulu Archipelago. At his suggestion I went to Mindanao to see the

Moros. The burden of their political complaint was their dislike of having Filipinos from the other islands put over them as rulers, members of the constabulary, and teachers. They preferred Americans, despite the fact that in the early days of the occupation when Americans governed Mindanao the Moros were far from tractable.

General Wood's aides had suggested that I visit the two outstanding Moro leaders, Datu Piang, who lived on the Cotabato River, and Datu Amai Manabilang, who lived at Lake Lanao in the northern part of Mindanao. To reach the former I went by launch with the American commander of the constabulary, Colonel Stevens, up a crocodile-infested tropical river to a small village called Delaoan, where we moored and climbed ashore over the roots of a big tree. As we walked up the village street, we saw coming slowly towards us an old man with a white beard, wearing a dirty shirt, an ancient pair of B. V. D.'s, and a soiled turban, apparently made out of a bath towel. In his hand he held a long spear which he used as a cane. Behind him were about fifty retainers, dressed in black clothes resembling those worn by pirates in the old days. Each one had a colored turban. This was Datu Piang. Although he was old and stiff and dirty, he was obviously a big chieftain. I soon realized that his was a keen, incisive mind.

When we reached his house, chairs were drawn up to a table, and we were seated while the fifty followers crowded into the room and filled up the doorway, gazing at us solemnly and silently. We exchanged compliments and the Datu had his servants bring us rice, chicken, eggs, and cocoanut water. As soon as the food arrived Piang got down to business. The Filipino governor of Cotabato Province, Guttierez, acted as interpreter. Piang complained because so little American money had come to the islands and asked why more was not invested in Mindanao. I told him that everything depended on what the politicians in Manila planned to do. This made him mad, for he snapped: "What do the Americans care about the Filipino politicians?" He went on to say that the Moros wanted their country developed and that I could tell the American people that he, Datu Piang, would promise them protection and co-operation so long as he lived. He insisted that the Moros wanted American control of Mindanao and said that they were opposed to American withdrawal from the Philippines. He then said something in Moro which Governor Guttierez translated as: "The old man, he's pretty frank. He says that if the Americans give the Filipinos their independence, the Moros will chase out every Filipino in Mindanao."

To get from Cotabato to Lanao meant an all-night trip by launch down the river and across the gulf of Mindanao, followed by an all-day climb on horseback over a slippery trail through a rain-soaked jungle. Only three or four Moros passed us on the entire trail. One of these was a distinguished looking gentleman with a long grey goatee, dressed from head to foot in bright yellow silk and carrying a baby-blue parasol over his head.

Our destination was Dansalan, on Lake Lanao. There we were met by the provincial governor, an American named Johnson. He had arranged for me to see Datu Amai Manabilang. The Datu's son-in-law, Datu Lawi, a dapper looking Moro dressed in army breeches and leather leggings, and wearing a six-shooter, took us to a side street and stopped before a large barn-like building. This had a narrow door opening on a flight of stairs. It was raining heavily, and as there were few windows in the building, the inside was dark.

At the head of the stairs we entered a room, about twenty by thirty feet in size, with a high peaked ceiling. The walls were hung with brass instruments of every kind, from spittoons and pots to cannons. Seated on the floor, and crowded into the corners, were many of the Moro chieftains of the neighborhood, together with their principal retainers. Most of them were in black, but a few wore orange, dark blue, or turquoise silk. Many of them had red turbans. As they belonged to the upper class, the Arab strain in them was marked. Their heads were long and narrow, whereas the ordinary Malay is round headed. Their noses were high, where most Malay noses are flat or small. Many of them had long, grey, goat-like whiskers, which are almost entirely lacking among the pure-blooded Malays.

Chairs had been placed for us near the entrance. In the center of the floor squatting cross-legged directly in front of me, was

Datu Amai Manabilang, obviously a very sick man. Governor Johnson had told me that he had been in bed for weeks but had insisted on getting up for this meeting. One of his retainers sat directly back of him to support him, and from time to time during the hour or more of our talk, the Datu sank back, speechless from pain. He was a fine-looking old fellow, with a vigorous frame despite his illness, and with a square jaw and a deeply lined face. There was not much light in the room, but such as there was shone on the Datu. In the increasing darkness back of him I could dimly discern the eager faces of his followers.

As the rain drummed on the roof the Datu opened the conversation by welcoming me as the President's son. From the start I tried to disabuse him. I explained that I was not the President's son but assured him that I would convey to the American people and to Governor General Wood whatever he had to say. As I realized that he did not altogether grasp my status, I drove home to him in the course of the conversation the fact that all that I could do was to report. I reminded him that General Wood was a friend of the Moros; but I insisted that it was the General, and not I, who could make decisions about their affairs. When finally he understood this, he and his associates were visibly disappointed. They had expected me to settle their troubles, then and there.

As we were getting nowhere at the end of an hour, and he was stirring up the other Moros with old grievances, I decided that the time had come to leave. So I asked the Datu what, in particular, he wanted done. He answered: "Give us American soldiers." I reminded him that the only soldiers available at the time were Filipinos with American officers and asked if that was what he wanted. He answered: "No!" and said that the Moros wanted American soldiers as well as American officers. I promised to give this message to General Wood and repeated that the General was a friend of the Moros and would doubtless come down to see them as soon as he could do so. I then wished him a speedy recovery from his illness and left with Datu Lawi.

When I transmitted Amai Manabilang's complaints to General Wood, he received them with the equanimity of one who had lived among the Moros for years, and who, much as he liked them, could not forget that in the early days a favorite Moro pastime was to take a pot shot from ambush at American soldiers who squatted in the brush to answer a call of nature. He explained that back of the dramatic talk was the fact that the Moros hated restraints of any kind, and that, when they had had American soldiers with American officers over them, they had carried on their feuds just as eagerly. But he said it relieved them to voice their grievances and that he would either visit Lanao soon himself or send down one of his aides.

On my return to the United States I wrote a book about the Philippines, published in the autumn of 1926. In it I described the strides made by the Filipinos in the first quarter-century of American trusteeship but indicated that many of the things which we had promised to do for the Filipinos remained undone and that a scant three decades had not been time enough to prepare the Filipino peoples for self-government. The politicos in Manila attacked the book bitterly because I stated in it that what they wanted was not the complete, immediate, and absolute independence which they demanded, but rather complete and absolute authority over the government of the islands, with American responsibility for their defense, and with unlimited American funds to meet their financial wants. When, in 1930, I was appointed vice-governor of the Philippines, their press was filled with denunciations of the book. They even staged mass meetings at which it was burned, and on one occasion, before burning it, beat the book with a sledge hammer on an anvil. One of the lesser politicos challenged me to a duel—which, at ten-thousand-miles distance, seemed reasonably safe for both of us.

Those of us who felt that we should not withdraw from the Philippines until our task of preparing the Filipinos for self-government was finished had logic on our side. But politics was against us. In 1934 the so-called Tydings-McDuffie Act was passed by Congress, naming July 4, 1944, as the date of Philippine independence. This date was postponed until 1946 as a result of the Japanese occupation.

Because of the growing tenseness in the Pacific and, in particular, the indications that Japan was preparing for war, I urged as early as 1935 that we advance the date of independence and that, when we got out, we should make it clear to the world that we were getting out "lock, stock, and barrel." I warned that Japan had embarked on a policy of aggressive expansion, having as its ultimate objective the domination of the entire Far East. "Whether we like it or not," I said in a speech before the National Republican Club in New York, in 1935, "we are responsible under the present laws for the protection of the Philippines until the end of 1944. We thus have ahead of us a period which is sure to be full of dangers for us." I added that "the only thing for us to do under the circumstances is to recognize frankly that we have made a mess of our relations with the Philippines and to shorten, rather than to prolong, the period of our occupation of those islands. Instead of holding them for ten years, as provided in the Tydings-McDuffie Act, we should, in my opinion, get rid of them in three years if possible, or at least in five years from today.... The longer we stay in the Islands the greater the danger of our being involved in a war."

Once more the Filipino politicians vented their ire. The very ones who were so bitter when I opposed immediate independence in 1926 were furious when I advocated it a decade later. What particularly outraged them was my contention that we should make their independence not only immediate but complete and absolute. Apparently they feared that others in the United States might agree that the American government should rid itself of all responsibility for the defense of the Islands. By their criticism, the Filipino politicos once more made it clear that what they really wanted was for us to have responsibility for their protection at the same time that we had no authority over the acts of their government. They wanted independence—yes—but they were determined that the United States Navy and Army should be obliged to continue indefinitely to stand between them and Japanese aggression—a natural and logical procedure from the point of view of the Filipinos, but obviously highly dangerous and disadvantageous for the Americans. The inertia of American political life worked in their behalf. The Tydings-McDuffie Act remained unchanged. In 1941 Japan attacked the Philippines, and we found ourselves forced to fight a long war to liberate them from Japanese control.

The conduct of the Filipinos during this ordeal was magnificent. They fought hard and long. Filipino men, women, and children performed acts of heroism not only in their own defense but in unselfish attempts to help Americans, even at the risk of death or torture by the Japanese. Prior to 1941, most Americans found it hard to appreciate the Filipinos' claim that America owed them a great debt. To us it seemed that till then the Filipinos had been the beneficiaries and the Americans had been the givers under American trusteeship of the Islands. But by their conduct in the war the account was more than squared. We now have an obligation which no fair-minded American can question—the obligation to stand back of the Filipinos if ever their independence is threatened. By their courage, their tenacity, and their bigness of heart in World War II the Filipino people have made all Americans their debtors. They are no longer our "little brown brothers," but rather our partners for permanent peace in the Pacific.

CHAPTER EIGHTEEN

CHINA IN CHAOS

W HEN I crossed to China from the Philippines in February, 1926, I met many Europeans, Americans, and Chinese to whom the forming of a correct estimate of the trends of the Chinese Revolution was a matter of utmost concern—for some, even, of life or death. My task was to evaluate their judgments and opinions.

The outstanding point on which my informants were agreed was that the revolution would last at least another seventy-five years. In retrospect this judgment, which my impatient Western mind then found hard to accept, seems sound. When I sought enlightenment about it from the urbane Dr. Hu Shih, then already hailed as one of China's greatest thinkers, he reminded me that the era of disorder and change initiated by the French Revolution lasted from 1789 until 1871, and that during the intervening eighty-two years France passed through Jacobinism, the Directorate, the First Empire, the Restoration, the Second Republic, and the Second Empire, accompanied by economic and social changes of a drastic nature. The analogy helps elucidate what was meant by those who said that decades would pass before China became a unified, modernized nation. If one took the short view, the chaos in the China of the twenties would seem utterly hopeless. But China, he reminded me, had been through periods of disordered reorganization before. Usually these lasted several generations.

The next point on which those with whom I talked agreed was that, apart from the changes of governmental forms implicit in the political revolution, Chinese traditionalism was being shaken as never before by the impact of modern industrialism. Chiang Mon Lin, chancellor of the Peking National University, sought to explain this to me by describing the village in the Yangtze Valley where he had spent his boyhood. The family unit was still supreme in the eighties and nineties, and daily living followed rigid patterns sanctified by tradition. The work and the social activities of the village were carried on as they had been a thousand years before. All was peaceful, and there was never any trouble. He quoted a native proverb that tigers, bandits, thieves, and ghosts were all in the same class—that is to say, they were nonexistent. Then came the first signs of a new way of life. Matches with phosphorous heads were brought in. People believed that these were kin of the goddess of lightning. Matches were followed by telegraph wires, which no one could explain. The best "reason" given in the village was that Li Hung-chang, under whose administration the wires were being strung, had been a spider in a previous incarnation and so felt compelled to weave his web over China. Then came railroads. Men who had never left their native villages began to travel. There was an exodus to the cities. Villagers returned with new ideas and aroused feelings of discontent among those who had stayed at home. Within a generation the Chinese sought to change one of the most conservative civilizations in the world into one of the most modern. Absolute monarchy had failed, so they tried constitutional monarchy. When that failed, they turned to a republic. When that also failed, there was chaos, confusion, and impotence, as had so often before been known in China when a dynasty was overthrown. Periodically the Chinese had had to fight foreign barbarians and, in the end, had absorbed them. But the barbarians who came from Europe in the nineteenth century differed in that they were cultured as well as strong. Even if they should be driven out, their ideas would remain. These new ideas had caused the current ferment.

On the prospects of industrializing China my informants differed. Then, as now, the views that struck me as soundest stressed the relative poverty of China in the sinews of industrial power. Its supplies of coal are neither widely distributed, readily accessible, nor of good quality. Its known iron deposits are localized. It lacks adequate reserves of other minerals essential in modern industry, such as copper and aluminum. Without an extensive system of good roads and railroads the economic modernization of China beyond the reaches of the navigable rivers and canals will continue to be slow, and no system of roads and railroads seems any more likely to be built now than it did when I was there a quarter-century ago. Hence, even if many Chinese had— or have—an urgent desire to substitute a machine-based civilization for the traditional China, rooted in agriculture, nurtured by skilled craftsmanship, and clinging to unchanging customs, they would find it hard to realize their ambitions.

Furthermore, pressure of population, so much greater in China than in Europe or America, makes it difficult to introduce into China the labor-saving inventions which are fundamental in modern economic systems. When transportation is largely by man power—on the backs of coolies, or in wheelbarrows or hand-drawn carts—the number of people who make their living from transportation is proportionately great. If trains and busses take the place of wheelbarrows and men's backs, the initial result is to deprive carrier coolies of their livelihood. The ensuing dislocation is calamitous, due to the shortage of other available jobs. No wonder, therefore, that the same sort of opposition to mechanization which developed in the early stages of the industrial revolution in Europe appeared in China—and has been even more stubborn.

Among the Chinese who sought to help me understand the problems of modernizing China was C. C. Wu, son of the celebrated Wu T'ing-fang, and high in the councils of the new Nationalist party headed by Chiang Kai-shek. Wu, who spoke more perfect English than the most scholarly Americans and Englishmen of my acquaintance, said that China's troubles could best be discussed under three headings, militarism, mandarinism, and imperialism. The first—militarism—was a recent development—the rise to military power of local bandit chieftains who seized entire provinces by violence and looted them. The second—mandarinism—was ancient and a great evil. It had its origin in the fact that, as government officials in the old days were never paid enough, they kept for themselves a portion of the taxes which they collected. The system was so enmeshed with corruption and graft that it made the task of establishing honest and good government in China extremely difficult. The third—imperialism—was also a great evil and threatened the survival of China as an independent entity. Not only had foreign nations imposed treaties on China requiring special privileges for foreigners, but several of the great powers sought exclusive domination over the trade of sections of China, and others even tried to annex Chinese territory.

Mr. Wu omitted to stress that much of what he called "imperialism" was a reaction to mandarinism. When the British and other foreigners sought to establish trade relations with China a century ago, they were faced with demands for "squeeze" and with restrictions and harassments imposed by local officials eager to "milk" the foreigners. The Chinese refused to permit foreigners to live in Chinese cities. They denied them the right to trade, save under rigorous restrictions. Foreigners could get neither justice nor protection before Chinese courts, and they found the legal and judicial system as corrupt as it was antiquated. If, therefore, they were to continue to trade with China they had to obtain rights commonly granted to aliens in civilized countries—the rights of residence and of travel, of doing business, of receiving the protection of the law and police, of having diplomatic and consular representation. In other words, the foreigners sought to be treated as equals in China, instead of tribute-bearing barbarians. Most of the treaties against which the Chinese were so bitter had been written to provide safeguards for foreigners in China—safeguards made necessary by the disordered conditions and the anti-foreign prejudices of its people.

Had not Mr. Wu's immediate purpose been to concentrate on the alleged evils of the "unequal treaties," he would probably have carried his analysis of imperialism further and would have discriminated between those powers which, like Britain and the United States, were primarily interested in commerce and investment in China and those which, like Russia and Japan, planned to control as much of China as possible. As a matter of fact, the pendulum had swung back and forth between Japanese and Russian efforts to dominate sections of China. In 1893 Russia was pressing China. In 1895 Japan declared war on China. In 1898 Russia acquired rights and concessions in Manchuria which had been denied to Japan two years before by the Western powers. In 1904 Japan took the offensive again—ostensibly against Russia but with the objective of seizing those portions of Manchuria which Russia controlled. Just before World War I, Russia gained ground. Between 1914 and 1921 Japan imposed the Twenty-one Demands which, if carried out in full, would have made China a vassal of Japan. She also occupied large parts of Manchuria and Mongolia. In 1923 Russia sought and obtained new concessions in Manchuria. In 1925 it was Japan's turn. This oscillation continued, with Japan proceeding with its plans of conquering China from 1931 onwards, and with Russia beginning to press forward with the defeat of Japan at the end of World War II, acquiring domination of China through the Soviet-controlled Communist party. Here was imperialism of the baldest kind—invasion, conquest, and control of China without a thought for the interests of the Chinese people. Compared to it the living and trading privileges which the British had won for themselves during the last century seemed not only harmless but actually beneficial to China.

During the winter of 1926 the demand for the abrogation of the so-called "unequal treaties," which Mr. Wu and others had described as such great evils, became a major issue in China. The stock argument in favor of abrogating them was that they impaired China's sovereignty and that until China regained full control over all the territory of the old empire it could not complete the modernization on which it was bent. Most vocal in this latest manifestation of China's age-old antiforeignism were the Western-educated Chinese students, who were supported by many American missionaries.

The emphasis of the Chinese on the "unequal treaties" and on the demand for the surrender to China of sovereignty over the few remaining foreign "concessions," as the foreign settlements in Hankow and elsewhere were termed, was in accord with the Chinese traditional procedure of striking first for what seemed

[167]

easiest to get. The antiforeign campaign was concentrated against the British, even though the Chinese knew that the Japanese had never abandoned that part of the Twenty-one Demands which called for virtual Japanese overlordship over all of China. The motive for this concentration was the realization by the Chinese that Great Britain, while obviously much stronger than Japan, was in the hands of vacillating sentimentalists with a predilection for appeasement. Hence the time seemed auspicious for a drive to bamboozle the British into surrendering their special privileges in China. Japan, in contrast, was ruled by hard-boiled, cynical militarists, whom it would be unwise to antagonize. A Chinese proverb states that a tree bows to the force of the wind, and already the blast out of the East was ominous.

Because of the resentment of the young Chinese against the foreign treaties, I made it a point to ask them to explain to me just what benefits would accrue to China from the abrogation of these treaties. From none did I get a convincing answer. In the process I was struck with one of the most engaging—and annoying—Chinese traits: their ability to avoid direct answers and to shy off a subject if they felt that the argument was not running in their favor. Often I thought of a drop of mercury on a saucer. Whenever you try to put your finger on it, it slithers away, and no matter how much you try, it continues to evade you.

Another favorite Chinese device is to talk in metaphors. The Westerner, as a rule, is at a disadvantage if he tries to meet the Chinese in this sort of mental fencing, as they are quick to drop a losing metaphor for one which seems more likely to be successful. In one such encounter, a group of young Chinese spent an hour elaborating the thesis that the treaties shackled China's freedom. When I asked how the treaties did this, one of them depicted a poor, small, weak old man in chains being attacked by a big, strong, young man. I suggested that, if the disparity was so great between the weaker and the stronger of the two, the chains were not important. He admitted that this was so but said that the weak man would at least like a try at the big man with the chains loosed. I then proposed that we remove the chains and put the man in the hospital, and I asked one of them how the patient should be treated. He laughingly declined to prescribe. I tried to get others to prescribe but had no luck. Finally David Yui, head of the Chinese Y. M. C. A., turned to me and asked me to prescribe. I replied that I had come merely as a friend of the patient to inquire how he was getting along. Yui then said, "Well, we appoint you doctor." I answered that, if that was the way the Chinese chose their doctors, the Lord should have mercy on the patient. The company seemed to think that the joke was on Yui, but I left them without learning the answer to my question.

The antiforeign campaign of the Chinese Nationalists in 1926 was used by the Soviets for their own ends. Russia's two skilled representatives in China, Borodin in Canton and Karakhan in Peking, remained in the background inciting youthful Chinese to the violence to which they were already inclined. The charge commonly made that the Russians spent millions to help the antiforeign campaign is exaggerated. A little shrewd advice here, a few words of praise there, the printing of a few pamphlets and broadsides accomplished much and cost little.

All the time that Russian agents were encouraging the Chinese to denounce foreign "imperialism" and foreign "interference" in Chinese politics, Soviet Russia was detaching Mongolia and attempting to cut off North Manchuria from China. It also resumed the control of the Chinese Eastern Railway, which it had previously surrendered, and furnished extensive military support to several war lords. Thus Russia was running true to form—one of the two most selfish and aggressive imperialist powers in China.

The reason for Russia's support of the Chinese Nationalists a quarter-century ago was simple: the success of nationalism in China would weaken the position of the Western nations in that country and leave Russia relatively more influential. Russia's support of Chiang Kai-shek was equally cynical and practical: he was the strongest war lord in South China and most likely to be able to force out the other foreign nations which would stand in the way of Russia's control of China. That Chiang planned to impose a modernized government on as much of China as he could dominate did not disturb the Russians, who felt able to control Chiang when and if he succeeded in extending his power over central and northern, as well as southern China, or to oust him if he failed to take orders from Moscow.

Both at the time and in retrospect, the obstacles which Chiang faced—difficulties of transportation, the traditional inertia of the Chinese people, and the expected military hostility of the war lords controlling other parts of China—seemed insurmountable. Success depended on the character and talents of the new Nationalist leader. The situation called for a man who was incorruptible, unselfish, politically shrewd, militarily able, an expert organizer and administrator, modern in outlook but sympathetic to Chinese traditions, and at the same time adroit as a propagandist and as an inspired and inspiring popular hero. Chiang seemed to fill the bill. It is to his credit that, however unlikely it was at the time that he would succeed where other Chinese war lords had failed, he came nearer than anyone else to establishing nationwide control over China. There is still dispute as to whether the Japanese invasion alone prevented the complete success of his plans. Certainly Japanese aggression helped to unify discontented and jealous Chinese factions behind Chiang. Equally certain is the fact that the cost of resistance against Japan was a big drain on the finances of the Chinese Nationalists. But it is also certain that, as soon as Japan was defeated, the Chinese Communists directed by Russia, quickly annihilated what was left of Chiang's armies, which suggests that Chiang's success had been in part, at least, due to the fact that he was the spearhead against the Japanese invaders and that, when Japan was defeated by the Western powers, a substantial reason for supporting Chiang disappeared.

The Soviet agent in Canton when I was there, Michael Borodin, was reputedly close to Chiang. For this reason I was particularly interested to meet him. He was a tall, powerful man, with a narrow head, dark hair, and a long, drooping, black moustache —looking, in fact, not unlike some of the early portraits of Robert Louis Stevenson. He spoke good English and began by assuring me that he had only one aim in life—to serve China. He was, of course, himself a Russian, he said, but Russia had befriended China and wished to help the Chinese find a way out of their troubles. He told me that he had been surprised to learn that the

Chinese were good organizers. Thanks to this quality, it would be possible in a short time to spread his program, which was bound to triumph by its appeal to the masses of the Chinese people. He then detailed the terrible sufferings of the Chinese at the hands of the wicked European and American imperialists. He laid down as a cardinal principle that foreigners must cease interfering in China's internal affairs. I asked him what the Russians were doing in Manchuria and North China. He repeated that the Russians wished to help China. I asked him about the Japanese in Manchuria and whether he thought that, if the treaties were abolished, the Japanese would withdraw from that region. His answer was that there would probably be chaos in China for a while when the treaties were scrapped and the foreigners withdrew but that ultimately there would be unity. He charged the foreign powers with aiding disunity actively and passively. He insisted that the foreign concessions must be given up, so that bandit leaders could have no place to deposit their funds and to seek shelter. I asked him why they could not deposit their funds in Japan and the Philippines. He replied that they could be searched and seized before leaving. He summed up the problem by saying that there was a basic difference of philosophy between the Americans and the Russians about China. The Russian theory was that the treaties must be abrogated before unity could be achieved, whereas that of the Americans was that the treaties could not be dropped until an orderly government had been established. Just before we parted, as he was getting more truculent about the foreigners in China, I remarked that I could not see that China would gain by throwing out western Europeans and Americans, only to fall under the domination of the Russians. To this he made no comment.

When I was in Peking I met Karakhan, then Soviet ambassador to China, and supposedly the "master mind" of Soviet imperialism in the Far East. He was at his zenith when I saw him, but in a brief time he fell from grace, was recalled, and soon went the way of others close to the Soviet inner council who had incurred the ill will of the all-powerful. His office was in the large splendidly furnished imperial Russian embassy building inside the legation quarter, where he sat under a big crayon portrait of Lenin—

the only nonimperial decoration in this obviously imperial office. He was a large, well-built, well-groomed man with an olive complexion and a blue-black beard trimmed in the best mephisto style. After some fencing we had a frank talk. His thesis was that nationalism was the great need of China, and that it was being stimulated by the antiforeign movement. He described the "cruel aggression" of the foreign powers, particularly the British. I asked him what the difference was between the "aggression" of the British in the Yangtze and that of the Russians in Manchuria. He replied that there was very much. Russia's interests, he said, were solely economic. He mentioned with pride that Russia had not gone to war when the Manchurian war lord Chang Tso-lin dismissed the Russian general manager of the Chinese Eastern Railway in Manchuria, whom he had arrested the previous December. Karakhan said that the Russians had no soldiers along the Chinese Eastern and that they submitted to the laws of the Chinese in that territory—a statement which later I found was untrue. I asked him how the Russians fared since they had surrendered the privilege of extraterritoriality. He said that when Chinese political interests were involved the new status left a good deal to be desired. I said that I had heard similar statements from other foreigners.

I then asked him what the difference was between the Soviets in Mongolia aiding one war lord and the Japanese in Manchuria aiding another. His reply was that Russia was seeking China's best interests. I remarked that the Japanese had made exactly the same statement to me about Japanese activities in China.

He asked me if I had been to Canton. I said, "yes." Had I seen any signs of bolshevism? I answered, "no." He said he was glad of this because most people thought about Canton in terms of "Reds." Then, as if in an aside, he said: "We don't want communism here."

After this he launched into a general attack on the imperialist powers and insisted that China must throw off the foreign yoke. He blamed the "unequal treaties" for China's woes. I asked him if the trouble did not lie in the policies of some of the powers rather than in the treaties. He said that the policies also were bad but that they were shielded by the treaties. He then made a plea that the United States should help a good government such as that of Chiang at Canton.

Karakhan, who was a soldier of fortune (his assumed name, translated, meant "Black Prince"), was, by virtue of his ambassadorial rank, the dean of the diplomatic corps in Peking, and enjoyed the occasions which this gave him to devil the other foreign diplomats—especially the British. Before his arrival the diplomatic corps had often acted as a body in protesting to the Chinese government about infringements on the rights of foreigners. But with this hated Mephistopheles at their head they rarely agreed on anything—a situation which brought suave satisfaction to the Chinese.

While Karakhan plotted with Borodin to concentrate Chinese antiforeignism against the British and paved the way for Russian control of China, three little Japanese in Peking quietly, unobtrusively, but diligently went about their business of preparing for the "new order" in East Asia. The most conspicuous was the least effective—the front man, Yoshizawa, Japanese minister to China. Guiding him was the framer and presenter of the Twenty-one Demands of 1915, Hioki by name, and working independently, yet in close touch with them, was a bullet-headed little Japanese general by the name of Banzai. To the foreigners they were sympathetic and understanding, implying that a united front was essential to the preservation of the rights of all foreigners in chaotic China. To the Chinese they stressed the fact that they were fellow Orientals, outraged by the arrogance of the Western barbarians in the face of China's just insistence upon its sovereignty. Under these shams they planned the conquest of China, welcoming disorder and disunion within the country at the same time that they approved Russian incitement of the Chinese to drive out the British and to quarrel with the Americans. Anything which weakened China or the influence of the Western powers would make it easier for Japan when the occupation commenced. At no time, apparently, did the Japanese consider the Russians as a serious rival for the domination of China.

I met all three of these little men under the most unfavorable circumstances—that is, as their guest at meals. Even had they been disposed to talk frankly, which was not the case, they would not have done so on such occasions. What I learned of their plans was from other sources—sources which erred primarily through underestimating the efficiency of the Japanese military machine. My informants had correctly assessed Japan's intentions but had failed to realize what a powerful military offensive the Japanese would launch when they started the occupation of Manchuria and North China in 1931. In this error they were not alone—as witness the persistence for another decade of the belief in American and British army and navy circles that Japan would be a "push-over" in the event of a war.

The Americans whom I met differed about the Chinese. Most of the businessmen leaned towards the views of the "old China hands" and were opposed to yielding the protections provided for foreigners by the treaties. The representatives of the State, War, and Commerce departments believed that the treaties should be maintained until a stable government existed in China. Some of the medical missionaries took the same view. Most of the religious missionaries and those connected with American-financed schools backed the Chinese Nationalists' demands that the privileges of foreigners in China be withdrawn forthwith. No one questioned the right of the missionaries to take such a stand, but many believed that they were naïve. The government people in particular disliked the readiness of missionaries to sign petitions drawn up by Chinese radicals expressly to embarrass the American and British legations. One such petition, circulated while I was in Peking, called, if I remember correctly, for the dismantling of the foreign forts at the mouth of the Hai River below Tientsin, and it was addressed to Senator Borah, then chairman of the Senate Foreign Relations Committee. As this subject at the time was involved in delicate diplomatic negotiations, it was obvious that the purpose of having American missionaries sign such a petition at this particular time and addressing it to Borah was to try to embarass the State Department. The missionaries, however, were not all in agreement about it, for when a group took the petition to one of the oldest and best-known missionaries, Arthur H. Smith, to sign, he read it over and (so he told me) said to those who brought it to him: "Gentlemen, there are only three things wrong with this petition. It's the wrong thing, at the wrong time, to the wrong man."

The missionaries were criticized on the ground that they were more often moved by affection than by judgment, and that they accepted the dreams and hopes of Chinese students as tantamount to the achievement of China's political modernization. Judging from most of those with whom I talked, there was truth in this criticism. But this should not blind us to the fact that the missionaries for decades indoctrinated a small but steadily growing group of Chinese with Western ideas and ideals, and that the ferment of these ideas in the last half-century has begun to shake China out of its millennial lethargy. Furthermore, rarely if ever has there been such an example of unselfishness as that of the men and women who went to China to do what they could to help the Chinese people. Some were stiff-necked, some bigoted. Many were blind to the good in Chinese civilization. But their purpose was to help, and they neither asked nor expected greater rewards than the affection and appreciation of those whom they taught. This they received.

Of the American officials in China the members of the consular service in particular struck me as outstanding. Most of them spoke Chinese and knew the country well. They understood and liked the Chinese and, almost without exception, were studious, diligent, and well informed. Some of our diplomatic officials also —notably Willys R. Peck and Nelson T. Johnson, the former subsequently minister to Siam and the latter to become ambassador to China—were sympathetic to the aims of the Chinese people and were helpful in their advice about Chinese problems. Of the Department of Commerce representatives, Arthur H. Evans, the acting commercial attaché, was as wise and knowing as he was genial and kindly—a shrewd student of China and an expert poker-player.

The most interesting American Army man whom I met in China was a lieutenant colonel in command of the Fifteenth Infantry, stationed in Tientsin. He was a graduate of the Virginia Military Institute and had an inquiring mind and balanced judgment. He was much interested in the Chinese people and realized the handicaps under which Americans in China lived if they did not know the language. This, he felt, was as true of the enlisted men and officers of the Fifteenth Infantry as it was of business-men and missionaries. But he was one of those rare men who, when they see that something needs to be done, go ahead and do it even if they are not obliged to do so. Accordingly, with the aid and encouragement of General William Connor, the commander of the American forces in China, this lieutenant colonel worked out a system of small cards each of which had on one side a phrase in English and on the other its translation into Chinese, together with the Chinese characters showing the phrase in writing. Several hundred of the commonest phrases which soldiers would use were put on these cards, with the Chinese equivalents on the back, and each soldier and officer in the regiment was given a complete set of cards and encouraged by prizes and games to memorize them. Within a comparatively short time the members of the Fifteenth Infantry were able to understand as well as to speak enough Chinese to get about the country. It was elemental Chinese —but useful.

The name of the lieutenant colonel who worked out this sys-tem, and who explained it to me, was George Catlett Marshall, at the time in his mid-forties, but already showing the rare gifts of leadership, good judgment, and understanding which were so valuable in his later services as chief of staff and as secretary of state.

CHAPTER NINETEEN

THE MANCHURIAN
STORM CENTER

O NE OF THE principal purposes of my trip to the Far East was
to learn what I could about a standard-gauge railroad which
the Japanese were building in the Chinese province of Manchuria
from the junction of the South Manchurian and Chinese Eastern
Railways at Changchun to a place called Tsitsihar, on the Chinese
Eastern Railway, west of Harbin. The Chinese Eastern, it will
be recalled, had been built by the Russians across northern Manchuria as a link in the broad-gauge Trans-Siberian Railway, short-
ening by several hundred miles the run from Lake Baikal in eastern Siberia to Vladivostok on the Pacific. Although it traversed
Chinese territory its economic and strategic value was to Russia
—not to China. Its main revenues came from through traffic. Control of this railroad enabled Russia to dominate northern Manchuria, in Soviet as in Czarist days.

For Japan to build a standard-gauge railroad paralleling part
of the Chinese Eastern there could be only one of two reasons—
either because the territory which it would tap could be profitably developed with resultant benefits to the Japanese-owned
South Manchurian Railway, or because such a line would be of
military value to Japan when the expected occupation of China
began in earnest. If its true purpose was strategic, the very fact
of its construction would be an important confirmation of Japan's
imperialist ambitions and might throw light on Japan's policy in
the next few years. The best way of finding the answer was the
simplest—to take a "look-see." When I asked the American director of public relations of the South Manchurian Railway, which

was supervising the construction of the new line, if I could go over it, the Japanese wisely interposed no objections. They realized, of course, that they could not admit that its purpose was military. Hence they insisted that it was nothing but a commercial line and, as such, was open to the public. The public relations man, by the name of Kinney, was a sensible, honest Minnesotan. He believed that frankness was the best policy in Japanese-American relations, and, while he admitted that some among the Japanese military leaders wished to occupy China, he did not think that such control was either necessary or desirable. The new line, he assured me, was not being built for military purposes but to open up a large sector of Manchuria for settlement by Chinese. Hence it would be a bona fide feeder for the South Manchurian. I had no reason to doubt the sincerety of his convictions, although I later questioned the soundness of his judgment.

Kinney arranged passage for me from Tientsin to Dairen (near Port Arthur) and accompanied me over the new line. We were to go from Mukden to Changchun by the South Manchurian, changing there to the Chinese Eastern for Harbin, and after a couple of days in that Russian center, take the Chinese Eastern as far as Tsitsihar (an overnight journey.) Thence we would drive by automobile to the railhead at the Nonni River, and by construction train back to Szepingkai, just outside of Changchun, and so return to Mukden. The journey would give me a bird's-eye view of a large section of Manchuria.

In contrast to the rest of China, Japanese-occupied Manchuria showed many outward signs of Westernization. The South Manchurian Railway had excellent American rolling stock, scrupulously maintained. Schedules were adhered to as rigidly as on our own transcontinental railroads. In the rest of China, trains were never on time, always overcrowded—often with passengers riding even on the roofs of cars—and invariably filthy. All along the South Manchurian Railway I was reminded more of America than of China or Japan, except for the omnipresent oversolicitude of Japanese officials about my comfort and for the repetition, wherever our train stopped between Dairen and Mukden, of a ceremonial which aroused my curiosity. At each station I noticed

[178]

a little group of Japanese in frock coats and high hats. As our train halted, a colonel got off the last car, carrying a flat package about fourteen by eighteen inches, covered with a purple silk cloth. After a few formal remarks, he would bow and hand this to the head of the local delegation, who received it with signs of great reverence, while the members of his entourage bowed low and clicked their heels. On inquiring, Kinney learned that the officer was on an official mission from the imperial household, bearing photographs of the Emperor, and that these photographs were being accepted with obsequiousness out of deference to the exalted status of the imperial person. I could not resist contrasting the awe with which the photographs were received with what would have happened if, when "Number Three" pulled into Gallup or Flagstaff, a representative of the White House had pre-

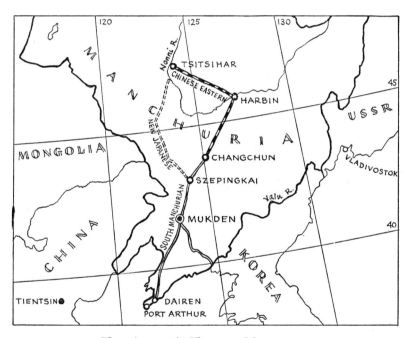

THE AUTHOR'S TOUR IN MANCHURIA
Japan's railroad building was for Manchurian domination

sented a local committee with the latest photograph of President Coolidge—the one, let us say, of him wearing patent leather pumps as he milked the family cow on his father's farm in Vermont.

I found Mukden a curious mixture of East and West—with the Western veneer imposed by the Japanese, instead of by Europeans or Americans. Like so many Chinese cities which had been "modernized," it was divided into a foreign and a Chinese section, the former lying between the railway station and the old walled city, which had been the capital of the Manchu dynasty. At the station was the chief hotel for foreigners—as drab and grubby as the worst American or European railroad hotel of the late Victorian era. Trains were shunting and puffing day and night—freight trains loaded with soya bean cakes from the northern prairies; others with *kaoliang* or millet; cars bound north with cans of kerosene and oil; local passenger trains crowded with Chinese in long, blue, cotton robes; Japanese express trains with Pullman cars to and from Korea—all to the incessant accompaniment of bells, whistles, klanks, and bangs so characteristic of the modern machine age. Traffic was under Japanese control, for the South Manchurian Railroad was the spearhead of Japanese imperialism and the main channel for Japanese trade with Manchuria.

Scarcely a mile away, within the walls of the Chinese city, there was noise of a different kind—the incessant babbling of Chinese tongues and the hammering of busy artisans. Vendors cried their wares in shrill tones. Wheelbarrows squeaked noisily. Occasionally a donkey would add his mournful voice to the never stilled din. With the patience so characteristic of the race, the Chinese isolated themselves from the world of the Japanese intruders, serenely confident that these foreign barbarians would be squeezed out or absorbed—as, in fact, happened inside of twenty years.

At Changchun, as in Mukden, Chinese were everywhere in the background, largely ignoring the presence of the foreigners. Here the two rival imperialisms and the two railroads—the South Manchurian and the Chinese Eastern—met. The contrast was illuminating. The Pullman train of the South Manchurian on which

we rode drew in precisely on time on one platform. Neat Japanese porters carried our bags to another platform, where, in theory,
the Chinese Eastern Railway's train to Harbin, connecting with
ours, was supposed to be waiting, and where sloppy Russian porters received our bags with indifference bordering on resentment.
As might have been expected, the connecting train of the Chinese
Eastern was nowhere in sight, and no one seemed to know or care
when it would be made up. The usual procedure was for a half-
dozen dirty Russian railroad carriages to be pulled into the station
at the convenience of the engineer. Instead of leaving on schedule,
the cars would be held there until every would-be traveler who
could be crowded into them had been packed on board and the
engineer had a last half-hour talk with his friends. The train would
then lumber northward at a rate of scarcely fifteen miles an hour
to Harbin, arriving at this Russian town in North Manchuria at
the engineer's pleasure.

After an hour or more, our train appeared, was slowly loaded,
and started its journey northward. At Harbin we found drosh-
kies at the station driven by bearded Russian refugees; Russian
signs everywhere; Russians of all classes and colors in the stores
and houses; Russian night clubs, looking just like their counter-
parts in mid-town Manhattan, run by sleek, overfed men such as
New York night club frequenters have often seen; Russian food
and drink, caviar and vodka; Russian music in the cabarets; and,
slinking like starved dogs through the streets, Russian orphans,
homeless, uncared for, surviving only through what they could
beg or steal or salvage. In the background, of course were the
omnipresent Chinese, but they, like the Chinese in Singapore,
were the hewers of wood and the drawers of water—a race
apart, living their own hard-working lives while the alien imperialists dominated the government.

From Harbin we took a westbound sleeper on the Chinese
Eastern and at two in the morning detrained in zero weather at
Tsitsihar. In a near-by rooming house run by some Japanese, Kinney and I slept for a few hours, and before dawn we started out
in an open flivver across the Manchurian Plain for the railhead
of the new Japanese railway beyond the Nonni River, about

thirty-five miles south of Tsitsihar. It was a frigid drive, under a metallic desert sky, and as dawn appeared I saw that the country was not unlike parts of western Texas—but a Texas with a cold, instead of a mild, climate and, for the most part, little more developed than Texas was before the Civil War.

We crossed the Nonni River on the ice and were met by Japanese railroad officials who invited us on board an American caboose car, attached to the end of the Japanese construction train. The caboose had the traditional potbellied iron stove, which quickly thawed us. Our Japanese hosts then urged us to have breakfast, which consisted of large quantities of caviar washed down with vodka. I never learned whether this diet had been chosen in order to make us so drunk that we could pay little attention to what we saw, or whether it was merely a Japanese idea of an American's favorite breakfast food. Fortunately my stomach has always been weaker than my head, with the result that I had to go slow on the vodka after the first few warming shots, and long before my head could get fuzzy.

The countryside was brown and drab in the cold spring sunlight. Here and there we passed fortified farms—some inhabited and some deserted. As we traveled southward, signs of cultivation increased, suggesting that a pioneer fringe was moving out along the railway, as happened in our own West when new rail lines were built. At occasional sidings we picked up a freight car of millet or soya bean cake. My Japanese hosts discoursed with enthusiasm about the volume of business which they anticipated, but anyone familiar with the enormous amount of freight which is deemed essential for the mere survival of our western American railways would have found it hard to visualize this project as having a great revenue potential. When, at last, we got back to Mukden, considerably the worse for the caviar and vodka, my impression was deepened that the prime purpose of this railroad was military—to forestall the movement of Russian troops into China when the Japanese occupation of that country commenced. Incidentally, it would still further strengthen Japan's military position in Manchuria in the years prior to the occupation and thus make it more difficult for the Soviets to extend their own military position there. If, in the process, the new road brought in new business, all the better.

I left Mukden realizing more clearly than before that Manchuria was one of the storm centers of the world, and that, even if there were no new direct clash between Russia and Japan for the domination of North China, Manchuria would be the point of departure for the Japanese militarists when they began to put their "greater Asia" policy into practice. We could not guess when the military movement would start, but we knew that the Japanese would follow plans carefully prepared long in advance. Theoretically the occupation of China would await a great crisis in Europe. In 1926 no such crisis was on the horizon.

Five years were to pass before the time was ripe. In the late summer of 1931 all of Europe was in an economic tail spin. When, in Budapest, I read in the *London Times* a dispatch from Tokyo stating that Japanese military airplanes had been flying over Japan dropping leaflets giving briefly the facts about Japan's expenditures in money and lives in Manchuria, I realized that this was no haphazard act. The only explanation that seemed rational was that the Japanese military leaders wished to build up a favorable reaction among the Japanese people for further expenditures of men and money in Manchuria. This could only mean that a major military operation was about to start. As so often before, it was impossible to guess the date. But we were not kept long in suspense, for on September 18th, 1931, came the report from Japanese sources in Mukden of the so-called "incident" in which Chinese were charged with murdering a Japanese guard at a railway bridge outside of Mukden. It was a typical "incident," ready made to serve as an excuse for the military seizure of Mukden, Harbin, Kirin, and way stations. The long-expected "day" had dawned. The occupation of China had started. The Japanese had chosen their time well, for three days later the Bank of England announced that it had abandoned the gold standard. Already the United States was in a deep depression, and Europe on the verge of bankruptcy.

In spite of the propitiousness of the time the Japanese deliberately moved slowly at first, uncertain as to what the British or

Americans would do. Just as Hitler had been prepared to pull back if he had met with armed resistance when he reoccupied the Rhineland, so the Japanese apparently would have halted their advance if Great Britain and the United States threatened to use force. But the only opposition took the form of legalistic protests from Secretary of State Stimson and Pilate-like silence from the British foreign secretary. Accordingly the Japanese armies moved south and consolidated their control. Another force attacked Shanghai from the sea a few months later. As the Japanese seized new strategic centers they continued to keep a weather eye on possible British or American interference and occasionally tested the readiness of the governments of these countries to get tough. By the end of 1937, when deliberate Japanese shelling of British and American shipping in Chinese waters met with nothing more rigorous than demands for indemnities, the Japanese knew that China was theirs for the taking. Great Britain was preoccupied with Hitlerism and the dangers of a new world war. The American people were unwilling to fight to save China from the Japanese. Not even when Chinese cities were bombed from the air and thousands of helpless civilians were killed did Japan risk more than a possible embargo on the shipment of scrap iron. As the army leaders prudently had been stock-piling this material for years, an embargo would not seriously hamper their armament manufacturing program. If stringently imposed it could even be held up to the Japanese people as "proof" of the hostility of the Americans—an argument which would be useful to prepare the people for the seizure of the Philippines and the Dutch East Indies, which was an essential part of the strategy of Japan's domination of Asia. They coveted the oil and rubber of the Indies and sought to drive the arrogant Yankees and the complacent British out of the Far East and the Pacific. With the huge indemnities which they would wring from America's slothful, luxury-loving people, the new order in Asia could be made to yield power, glory, and wealth to the Nipponese. They were convinced that American youth was so decadent that it was unwilling to undergo the rigors of military training. Hence no effective resistance to their plans was conceivable. The tide of Japanese victory which started from Mukden would sweep west and south until all of Asia and the Pacific Ocean was under the flag of the rising sun.

That was the plan and intent of the military leaders of Japan. Instead, in less than two decades they brought ruin to their country and saw their dreams of empire shattered by the reality of American fighting strength from Midway and New Guinea to Okinawa and Hiroshima. The softness of American democracy proved too tough for the hardness of Japanese militarism. From the incident outside Mukden in 1931 to the signing of the capitulation on the bridge of the *Missouri* in 1945 almost every one of the major calculations of the Japanese militarists had gone awry. Before 1931 we had all marveled at the speed with which Japan changed from a backward isolated state into a great world power. Since 1945 we have marveled at the rapidity and completeness of its collapse. In part this was due to the disproportion between the strength of Japan and the United States. But most of the blame lies on the military leaders, arrogant, overconfident, brutal, short sighted—the architects of Japan's defeat.

CHAPTER TWENTY

BACK TO BUDAPEST

I RETURNED to New York in May, 1926, with much background material for the editorial page of the *Times* and enough extra to fill two books, *The Philippines, A Treasure and a Problem*, published late in 1926, and *The Restless Pacific*, published in 1928. They were followed, in 1930, by *America and England?*—an attempt to appraise the relative influence of the United States and Great Britain in the years ahead. There might have been more volumes on America's foreign relations had I not, in the autumn of 1930, been sent to Budapest as United States minister to Hungary. I was thirty-seven years old at the time—one of the youngest ministers in the foreign service.

The experience during the Armistice following World War I had given me a useful ethnic, historical, and political background of central European affairs. My interest in the economic aspects of international relations in the intervening years also proved valuable. The Undersecretary of State, Joseph P. Cotton, told me before I left Washington that, in addition to obtaining information about Hungary, the department wanted me to study the economic conditions in the neighbor nations and co-ordinate this information in compact, nontechnical form. This had to be done without letting my colleagues in the adjacent capitals know that I was acting under instructions, as the implication would have been that they were remiss in not sending adequate reports to the department. Thanks to the fact that none of them shared my interest in financial and economic problems, the material which I obtained about conditions in the countries to which they were accredited was for the most part supplementary to what they were transmitting. This broader scope for my mission gave it an added interest—all the more so in that, within six months of my arrival in Budapest, central Europe was shaken by the greatest bank panic of its history—the collapse of the Viennese Credit-Anstalt—followed by a wave of withdrawals of credits and the imminent collapse of currencies throughout central Europe.

Before leaving for Budapest I had several sessions with Jeremiah Smith, the able, salty New Englander who had salvaged Hungary's finances for the League of Nations. He had done an admirable job in Hungary and had won the awe of the Hungarian people because of the frugality and austerity of his way of living, and their love because of his untiring devotion to Hungarian interests. When he reached Budapest the Magyars were prepared to receive him as they would a foreign potentate. They had assigned him an elaborate apartment in the Royal Palace. A large staff of servants had been assembled. When it was learned that he was a bachelor it was also arranged that he should have all the comforts and consolations to which, according to Hungarian custom, an unmarried man was entitled. "Jerry" Smith refused the offer of the palace apartment, taking, instead, two small rooms in a hotel. He dismissed the servants and declined the other forms of hospitality awaiting his pleasure. He went to his office early, left late, worked in his hotel all evening, and rejected the countless invitations to teas, dinners, and lunches which were heaped on him. Nothing like this on the part of a high official had ever been seen in Hungary.

Smith outlined in detail Hungary's financial troubles in the past and suggested watching current aspects closely. He briefed me on sources of information. One man in particular he recommended—Eugene Havas, a young Hungarian financial expert who was the Budapest correspondent of the *London Economist*. Throughout my stay in Hungary Havas was most helpful in obtaining information for me about Hungary's finances. I had the added advantage of having as my house guest for many months Royall Tyler, formerly Smith's assistant, who was sent by the League of Nations in 1931 to supervise Hungary's finances. He

[187]

was one of the few Americans who spoke Hungarian fluently. His contacts were wide, and his discrimination in appraising information was excellent. Thanks to my constant contact with Tyler, Havas, and a few others who knew the situation, I was able to warn the Department of State in detail about the coming crisis, months before the collapse of Hungary's finances.

Despite the dismemberment of Hungary after World War I, Budapest in the thirties was still a gay capital. It was not, of course —and never had been—a cosmopolitan center like Vienna, rich in tradition and in monuments of past greatness. Rather was it a provincial town, with few old historical landmarks. The more I saw of Budapest the more I realized that the skyline of Buda, dominated by the Royal Palace, was symbolic of the nation—an imposing façade designed to give the illusion of magnificence and strength. The palace was an impressive tribute to the Hungary of the Magyars' dreams—a spacious and imposing residence for a great emperor or all-powerful king of a mighty nation. But it was—and had been since it was built—an empty shell in which no king had lived for more than a night. The modern statues of Hungary's historical heroes on the bastion adjoining the palace were arresting—from a distance. But they represented Hungarian heroes of old as modern propagandists would like them to look— big, strong, fierce warriors, riding great Roman steeds—whereas in actual life they were probably no larger than their rather small, stocky descendants, and rode the same kind of tough, scraggy ponies still to be found on the Hungarian plains—as different from the Roman and the imperial Austrian horses as mongrel hound is from blooded bird dog.

Externally the Hungarians—especially those of the upper class —were Westernized. But in many ways they retained Oriental traits—the love of face and appearance, the unquestioning acceptance of caste and position, the preference for pleasant pretenses over unpleasant truths. The lines between the classes were sharply drawn. At the top were the Hapsburgs and the so-called "mediatized" families—Windisch-Graetz, Hohenlohe, Kinsky, Festetetich, Salm, to name but a few—who were *ebenbürtig* and hence regarded as of sufficiently exalted lineage to intermarry with the Hapsburgs. Graded into them (and intermarried with them) were the magnates or great landed aristocrats, most of whom owed their large estates and the title of "count" to the Hapsburgs—names like Andrássy, Almassy, Apponyi, Batthyány, Bánffy, Palffy, Károlyi, Pallavicini, Széchenyi, Zichy. Beneath these in rank, but often above them in ability, were the members of the gentry or untitled nobility, who had only small estates, and who traced their ancestry to early Magyar chieftans. Sandwiched in between the gentry and the peasants—and only in existence for the last two or three generations—was a middle class, almost entirely of Jewish origin, which had furnished Hungary with nearly all of its bankers, industrialists, merchants, lawyers, artists, writers, and musicians. The upper classes were rightly termed "privileged," but the peasants who worked for a great count or the servants who maintained his household and cared for his possessions were proud to be his retainers. I have seen peasants kneel by the roadside and take off their hats in reverence when the lord of the manor rode by.

Those who have had contacts with the Magyar peasants have been struck by their industry, diligence, sobriety, and self-discipline. Theirs is, in fact, one of the best stocks in Europe. It is not their fault that for generations they were denied the opportunity to obtain even an elemental education. Similar conditions prevailed down to the end of the last century throughout all of eastern Europe and even in large parts of Italy. As late as 1930, most of the Hungarian peasants were living under conditions but little removed from those of the serfs in Russia of the nineteenth century. I visited some of the large estates in Hungary. One I remember in particular had been rented from the Czernin family. The farm hands who worked it received annual pay and allowances consisting of the free use of a small two-room house per family, with about two acres of land for gardens, geese, and pigs, a small amount of firewood per year, and a total cash wage per year—not per day or week or month, but per year—of about seven dollars. This was in 1932. Most of them could not afford a kerosene lamp. None wore shoes except in winter. Yet they were healthy, apparently contented, and seemed to feel no resentment because of the disparity between their own sub-slum living conditions and the hundred-room country houses of the landed nobility which were maintained by large staffs of underpaid servants.

The extent to which peasants and servants derived prestige and satisfaction from "belonging" to one of the great families was repeatedly borne in on me during my two and one-half years in Budapest. It was, of course, a survival of feudalism. I soon found, in this connection, that I was a trial to the legation chauffeur because of my insistence on opening the door of my car on arrival at my destination. Repeatedly he made cordial and polite efforts to teach me the error of my way, but finding that I was impervious, he resorted to the expedient of having the handle of the door tightened in such a manner that I could not open it from the inside. The reason was that he lost face through working for a man who was so ignorant of the conventions as to try to open a door himself, instead of waiting for an attendant to do so. This silent struggle between us continued throughout my stay. Whenever the handle began to loosen up so that I could get out by myself, he had it tightened.

I soon found that anyone taking over the position of minister or ambassador is always in a delicate—and sometimes an embarrassing—situation. He steps into an organization which is well established and is crystallized into cliques. The outgoing chief of mission is missed by a good many of the staff. Even those who did not like him had adjusted their working methods to his. The incoming chief may disturb their routine. It follows, therefore, that beneath the perfect outward courtesy and apparent deference with which the new man is received there lies resentment, uneasiness, and hypersensitiveness. When the new chief is an outsider—a political appointee, rather than a career diplomat—he faces, in addition, the barrier of professionalism. He does not "belong." With the utmost politeness he is continually made conscious of this fact. To do this without being rude requires tact and suavity—two qualities which most foreign service officers have mastered. The staff takes over policy-making as well as routine and assures the new chief that this is "according to Hoyle."

From the point of view of the success of the mission the procedure has much to be said for it, as it results in the subjection of
the inexperienced political appointee to the guidance of experts.
If he is wise he accepts this—at least until such time as he is able to
orient himself and has learned enough to form intelligent reactions of his own.

In my case a few allowances were made because I spoke French
and German fluently and had been for two years in the embassy
in Paris. Furthermore it was known that I had written articles
urging the strengthening of the foreign service. But to counteract
these points in my favor was the fact that I lacked the indis-
pensable requisites—or accomplishments—of social popularity in
a diplomatic capital. I did not play bridge. I did not shoot. I did
not ride. I did not play golf. I had—at the time—no wife to compensate for these deficiencies. But with a mixture of determination, patience, and the most urbane courtesy, the secretary of the
legation, "Kippy" Tuck, subsequently ambassador to Egypt, who
had been devoted to my predecessor and regretted his transfer to
another post, undertook my official and social indoctrination. I
appreciated his help, found his advice on social matters valuable,
and was pleased to realize, when he was transferred after being
with me for more than a year, that he had a feeling of confidence
in me which at the beginning he notably lacked. His successor,
Rudolph E. Schoenfeld, later minister to Romania and ambassador
to Guatemala, like Tuck at first treated me with polite tolerance
—especially my preoccupation with financial and economic matters. In time he became as deeply interested in this field as I was.
We parted with genuine respect and affection for each other.

I found the formality of presenting my letters of credence to
Admiral Horthy, the regent of Hungary, interesting. The hour
was set at 11:30 in the morning, and the uniform full evening dress
with black waistcoat. The staff of the legation, which was to accompany me to the presentation, assembled at the house. We had
been there only a few minutes when the Regent's aide-de-camp
was announced. I waited in the library, and Secretary Tuck went
out to bring him in. As I stood in the door of the library, the A.
D. C., wearing the formal dress uniform of a naval officer (Hun-

gary, of course, had no navy), drew up very stiffly, saluted, and in a loud voice said: "In the name of His Serene Highness the Regent of the Kingdom of Hungary I have the honor to summon you in solemn audience to present your letters of credence." Then, relaxing, he added: "We have three or four minutes before we must go."

We had some sherry and then drove to the palace. There a guard of honor was drawn up and two men in uniform ushered us into a marble hallway, where the official master of ceremonies was waiting. He greeted me formally, turned about, and led the way up the main stairway. On every other step stood a guard in a full-dress, reddish-purple uniform. Each had a saber or halberd. I followed the master of ceremonies with the Regent's aide at my left. Behind us was an officer in red and white uniform, and behind him the legation staff.

At the top of the stairs I noticed a change in the color of the uniforms, the guards wearing red tights and white capes. We walked down a long corridor, with men in red and white every six feet. At the end of the corridor stood an officer in a pink uniform.

Here we were ushered into the Regent's anteroom, where the court chamberlain received us. He wore a coat bordered with fur and embroidery, and high black boots, as if he had stepped out of a seventeenth-century painting. Behind him, also in seventeenth-century court costume, was the Foreign Minister. At the appointed moment the Foreign Minister, walking on my left, accompanied me into the audience room, which had a bare floor and little furniture. At the opposite end stood the Regent in an admiral's uniform. Red faced, bluff, stocky, he looked like a typical sea dog. I walked up to within six feet of him as he stood stiffly. Then he suddenly stepped forward and shook hands with me.

According to instructions I read my speech to him and handed him my letter of credence. He read me his answer in English, after which we shook hands again and had an informal talk. He asked about my previous visit to Hungary and told of his disappointment that he had never been to the United States. He said that he had been delegated to represent the Emperor at the opening of the Panama Canal but that the war intervened. He then turned to hunting, of which he spoke at length. During a pause I asked if I might present my staff. When I had done this we took leave of him and the Foreign Minister and, reclaiming our coats and hats, walked down the long corridor between the guards in their extravagant costumes and were driven back to the legation.

On the numerous occasions during my two and one-half years in Hungary when I talked with the Regent, either at official functions or at "shoots," he fell back on two perennial topics—shooting, and the terrible threat to Hungary from the Russians. He could outshoot nearly all the Hungarian aristocrats, who made it virtually a life work to hunt pheasants, hares, woodcocks, and other animals. Furthermore he was wise enough to recognize the importance of keeping himself in good physical condition and welcomed the opportunity to take part in a "shoot" for the diversion and exercise which it gave him.

At the time, it seemed to me—and to my colleagues in the diplomatic world in Budapest—that the Regent's fears of Russia had become an obsession with him. Over and over he insisted that it was Russia which presented the greatest threat to Hungary and to the Western world and that it was against Russia that, sooner or later, we would have to unite. In the early nineteen thirties this seemed a fanciful phobia. And yet, in retrospect, his fears have proved amply justified. More even than the Nazis, the Soviet Russians have turned out to be Hungary's worst enemies, crushing the spirit of the nation at the same time that they have reduced the economic level of the people to pre-feudal poverty. The Hungarian peasantry and gentry are tough. They have been subjected to many brutalities at the hands of barbarian invaders. In time they may recover. But the black years are now upon them—the black years against which the old sea dog on horseback, who ruled Hungary's kingdom when it had no king, warned so often—and so unconvincingly.

CHAPTER TWENTY-ONE

DIPLOMATS, ARCHDUKES, AND ARISTOCRATS

SOCIAL LIFE in all diplomatic posts takes too much time, especially the entertainment of fellow diplomats. Custom decrees that the head of each diplomatic mission must periodically invite the heads of other diplomatic missions to lunch or dinner or tea. To decline these invitations except for valid cause would be a serious breach of etiquette. Lunches and dinners at least serve the useful purpose of providing food. But the teas and large receptions do not have even that redeeming feature. I know of few more futile pastimes than milling about in a large crowd of people most of whom are bent on getting in touch with someone at the opposite side of the room, and who, if you detain them, react just as a cat does when its owner demands responsiveness at a moment when the cat's attention is riveted on the dish of pig's liver which it believes to be in the kitchen.

The dean of the diplomatic corps—by custom the chief of mission who has served longest in the post—was, when I was in Budapest, a charming, stereotyped old-school Austrian, Count Calice, whose father and grandfather before him had been in the Austro-Hungarian diplomatic service. He was invariably helpful, friendly, and "correct" in the French meaning of the word—that is to say, precise, accurate, and conventional in his statements, never volunteering any elaboration unless requested to do so. Count Calice was an accomplished violinist and had a thorough knowledge and deep love of music. This became a bond between us, and we spent pleasant hours playing Beethoven trios, he as violinist, I as cellist, and one of his staff as pianist. He spoke faultless English, was stiffly courteous, and to direct questions was always cordially responsive. But I do not recall that he was either keenly aware of, or even interested in, the problems of Hungary.

Not so the Belgian minister, Viscount Davignon, who was to become Belgium's ambassador to Germany just before the outbreak of World War II. Outwardly he had the earmarks of the old-fashioned professional diplomat. He cultivated a pose of apparent fatigue and boredom and showed a marked preference for picking his friends among the legitimist members of the Hungarian aristocracy. But beneath this pose was an excellent, orderly mind, a freedom from wishful thinking, and a keen awareness of the dangers inherent in the threatening economic crisis. Furthermore, he was the only one of the "colleagues" who had a sense of humor, albeit even this failed him when things pertaining to any of the diplomats came up for comment. When, at a dinner attended by the chiefs of mission without their wives, some of them showed the influence of too much wine, I sought out Davignon and remarked that it would be fun if someone once were to decline to take fellow-ministers *au grand sérieux*. He fixed a baleful eye on me and said ruefully but with finality: "That would be quite impossible," and continued to view their antics with mournful solemnity.

It was usual for the archdukes in Budapest to invite members of the diplomatic corps to lunches or teas. The Archduchess Isabella also asked them to play poker, which she relished. As I enjoyed the game I went occasionally to her house to make a fifth or sixth. She was a woman of intelligence and force—in contrast to nearly all other royalty, and certainly to the other Hapsburgs at that time living in Hungary. She was born princess of Croy, a member of a Belgian family which had intermarried for generations with European royalty and nobility. Her husband, the Archduke Frederick, was still alive when I knew her but lived in seclusion on one of his estates near Esztergom and never appeared at any of her parties.

Isabella was a large, heavy woman in her mid-seventies, with a broad face, a square chin, a prominent but finely chiseled nose, and eyes which she kept closed much of the time due to prolonged eye trouble. She always wore magnificent necklaces and other jewelry—my mother estimated that when she came to dinner one night she had on at least a half-million dollars' worth of diamonds, emeralds, rubies, and pearls. She spoke English, French, and German with equal colloquial fluency, and also Italian, and, I believe, a little Hungarian, although, as she had lived in Austria until the end of World War I, her knowledge of Hungarian was probably sketchy. Despite her weight and age she loved shooting. The morning of the day I first met her she had knocked down thirty-five pheasants, which for a very stout old lady with failing eyesight was not a bad record.

The former German chancellor, Prince von Bülow, in his memoirs, tells the story that Isabella had made up her mind that her eldest daughter was to marry the Archduke Franz Ferdinand, who became heir to the Hapsburg throne after the death of the Archduke Rudolph. When Franz Ferdinand was a frequent visitor at her home in Vienna—I believe she lived in the Belvedere palace—Isabella was much pleased and did everything to encourage his attentions to her daughter, under the careful chaperonage of one of her ladies in waiting, the Countess Sophie Chotek. After this had been going on for many months, Franz Ferdinand asked his great-uncle, the Emperor Franz Josef, for permission to marry the Countess Chotek. Isabella, according to von Bülow, was furious and not only dismissed her lady in waiting but did all in her power to persuade the old Emperor to forbid the Archduke to marry her. But Franz Ferdinand was not to be deterred, and even when the Emperor, as head of the house of Hapsburg, ruled that she could not become empress and that none of their heirs could inherit the throne, Franz Ferdinand insisted on marrying her. She was given the title of duchess of Hohenberg when they were married and, a few years later, was murdered with him at Serajevo.

As poker partners Isabella often invited one of the other diplomats—usually the Greek or the German minister, who enjoyed the game—and, on occasions, a Countess Károlyi, who seemed to be as determined a character as Isabella, and inclined to be cantankerous. There were also two "steadies"—both ladies in waiting—

ALBERT APPONYI
Who preached that no settlement in Europe lasts forever

who were perfect examples of the professional hangers-on whom one had always heard were attached to the old courts in Europe—hard-eyed, painted, sharp-clawed women who earned their keep by their skill at cards and by pandering to the weaknesses of the guests of the great—and of their employers. When either of these ladies lost—which happened rarely—she seemed to draw into her shell like a turtle, and blinked her beady eyes as she watched the pot gathered by someone else. When she won, her boney fingers would rake in the chips and caress them greedily as she sorted and stacked them.

My diary entry written the day after my first poker party at Isabella's gives a few side lights: "At 9:30 I went to play poker with Izzy. Costume tux. She was not quite ready when I arrived, but came out into the hall in a few minutes, where the poker table had been arranged, and sat down on a sofa and drew a rug over her, and then organized the game, told us where to sit, and what the stakes were (fifty pengö worth of chips), etc. Mostly jackpots, with a stripped deck, dealing to the right. I sat on Izzy's right, and she played a good fast game, and very cheerful. She took her turn at everything, including shuffling, and did some pretty fancy and successful bluffing. Also loved to pick up my cards for me if she was out, and insisted that she brought me luck (which I needed, as I lost steadily after the first half hour.) At about 11:30 Gabby [the Archduchess Gabrielle] came in, back from *Tristan*, and joined us. A really charming woman, with a keen face and a merry eye. Item: Gabby carried an old brown bag from which she took some sandwiches that she had evidently taken to the opera. Towards midnight the old girl began to nod, and so the last three rounds were played, and a change pot. I was down 180 pengö. Walked home."

When Isabella was losing she became downhearted. When she won she was gay. Occasionally she would get bored with regular draw poker and would call for a round of roodles or dealer's choice. She was particularly delighted when, on one such occasion it was my turn to deal, I proposed a hand of "spit in the ocean." She translated the name into French—"*cracher dans la mer*"—and into German—"*in See spucken*"—and seemed to relish its sound in all three languages. Thereafter, quite often she herself proposed this variant and always translated it into whatever language at the moment we were not speaking—German and French were usually used at these games.

The diaries and letters contain numerous references to "Jo & Gussie"—the Archduke Josef and his wife, the Archduchess Augusta. They were friendly, dull people, made even duller by the restrictions which had surrounded them from childhood—restrictions as to whom they might see and the things which they might do. As all archdukes took precedence over everyone other than royalty, it followed that if more than one Hapsburg couple was present they always sat together. Thus, when Isabella invited Josef and Augusta and their daughter to lunch, as she did on one occasion when I was present, she had the Archduke Josef on her right, and beyond him her daughter Gabrielle and next to her, Augusta. Had there been any other Hapsburg man present he would have been seated on Isabella's left, but as there was none, and as I was the ranking diplomat at that particular luncheon, this position was assigned to me. I had not had a chance to find out who was sitting on my left. She was a plainly dressed, very shy girl in her early twenties. To make conversation I asked her if she had been skiing—the snowfall was good at the time. She answered "No." I then asked if she had been at a large ball which one of the foreign diplomats had just given. She answered "No." Had she seen such and such a movie? No. Did she like the opera? She never went. Was the swimming good at the Gellert pool? She had never been in. Did she play much tennis? No. After a few more attempts to find out what she did—partly in hopes of finding out who she was—it dawned on me that she must be the Archduchess Magdalena, the daughter of Josef and Augusta whom I had never met. Only an archduchess could be cut off from so many normal activities and interests of youth.

Augusta was a daughter of the King of Bavaria, and a granddaughter of the Emperor Franz Josef. She was an enormous woman with prodigious energy—she rode horseback or swam each day, and with much pride she showed me her rowing machine, on which, she assured me, she spent a half-hour each morning. But she was the human counterpart of the California privet, which in most plant catalogues is described as a "gross feeder." She took three or four helpings of everything, and at her own table she not only washed them down with wine but always had one or more large mugs of beer. She was so fond of sweets that several desserts were served to her which were not offered to her guests—and she took large helpings of each. After lunch or dinner she always pulled out a big black cigar and puffed it with evident relish. Her chief diversions were the movies and the opera. Each afternoon she spent at the former, and each evening at the latter, usually having a snack served to her in her box so that she could pull through until the next meal. When the Archduke Josef showed me a portrait of the Empress Elizabeth, famed for her beauty, and I glanced at Augusta, it was hard to believe that this heavy, red-faced, blowsy creature was Elizabeth's granddaughter.

It was in the tradition of the old dual monarchy that hunting was the principal interest not only of the archdukes but also of the Hungarian aristocrats—so much so, in fact, that I noted in my diary early in my stay in Budapest that "apparently one has to shoot one's way into Hungarian society if one wants to get there." The game on the great Hungarian estates—particularly the pheasants and hares—formed an important item of revenue. The custom was to permit shooting on only three or four days at a time, and then to invite ten or a dozen expert shots. From fifty to two hundred beaters were employed, stationed at various strategic spots on the estates, with instructions to move in a line slowly towards the guns, driving the game ahead of them. In the days of Genghis Khan a similar procedure was followed as part of the military training of his forces, with the difference that the beaters first formed a large circle and slowly moved in towards the center, imprisoning and killing all animals that could not fly. But as practiced in Hungary and on the great estates in parts of Poland until World War II, the killing was reserved to the aristocrats, each of whom usually had with him at least two guns and always one or two gunbearers who loaded for him and carried the hundreds of shells which he required. On occasions a good shot would get upward of a thousand animals in a day—the Archduke Josef once told me that he had shot twenty-three hundred pheasants and hares in the previous two days.

The custom was to allow each beater to take home a hare—his wage for the day. The rest were sold. The peasants seemed to enjoy the outing as much as did the shooters and, of course, preferred to drive for men who were good shots. When, as was usually the case, the good shots were also the bearers of famous names, the peasants liked it even better. As far as I could see, the attitude of the magnates towards the peasants was one of genuine benevolence and paternalism. But the difference in points of view between the feudalism of eastern Europe and our own Western world was brought home to me by mere chance when I had been invited by the Regent to take part in a wild-boar hunt in mid-winter. I knew that I would have to stand for hours in the snow, and so not only had dressed accordingly but had brought with me a knapsack in which, among other things, I had a thermos filled with hot tea with rum in it. After the first hours in the cold, early morning, I made signs to the gunbearer who had been detailed to go with me, and who spoke no German, to hand me the knapsack. After taking a cup of the hot tea, I did what any American would have done without giving it a thought—offered a cup to the bearer. He looked at me with great surprise, and as I smilingly held it out to him, he removed his hat and continued to hesitate to take the proffered cup, acting almost as if he expected me to snatch it away as he was about to reach for it. It was obvious that this was the first time that he had ever been offered anything by those whom he was attending. When finally he took the cup and drank it, he still seemed incredulous, as if I had done something that just was not done by our best people, and as if he might be reproved for abetting my unconventionality.

On several occasions after attending one of the shoots I noted in my diary the difference between members of the gentry like Horthy and his brother, and the aristocrats. Both Horthys were men of force, energy, and character—simple, practical, and intelligent at the same time that they were well bred and courteous. I noticed, for example, on a shoot which the Regent gave for the Maharaja of Patiala, that Admiral Horthy, who accompanied the

Maharaja on horseback to a new shooting stand where the Maharaja dismounted, himself took the Maharaja's horse back with him because it was the simplest and most natural thing to do, rather than to wait for a groom.

In contrast to the Horthys, the heads of the big magnate families seemed to be survivors of a social system which was rapidly dying. This impression was heightened by the fact that they all wore hunting coats which dated from the last century, buttoned tight in the neck, and with long full skirts. Each carried a little muff. Those whose hats were not full of feathers wore fur caps. Without exception they had charming manners, spoke several languages fluently and with little or no accent, were courteous, and, of course, were excellent shots and horsemen. Undoubtedly they had personal courage. They could hardly be described as weak. But they seemed to be physically spent, as if they found the futility of their existence exhausting. They went from one estate to another, shot from dawn till dark, and unless the bag of each gun ran into the hundreds, they felt that they had failed their host. Not only did they live for shooting, but shooting was their only interest. Wickham Steed, the famous editor of the *London Times*, who had for years been correspondent for that newspaper in Austria and Hungary, noted in his volume *The Hapsburg Monarchy* a story told about one of the Czernins who, taking stock of his life as he lay on his deathbed, considered what he would say when the Lord asked him what he had done in his years on earth. "Just shot hares, Lord. Shot hares. Shot hares. Shot hares." This is the life story of many a Magyar magnate.

Lest these generalizations about hare-shooting aristocrats seem too all-embracing, it is only fair to mention some of the exceptions with whom I came in contact, whose achievements were widely recognized. Outstanding because of his intelligence and integrity was Count Paul Teleki, to whom I have already referred in Chapter Twelve. Where other Hungarians sought to convince by impassioned speeches and extravagant arguments, he was cool, clear, and frank. He neither evaded nor denied facts which more biased Hungarians would have brushed aside angrily because they affected Hungary's claims adversely. A meeting of minds with

Teleki was easy in that by intellectual discipline he was a western European—one of the few in that predominantly Oriental section of Europe. This is remarkable in that his father's family was of Transylvanian origin—and Transylvania was physically and spiritually a part of the Orient. His mother was a Greek—a member of one of the Greek Phanariot families which for generations had served the Turks as overlords in eastern Europe. Out of the union of the two blood streams came an intelligence that was as forthright as it was honest. It was characteristic of this earnest, truly good man that, when he was prime minister of Hungary during the first year of World War II and it became clear that Hitler would overrun Hungary, he committed suicide as a way of dramatizing to the nobler element among his people the shame which this course implied. A man of lesser integrity would have bowed to the inevitability of overwhelmingly superior brute strength. To Teleki the prospect of Nazi domination of Hungary was intolerable. He could not stave it off. He would not be a party to compliance. In consequence, suicide was the only form of protest left to him.

The most distinguished of the Hungarian aristocrats, both in character and intellect, was Count Albert Apponyi, then in his mid-eighties. Tall and lean, he had an eagle's eyes and beak-like nose, a long grey beard, and upstanding grey hair. Although a passionate Magyar he yet was cosmopolitan in his outlook, steeped in the history and the traditions of Europe. He loved Budapest but was equally at home in Vienna, Geneva, Paris, or London. Not only did he speak seven modern languages fluently, but also Latin, which, in his youth, was still used as a spoken tongue by the upper classes in eastern Europe. He had the broad outlook of a man who had observed Europe closely for sixty years, and he had known most of the great figures in this period. His was the long view, which was enlightening to one who, like myself, was imbued with the American tradition of haste and finality. I remember his saying that in his own lifetime he had seen the Second French Empire rise and fall, the German Empire rise and fall, and the Austro-Hungarian Empire revivified and apparently made new and strong, only to collapse within a few decades. Why, then, believe that political matters were finite or that treaties were immutable and would last forever?

It was generally said of Count Apponyi that he was a liberal. This is more than can be said of most of his associates among the Hungarian aristocracy. One of them—also a count—who had been one of the undersecretaries in the Austro-Hungarian foreign office when the ultimatum was presented to Serbia following the murder of the Archduke Franz Ferdinand at Serajevo in 1914, lectured me one day about the "brutality" of the Serbs. I was aware that he was reputed to have had a part in the so-called Friedjung forgeries through which the Austrian foreign office sought to justify before the eyes of the world a policy of "punishing" Serbia as early as 1909. I also knew that he was supposed to have done everything in his power in 1914 to encourage the Austrian foreign office to bring about a situation in which the Serbs would have to fight. When he paused in his diatribe against the Serbs I said to him: "In the light of what has happened since 1914—including the breakup of the empire and the death of millions of men in the world war—as you look back upon the action of the Austro-Hungarian foreign office in presenting the ultimatum to Serbia in July of 1914, do you think that a different course should have been followed?" Without a moment's hesitation he replied: "If I had it to do over again I wouldn't change one single thing. We had no alternative but to do what we did." Not even the fact that he was not very intelligent made up for the callousness of the reaction. It seemed to me to represent the blindness and stubbornness of Bourbonism at its worst. To the extent that he was only a subordinate, and that the policy had the support of others from the Emperor Franz Josef and the German Kaiser down, my reaction was unfair to him. From the Russians or even the Germans before 1914, as after 1933, such callousness was to be expected. But the very qualities which had made Vienna one of the most civilized cities in the world—the tolerance, the graciousness, the easy-going good humor, the philosophical resignation of the Austrian people—made it hard to visualize Austrian officials, even though Hungarian by birth, continuing to be proud of their share of the responsibility for World War I.

More typical of the easy-going attitude of the old court nobles was a story which one of them told me about an experience of his during World War I. He must be nameless lest, through the perverted sadism of the Communists, the incident might be used by them against some of his heirs. This man, head of one of the great aristocratic houses, was cultivated, gifted, charming, an excellent horseman, an expert shot, musical, a connoisseur of the arts. But he was also lazy, with an easy-going disposition, and with a large measure of the spirit of "live and let live." At the outbreak of World War I he held an important diplomatic post in one of the Allied nations, and on his recall to Vienna he joined the army and was assigned as aide-de-camp to one of the archdukes who was in command of the Austrian troops operating in the Trentino. This territory, although largely Italian in population, had been an integral part of the old Austro-Hungarian Empire. There was little or no fighting in the area at this time, but the Austrian general staff was bothered by the surreptitious publication of an Italian language newspaper which incited the Italian-speaking population in that part of Austria to join with their Italian brethren across the line. Several times the paper was suppressed, only to reappear shortly in another part of the Trentino.

As the publication began to influence the local population against the Austrians the headquarters decided that drastic steps would have to be taken. Accordingly my informant, at the time a major on the staff, was ordered to take a detachment of soldiers and find and arrest the two men suspected of being the publishers of this seditious sheet. He told me that the assignment was distasteful to him—that he felt that it was only natural for these Italians inside Austria to sympathize with the Italians who were fighting Austria. He went to Trent and found one of the men, who was placed under arrest, and later tried and executed. For several weeks nothing further was seen or heard of the offending newspaper, and my friend felt that he had achieved his purpose. But shortly the newspaper reappeared, this time in a more aggressive form. Once more he was sent to find and arrest the publisher. Once more he set out on his mission feeling sorry for his intended victim. He found the house in which the printing press was located and surrounded it. But the good-natured aristocrat carefully left the rear door unguarded. His men broke in through the front and searched the house. They confiscated the press and the latest edition of the paper. But the editor escaped.

As my friend told me this, he asked: "Do you know the name of the man who escaped?"

Obviously I answered: "How could I?"

"His name," he said—and he paused—"was Benito Mussolini."

As I sat in the window seat of this magnate's palace in Budapest and looked at his kindly, cultivated face I realized once more the enormous power of individuals in the shaping of history. Had this representative of the old court aristocracy not been so easy going, and had he carried out literally the orders given him, Mussolini would have been shot then and there and the history of Europe might have been distinctly different. But the iron was in Mussolini's soul, rather than in the soul of this amiable cosmopolite.

CHAPTER TWENTY-TWO

A PREVIEW OF MACARTHUR

VISITING FIREMEN have always been troublesome for American diplomats. During my years in Budapest comparatively few civilians in search of "honors" besides President Butler of Columbia University turned up. But my freedom from this phase of diplomatic representation was more than compensated by the circumstances attending the visit, while on a holiday, of General Douglas MacArthur, who at the time was chief of staff of the United States Army. From my military attaché, who lived in Vienna, I first had word of the General's intended visit. As it came at a time when most of my contacts with the Hungarian government in behalf of Americans had been for the purpose of helping American bankers obtain repayments on loans which they had pressed on reluctant Hungarian creditors, the coming of a high ranking official who, obviously, had no financial favors to ask of the Hungarian government, and who represented American public life at its best, was welcome. In his own right Douglas MacArthur, when he was chief of staff, was already one of the most distinguished officers of the American Army. Accordingly, as soon as I knew his schedule I arranged to present him to the Regent and the Minister of War and planned a number of lunches and dinners in his honor.

About ten days before his expected arrival I had word from the military attaché in Vienna that the General's aide had telephoned to ask me to request the Hungarian government to send a private railroad car to Vienna to take the General to Budapest. As the Hungarian government was facing bankruptcy it seemed to me inopportune to ask it to undertake the expense of a private car for General MacArthur—all the more so in view of the fact that the General was not coming to Hungary on a mission, but merely on a vacation, and, incidentally, to receive in person a decoration that had been promised him. Furthermore, whenever I traveled to or from Hungary, even on government business, I, as American minister, went second class because the government did not pay me enough to travel first class. I saw no reason why another American official, vacationing in Hungary, should require a special car to bring him to Budapest, even though he was chief of staff of the American Army. Accordingly I asked the military attaché to tell General MacArthur that I did not feel justified in passing along his request to the Hungarian government.

Three days later there was another telephone call from Vienna. This time General MacArthur's aide sent word that the General would like me to ask the Hungarian government to provide a private railway car to take him from Budapest to Bucharest, the capital of Romania. To my nonmilitary mind the same arguments that applied against requesting a private car to take General MacArthur from Vienna to Budapest applied to asking for a car to take him from Budapest to Bucharest. Furthermore, I realized that if a Hungarian railway car were sent into Romania it might not be returned, and that, therefore, the legation might find itself involved in a quarrel between the Hungarian and the Romanian governments about rolling stock. So once more I sent back word to the General that I was sorry, but that I did not think it proper for the legation to comply with his request.

Two days later came another telephone call from MacArthur's staff, relayed by my military attaché in Vienna. Would I obtain clearance from the Hungarian government for a Romanian private car on which the American minister in Bucharest was coming up to Budapest to meet the General and take him on to Bucharest? Because such a request should properly have come from the legation in Romania, I telephoned Bucharest and asked the American minister, Charles Wilson, if General MacArthur's request had his approval, and if he wished me to intercede with the Hungarian government. Wilson—an old friend—began burning up the wires. When he had calmed down sufficiently I learned that, through his military attaché, he had received MacArthur's request that the Romanian government be asked to furnish a private car; that he had replied that he disapproved the request and would not transmit it; that he had no intention of coming up to Budapest to meet the General; and that he saw no reason why the chief of staff of the United States Army, traveling on leave, could not use a compartment on the *Orient Express*, just as would any other American official, including the secretary of state, even if he were on an official mission. As this was just what my own reaction had been, I called up the military attaché in Vienna and asked him to relay to General MacArthur my regret that I could not ask for clearance for a Romanian private car to take him from Budapest to Bucharest.

As the General's visit was to be brief, plans were made to enable him to see as much as possible and to meet the principal officials. Even such details—all-important in the eyes of the Hungarians—as where he should sit at official functions were checked in advance and prearranged. As is usually done, the local protocol was followed, which, in Hungary, was the court procedure as laid down in the days of the Emperor Franz Josef. A few days before the General's arrival I had a telephone call from the chief of protocol at the Foreign Office to say that word had been received through the Ministry of War to the effect that General MacArthur would like to take precedence over the American minister at official functions. The Foreign Office wished to know if I concurred in this proposal. I asked the chief of protocol whether, under Hungarian procedure, a minister of a foreign government accredited to Hungary or a visiting dignitary of that government was regarded as the ranking representative of the foreign government. The reply was that only if the head of the foreign government in person or, on occasions, the foreign minister of that government, visited Hungary would he be considered as outranking the accredited minister of that government. I remarked that I was unaware of any American ruling according to which the chief of staff of the United States Army on leave of absence would outrank the American minister or ambassador to the country which the chief of staff was visiting. The chief of protocol expressed his relief and said that, according to Hungarian custom, it would be most unusual to accord such special precedence to a foreign military dignitary, and assured me that the inquiry would never have been made if the suggestion had not come from the General's own staff. Nevertheless we agreed that, except at official functions at which I represented the American government, he would be given first place.

In due time I had word that General MacArthur had decided to motor from Vienna to Budapest, and was expected to arrive at the Hotel Ritz at about 11 P.M. on September 20. Because of my respect for the office of chief of staff, and because, as head of the American mission I had made numerous official arrangements for him, I went to the Hotel Ritz that evening to await his arrival —the only American official visitor, incidentally, during my entire stay in Budapest for whom such an exception was made. When we were introduced, his coolness bordered on rudeness— which I attributed to the natural fatigue of a long automobile journey following a busy day in pursuit of decorations. Accordingly I suggested that if he would care to call at the legation the next morning I would be glad to confirm the details of the engagements which I had made for him.

At the appointed hour he arrived. Very formally he took note of the appointments made for him; he was to lunch with the Regent; there would be a dinner for him at the legation, etc. When I had finished outlining the schedule there was a pause. Then he said to me:

"Oh, by the way. If you don't mind, I think I'll take up with the Ministry of War the matter of obtaining clearance for a private car to be brought to Budapest from Romania to take me to Bucharest."

For a moment I found it hard to believe that, after being turned down three times, he was making for the fourth time this request which I had so plainly indicated could not be granted.

I paused while I gagged my natural indignation and very softly said to him:

"I'm sorry, General, but I think you'd better NOT."

As I emphasized the "NOT" with finality his face flushed, and even the back of his neck. Obviously he resented being denied his own way. But he behaved like a good soldier and a gentleman. "All right," he said, after a brief pause, "if that's the way you feel about it, I won't."

From that moment onwards he was helpful, co-operative, and understanding. He said the right things to the right people. He went out of his way to be agreeable to the Hungarians. When I suggested that a word to so-and-so would be appreciated he at once made the appropriate remark. His fine appearance, his distinguished record, and his very genuine ability impressed everyone. Altogether his visit contributed materially to better relations with Hungary. He was presented with the decorations which he coveted, and left in a first-class compartment for Bucharest, where more honors were shown him, and where, likewise, he won friends for America and admiration for his own fine soldierly qualities.

CHAPTER TWENTY-THREE

IN THE NEIGHBORING
CAPITALS

FOLLOWING instructions from the State Department I kept in touch with events in the neighboring capitals. Most fruitful was Vienna, still a great financial center, and closely tied to the former parts of the old empire, despite its divorce from them. The pan-German movement, which was to end in the union of Austria and Germany, was already strong in Austria before Hitler became its leader in Germany. Through my military attaché, Colonel Baer, who lived in Vienna, I kept in touch with the heads of the Nazi movement in Austria. I lunched or dined with two or three of them on a number of occasions—all of this was before Hitler came to power in Germany—and I was interested to see that they were steadily gaining in influence. When I lunched with them a few days after Hitler became chancellor I found them puzzled as to how his advent might affect their plans. A month later, however, they were going about their propaganda with such confidence that it was apparent that they had the approval of the new German government. During my last visit in Vienna, in April, 1933, the Austrian Nazi party was not yet politically powerful, but it was apparent that within a short time the Nazi movement in Austria might be formidable. When I suggested this to Americans in Vienna they were skeptical. My prediction was based on knowledge of the fanatical character of the leaders and on their reports about how they had arranged in the provinces that persons with radios not only should listen when Hitler and his agents in Austria broadcast, but also should invite the young men and women of the neighborhood to listen. The appeal of the

German Nazis at that time was largely directed to the discontented youth of the country. It seemed logical that the promises which Hitler's followers were so successfully holding out to the German people would also appeal to the Austrians. Within a few months a powerful Nazi party was functioning in Austria, and in little more than a year this party failed to obtain control of Austria by a *coup d'état* only because someone blundered and needlessly murdered Dollfuss.

I had no direct contacts with Hitler, but one of his passionate followers and intimates, "Putzi" Hanfstaengl, had been a close associate of mine at Harvard, where he and I had formed the so-called Harvard Opera Association, which offered opera tickets to Harvard undergraduates for very small prices. Hanfy was a tumultuous, gifted fanatic, with an exuberant passion for music. He would play the piano for me by the hour—largely from memory—Wagner, Strauss, anything and everything that I called for —and then would take me to a German rathskeller in Boston where, after large quantities of food and beer, he would lecture me about international affairs, art, or philosophy. Always he was good company, but he lacked balance and judgment. So deep was my impression of this side of his character that, when I heard that he was one of Hitler's intimates, the conclusion was unavoidable that Hitler must be a thoroughly unstable person. I knew that Hanfy was convinced that the Germans were the master race. He dramatized the role of Germany in the world as that of a combination of Parsifal, Siegfried, and Hans Sachs. To what extent he fired political mysticism of this sort in Hitler I do not know. But the more I thought of Hanfy's potential influence over Hitler the more it seemed unbelievable that any political leader who was hypnotized by such a man could become formidable. Least of all was there reason to believe that a maniac such as Hitler could hypnotize the German people as he soon did. This judgment was one of many which proved badly mistaken. Hitler turned to Hanfy for relief and entertainment, apparently as fascinated by Hanfy's passionate outpouring of music as I had been. In time they parted company. Hitler's fanaticism became too much even for the fanatical Hanfy.

[212]

GENERAL DOUGLAS MACARTHUR
A brilliant soldier, he always loved medals and personal adulation

While my visits to Vienna were frequent, I also made a point to go to Belgrade, Prague, and Rome. The American minister to Yugoslavia, Dyneley Prince, was an old acquaintance. He and his wife had many ties with friends and relatives of mine in New York. He spoke various local dialects of Croatian and Serbian, as well as Polish, Czech, Russian, French, German, and a dozen or more American Indian languages. When I visited Belgrade he volunteered that most of the people whom I might see would have little interest for me. The country, he said, was run by a dictator, and the dictator was King Alexander. Accordingly he arranged an appointment with him for me.

I found the King to be a man of rather limited intelligence, friendly and interested, but in no sense a man of the world. Like so many Serbs he was stubborn, upright, narrow, stern, and unimaginative. The audience was held at his palace outside Belgrade —rather like the Long Island house of a New York banker. In the entrance hall I was shown a door and told to open it. I found myself in a comparatively small library with large windows looking out into gardens beyond. A man in uniform sat behind the desk and rose as I came in. I recognized him at once as the King, but was somewhat surprised that no one was there to make any introduction. He was affable and interested and spoke good French with a bad accent. He talked mostly about Italian policy, blaming Italy for many of the troubles in central Europe, and saying that he could not understand the Italians' policy except on the grounds of their desire for prestige.

Competent observers assured me that the King's policy with respect to the Croatians had created such bitterness that his life was in serious danger. It was no surprise, therefore, to learn eighteen months later that he had been murdered by Croatian agitators. On his death his cousin, Prince Paul, became principal regent. I saw him twice—once at his summer place in Bled and again at a lunch at his palace in Belgrade. Whereas Alexander was a Balkan, Paul was a Westerner. Alexander had been brought up and remained a soldier. Paul was a graduate of Oxford and a keen student of political problems. During my two visits he cross-questioned me closely about conditions in America and showed a better-than-average understanding of our problems. We did not, of course, speak about Yugoslav affairs, and I could therefore only surmise that his attitude would differ from that of the King primarily because he was Western.

I also visited Czechoslovakia. Beneš was still the leading figure there. I had met him in 1923 and found him very interesting. But when I saw him on this visit to Prague, a decade later, I had the impression of a tired man who had lost touch with realities by becoming too firmly wedded to theories and "solutions." As the originator of the Little Entente—the understanding between Romania, Yugoslavia, and Czechoslovakia—he tended to continue to think in terms of fixed groupings. It is a measure of the extent to which his thinking had become frozen that as early as the beginning of 1933 he described the European situation as one in which a new rivalry was forming between Italy and Germany, and he insisted that Italy was strongly opposed to the union of Austria with Germany. As a matter of fact Italy and Germany soon became close partners, and if Mussolini in reality opposed the *Anschluss*, he was peculiarly inactive in translating his opposition into effective speech or action. Beneš also remarked that Hungary was not anxious to be absorbed in the German orbit. While this had a larger measure of truth in it, Hungary, in fact, also soon became an active partner of Germany's, even though a substantial portion of the people of Hungary regretted that this course seemed to be unavoidable. If Beneš had any doubts as to the ability of his own country to escape the German maw, he did not mention them. Even after Hitler came into power Beneš continued to fear the restoration of the Hapsburgs more than he feared the union of Austria with Germany. He was one of many who underestimated Hitler's capacity to take what he wanted. For this he does not deserve too great censure, for, like many other devotees of reason applied to international affairs, his logical mind found it hard to envisage the triumph of unreason. When, five years later, Chamberlain sold Czechoslovakia down the river, the British statesman was not alone in believing that this concession to the beast of Berchtesgaden would bring "peace in our time." Apparently many leaders in Europe were unable to conceive that

Hitler would go from one monstrous demand to another and would deliberately bring on a world war.

Beneš was always more impressive as an idea man than as a leader. He lacked the egotism, the vigorous personality, the dramatic powers, and the ruthlessness which seem standard equipment for men of the leader type. In contrast, Mussolini had all the characteristics of the typical *duce*. He was power and will incarnate, the inspirer of millions, and the restorer of a disillusioned and beaten nation. His political philosophy centered about the use of force to modernize his country—a concept as old as hoary paternalism, and as lacking in faith in humanity.

When I was in Rome our ambassador, John W. Garrett, who had been my chief when I was in the embassy in Paris during the first two years of World War I, arranged for me to have a talk with *il Duce*. The interview took place at the Palazzo Venezzia. At precisely 4:30 a secretary ushered me through a small door that led into the ballroom of the palace, and she at once withdrew. The room was about one hundred and fifty feet long and fifty feet wide with a thirty-foot ceiling. The only bright light was over a desk in the corner diagonally opposite the door through which I had entered. A long, narrow carpet led to the desk. Mussolini did not look up till I stood in front of him. He then rose, walked around the desk, shook hands, and asked me to be seated.

As I had been warned that he liked to speak English but that his English was bad, whereas his French was good, I took the bull by the horns and started the conversation myself in French. When I remarked at the outset that conditions in Vienna, where I had been the previous week, were uneasy, he interjected: "Not without reason," and then proceeded to discuss the Austrian situation, and from this branched into possible solutions of the central European problems as a whole. I was struck with his detailed knowledge of the ethnic complexities in the territory of the former Austro-Hungarian Empire, and with his familiarity with the economic relations of the succession states. While I had expected to find a man of great personal magnetism, I had not thought he would be either particularly well informed or intelligent.

Twice in the course of our talk he warned me that Americans did not and could not realize how deep-seated were European hatreds and how difficult it was to soften or eradicate them. He brought this up in connection with the question of boundary revisions and remarked incidentally that he believed that the leaders in prewar Hungary had made a mistake in thinking in terms of a state rather than a nation. They had considered the various minorities governed by them as being Hungarian instead of thinking of the Magyars as forming the true Hungarian nation. When I pointed out that there might be opposition even to minor modifications of the boundaries in situations where these changes were ethnically sound, he asked if it wasn't better that the big nations force minor sacrifices on smaller ones than risk a new war. Incidentally, he remarked twice, with the greatest emphasis, that it would be impossible to localize a conflict between any two states in Europe and that a new war would be fatal for Europe.

From the Balkans he turned to Germany—Hitler's election had given the Nazis the majority in the Reichstag eight days previously—and remarked that he looked on this event as a safeguard for peace, owing to the fact that Hitler could not afford the diversion of a war. "I speak from experience," said Mussolini, "when I say that Hitler must concentrate his entire attention for the next three or four years on consolidating and organizing his country."

During the preceding month Mussolini had been having many difficulties with the French. He was outspoken about how hard it was to come to any agreement with them. He scoffed at the popular idea that the Italians and French were close kin. Not only did they come of different racial stock but their philosophy was different. Where the French were cynical and hard, the Italians were open and friendly. Whenever the French criticized Italy the Italians took offense in spite of the French explanation that they criticized their own people in the same manner.

When, finally, our long interview drew to a close he walked with me down the long carpet to the door. Pausing by a window, he spoke with enthusiasm about the excavations that he was having carried on at the Forum and suggested that I see them. I had the distinct impression that they were of deep interest to him because of his concept of himself as the reincarnation of the rulers of ancient Rome who had built and remodeled the Forum. In fact, as I look back on this talk with him, and on his subsequent acts, his consciousness that he was the heir to the Cæsars—which, in a restricted sense, of course he was—seems to have been the dominant force in his life, responsible not only for his rise but for his fall. Had he not been so zealous to recreate the Roman Empire he would not have launched such vain expeditions as that against Ethiopia and, later, against Albania and Greece, which led to his ultimate defeat, rejection, and ignominious death—an inglorious Cæsar, if ever there was one.

As I backed through the door he turned and walked slowly down the long carpet towards his desk. Throughout the entire interview he had not once smiled. Never before or since did I meet a high official who was so somber and humorless—which in itself was a portent the significance of which I failed then to grasp.

CHAPTER TWENTY-FOUR

GOODBYE TO EUROPE

WHEN F. D. R. was nominated in 1932 I knew that, if he won, I would be out of the foreign service. Mine had been a political appointment. I was a Republican. F. D. R. had many political debts to pay. He owed me nothing. When, according to custom, I submitted my resignation on March 4, it was accepted, and my return to the United States was set for May.

So ended two and one-half years as American minister to Hungary. During this time I had had the opportunity to study intensively a nation in the throes of bankruptcy and a group of nations struggling to survive one of the world's greatest economic depressions. On these subjects I sent frequent dispatches to the Department of State. Today these dispatches are of no interest except to a research student. At the time they were pertinent and even appreciated—which in a bureaucracy is rare. In retrospect this, which was the really important phase of my work in Hungary, was of less lasting interest than were the glimpses which I had of the remnants of European feudalism, and of the way of life that had centered about the court in the old double monarchy. I had the chance during these two and one-half years to become more aware of the invisible line that runs from the Baltic through the Balkans, dividing Europe in two, much as it had done ever since the Roman Empire split into two parts fifteen centuries ago. In the Balkan Peninsula it approximates the line that separates the Roman Catholic and the Greek Orthodox religions (with a generous intermingling of Mohammedans with the members of the Eastern Church). Its demarcation is not rigid, nor can it be precisely traced. But east of the line the people are, for the most part, backward, living on an incredibly low economic plane, with little or no schooling, and with no traditions of political democracy. West of the line, varying forms of western European culture have been long established. Education is widespread. The practice of effective political participation by plain citizens is progressively stronger as one goes to the west and north.

Since the end of World War II most of Europe east of this line, so long accustomed to autocracy, has been buried in the mud of imposed uniformity by the heel of Russian tyranny. But no one who knows eastern Europe mistakes the passive submission to the Russians' dictates for an abandonment of cherished national ideals and dreams. The peoples of the small nations of eastern Europe have long been forced to submit to alien domination. Within the memory of many persons still living the Turks controlled what we now know as Romania and Bulgaria, as well as a large part of Yugoslavia. Poland was long split up among Russia, Austria, and Germany. Even the northern provinces of Italy were ruled from Vienna until 1867. Thus the wisdom of old Albert Apponyi's remark is, if anything, even more apparent than when he made it twenty years ago—that nothing is finite in European politics, and no treaty remains in force forever. Conformity to the arbitrary dictates of alien rulers can be imposed by brute force, but true unity can only be achieved by consent, and then only if each group not only retains its separateness but grants the same privilege to all other groups, regardless of their cultural or political ideals or their geographical location. Only by the widespread acceptance of something akin to federalism does there seem to be hope for a European union.

In 1933 such a union seemed utterly remote, despite the preachings of Count Koudenhove-Kalergi—the son of an Austrian father and a Japanese mother—and despite the hopes of the supporters of the League of Nations. Germany under Hitler was beginning to prepare for the resumption of the war and for a new bid to dominate the world. It was obvious that it could only succeed by force, as not only western Europe but all of the countries south and east of Germany would never submit to German overlordship except under military compulsion. It was the dynamic impetus of separatism—of countervailing rivalries, of jealousies between neighbor nations, of the delusions of the superiority of one race or group over another—which dominated the picture of Europe that I carried with me back to America.

When I reached New York I telephoned to Washington for instructions and was asked to report to the State Department at my convenience. There I was told that, although it was customary to make a formal call on the President, the White House was now very informal and that the best thing was to ask the President's secretary, Marvin McIntyre, for an appointment. I explained to him that I had nothing that demanded F. D. R.'s attention and suggested that I could drop in for a few minutes in the evening or at some time when he was not otherwise occupied. McIntyre disappeared into the President's office and returned grinning. "F. D. says if you've got a bathing suit come at five-thirty and have a swim in his new pool," was his message.

Shortly before five-thirty I tucked a borrowed bathing suit under my arm and walked over to the White House. A policeman with his coat open stood outside the portico. He eyed me carefully and out of the corner of his mouth said, "Got an appointment?" When I replied, "Yes, at five-thirty," he pointed over his shoulder with his thumb to the entrance of the White House.

I walked up the steps and into the large reception hall. No one was in sight. Looking towards the East Room I spotted a Negro reclining on the small of his back. When he saw me he got up and asked me what I wanted. I told him that the President had invited me to come for a swim at five-thirty. "Wait a minute," said he, and going to the usher's office, returned with a young man in shirt sleeves to whom I repeated my story. He took me in to one of the small waiting rooms and said that as we were to have tea on the veranda I might prefer to wait outdoors. In a few minutes the usher, who had left me alone on the porch, returned, announcing: "the President of the United States."

Dressed in an old grey flannel suit with a soft shirt, F. D. R. was wheeled in, looking a little tired under the eyes, but in excellent health. He was as cheerful and friendly as ever and full of inquiries and gossip about relatives. When tea was finished we adjourned to the new swimming pool, followed by two ladies who had been on the White House veranda at tea. Only Franklin and I went into the pool, despite the very hot weather, and as we swam around he talked at length about domestic affairs.

Vigorous, charming, plausible, he was full of the fun of life. As I watched his handsome head over the waters of the pool and listened to his genial comments I kept saying to myself: "It's not possible. This delightful, youthful-looking man in this pool cannot be the President of the United States." Then, as in the years to come, a German adjective, *leichtsinnig*—which is hard to translate—came to mind as particularly applicable to this side of his character. Some of the dictionaries define it as "frivolous," which is too absolute. Rather does it imply a sort of light-hearted nimbleness, a mercurial capacity to react to surface indications without ever looking deeply.

I dressed faster than Franklin. Going out of the enclosure which covers the pool, I saw an unkempt policeman with his coat open leaning against the wall of the White House. A few minutes later, when the President was wheeled back to the White House, the policeman disengaged himself from the wall and saluted him. I said goodbye and, tucking my wet bathing suit under my arm, walked out of the front door of the White House, a private citizen again.

As I went up Pennsylvania Avenue, I couldn't help smiling as I pictured the formalities that would attend a retiring Hungarian minister to the United States calling upon the Regent of Hungary upon terminating his services. Perhaps the fact that I had so recently watched the redcoats with their beaver hats marching up and down in front of Buckingham Palace made the New Deal White House seem somewhat unconventional. Certainly the contrast left no doubt in my mind that Budapest was many thousands of miles away and this particular chapter in my life was ended.

CHAPTER TWENTY-FIVE

F. D. R., MASTER OF POLITICS

IN THE AUTUMN of 1933 I joined the staff of the *New York Herald Tribune* as editorial writer. Under the inspiration of Helen Rogers Reid, the able and liberal-minded wife of the publisher, the paper was fighting for enlightened progressive Republican principles as opposed to the blind reaction of the old-line G. O. P. bosses. After the political truce following F. D. R.'s inauguration, the *Herald Tribune*, as the leading Republican journal in the country, took its place as a constructive critic of the New Deal. It regarded thoughtful opposition as an essential part of the democratic process, focusing attention on controversial aspects of proposed measures, and helping to mold opinion.

Because F. D. R. so completely dominated the political scene, interest centered in him as much as in the New Deal. Before 1933 the country knew little about him except that his record as governor of New York was good, and that he was an astute politician who had capitalized the popularity of the family name. He was skillful in the give and take of personal relationships which is the essence of good politics. In addition he radiated charm. His friends admired greatly his courage in overriding the handicap of being stricken with infantile paralysis in his fortieth year. His eager interest in people, together with a quick facility in picking others' brains, gave visitors the impression that he was at home in their special fields. A trick of agreeing affably with everyone led the undiscerning to look upon him as wise and understanding. But none who knew him well believed that he thought things through. Walter Lippmann summed up their reaction when he wrote in June, 1932, that "his mind is not very clear, his purposes are not simple, and his methods are not very direct."

In view of F. D. R.'s political skill his lack of depth was not necessarily a serious defect. Few presidents have shone as thinkers or deep students of history and economics. But the less his own capacity to think deeply, the more important was the judgment of those whom he picked as advisers. The list is not impressive. Tugwell, Berle, Moley, Morgenthau, Wallace, Murphy, Biddle, Bullitt, to name but a few, inspired as little confidence as any group that ever battened on a president. In the prewar cabinet only three members—the diligent Cordell Hull, the irrascible Harold Ickes, and the humane Miss Perkins—were persons of distinction outside the offices which they held. Important leaders in the Democratic party were excluded, with the exception of the loyal Roosevelt-before-Chicago generalissimo, James Aloysius Farley. While no cabinet member lacked fitness in the sense that Harry Daugherty or Hubert Work did, F. D. R.'s prewar cabinet, man for man, lacked the stature even of Warren Gamaliel Harding's cabinet. Certainly it was in striking contrast to the cabinet of the elder Roosevelt, in which figured such great Americans as John Hay, Elihu Root, and William Howard Taft, as well as such lesser known but able public servants as James R. Garfield, Robert Bacon, Paul Morton, and George von Lengerke Meyer. This also, as we were soon to learn, was symptomatic, indicating in F. D. R. a definite distaste for men of ability.

Although my contacts with F. D. R. had never been close, I had heard much about him from family and friends. Everybody stressed his charm, his good looks, his fine work as assistant secretary of the navy in World War I. At Harvard he had been popular among the residents of the "gold coast," as the socially fashionable part of the undergraduate world of Cambridge was called, and was one of the editors of the *Crimson*—a position which required initiative, energy, and skill in dealing with his fellow students and the faculty. The only criticism of him that lingered when I reached Cambridge a few years after his graduation was that he was "too much of a politician"—which, in the college

[223]

world, meant that he was unusually successful in club and class politics.

One of the outstanding impressions I have of F. D. R. is illustrative of his reaction to his physical handicap. I was spending a week end at his summer place at Hyde Park when he was still governor of New York. He wanted to show me his new swimming pool and had sent for a little runabout which had been arranged so that he could drive it himself without using his legs. His mother and I stood on the veranda watching his son Elliot and Gus Gennerich, the state trooper who acted as his personal bodyguard, carry him down the steps and place him in the car. As they turned and left him he lost his balance (his powerful torso was much heavier than his crippled legs), and he fell over on the car seat. I doubt if one man in a thousand as disabled and dependent on others would have refrained from some sort of reproach, however mild, to those whose carelessness had thus left him in the lurch. But Franklin merely lay on his back, waved his strong arms in the air, and laughed. At once they came back and helped him to his seat behind the wheel, and he called me to join him. For a moment I had seen the true spirit of the man. He was not putting on an act. Rather was it the instinctive reaction of a brave and gallant gentleman—as illuminating as it was moving and inspiring.

As we watched the New Deal get under way, we on the *Herald Tribune* were even more uneasy about F. D. R.'s methods than his aims. The New Deal technique was basically changing the American political system by greatly enhancing the power of the executive branch of the federal government, both with respect to Congress and to the states. The system of submitting to Congress so-called "must" legislation and at the same time vilifying all who differed with or criticized New Deal measures resulted in laws being written by presidential aides and rammed through Congress with little or no discussion. This was a drastic departure from the traditional process of working out legislation and debating it fully in Congress. While this new procedure was probably justifiable—and certainly expedient—in the early days of the national emergency immediately following F. D. R.'s inauguration, the practice was continued for years. After 1936, New Deal

strategists put forward a new concept which was even more subversive of our traditional practices of government—the idea of
the "mandate." The President had been given such an overwhelming vote of confidence that he had, in effect, a blank check or a

N. Y. Herald Tribune Syndicate

CARLISLE'S "TOO MANY HORSES"
A master politician like F.D.R. was needed to handle the team

[225]

blind endorsement for anything that he might wish to do. Post-master-General Farley expressed it with cynical frankness in May, 1937, when the possibility of a compromise over the President's plan to pack the Supreme Court was being discussed: "There's no need of talking compromise. *The Democratic senators were elected on the basis of supporting the President's program. It's up to them to support it now.*" (The italics are mine.) As the *Herald Tribune* commented editorially on May 16 of that year, this attitude could be summarized by the simple statement: "Mr. Roosevelt knows best what the country needs. Pass the bill, Senators!" The duty of legislators, under this New Deal concept, was not to exercise either judgment or initiative with respect to laws, but merely to ratify. To us this sounded like a precept taken from the practice of Mussolini or Hitler.

In two other major fields—relief for the unemployed and assistance to needy farmers—we were also disturbed about methods. It was apparent that when the federal government undertook to hand out directly billions of dollars for much-needed relief, personal ties would be created between the administration and millions of voters. The support of these millions could be indefinitely assured to the administration in power by the simple expedient of merely suggesting that, if the opposition party won, it would cut federal relief payments. Such a large body of voters could thus be bound to the administration by their pockets that party opposition might cease to be a practical possibility. A similar danger existed in the payment of subsidies to farmers.

In retrospect much of our criticism of the New Deal methodology seems sound. But we made the tactical mistake of writing about it in terms of logic and reason. We brought out the contrasts between his campaign promises and his later performances, unaware that most people were more interested in his latest promises than they were in old ones which he had made but not kept. For example, during the 1932 campaign he had urged the reduction of federal spending and had excoriated Hoover for his "extravagance." Once in office F. D. R. spent at the rate of from two to three times what Hoover had spent, and when he promised to spend more the people applauded. He had urged a balanced budget. Yet by 1934 he was spending three dollars for every two that the government took in, and the people approved deficit financing. He had advocated the preservation of a sound currency. When, within a few months, he devalued the dollar his followers praised his sagacity. He had stated that "no responsible government would sell to the country securities payable in gold if it knew that this promise, yes, this covenant, embodied in these securities was worthless." Yet within five months he had done this very thing, and when Republicans pointed this out they were bitterly attacked by the administration with the approval of a large portion of the people.

In our old-fashioned way we had felt that a president who so cynically did the very things for which in the campaign he had bitterly attacked his opponent, and who cared nothing about fulfilling his own promises, was degrading the office. But he was smart enough to know that in politics the promise always has a greater appeal than the performance—especially if the promise is made with fervor. The number of persons worried by F. D. R.'s inconsistencies was small compared with those who thrilled to the vibrant accents of his warm voice over the radio as he opened his appeals for confidence with the heartening words: "My friends." When we comforted ourselves with the assurance that the American people could not be "bought," we failed to realize that the number of the voters who were actually being "bought" was unimportant compared to those who were being hypnotized by the greatest political snake charmer in American history.

The truth is that F. D. R. was, in fact, the ablest politician who ever occupied the White House. He knew that the people wanted reforms—that the idea of a welfare state was gaining popularity. So he set himself at the head of the reform movement, ready to experiment with any nostrum that might win votes. He knew, as did all experienced politicians, that any scheme to "soak the rich" was sure to be popular, and that a president who attacked Wall Street as the nation's personal devil would receive widespread applause. Hence by denouncing the "money changers" for what had been in fact the greatest mass gambling orgy in the history of a country repeatedly given to widespread speculation, he was sure to get off to a good start. Enough ill will adhered to the bankers for having closed out loans as the stock market crashed in 1929 to make them even more vulnerable in 1933 than in past history. Their failure to stem the stock market collapse and the ensuing panic was adroitly used as a justification for trying economic experiments opposed by all sound economists. Devaluation of the currency, partial repudiation of the debt (through refusing to honor the government's pledge to pay its obligation in gold), purchasing silver at inflated prices—these and other expedients so often tried in times of financial crises he embraced with enthusiasm, deaf to those who pointed out that they were mere palliatives, not cures. His skill lay not only in his willingness to shift from one panacea to another but in his agility in winning support in Congress for each new move.

The ability to master politicians is an essential requisite for a president. Without the effective co-operation of Congress no president can do much. If Congress opposes him his only chance of achievement is by arousing popular support. In F. D. R.'s case Congress was a rubber stamp, and public opinion was enthusiastically on his side in nearly every major issue except the court-packing fight. Never has a president had such overwhelming confidence. A large majority of the voters of the country felt that F. D. R. was their personal friend, that he had their interests at heart, that he knew what to do. To anything that he wanted they replied cheerfully, "O. K., chief," glad to leave their troubles on his doorstep.

In retrospect the most serious blunder which the Republican opposition made was to demand consistency of objectives and adherence to long-tried principles of government at a time when few saw clearly what lay ahead or what policy would be best in the long run. The majority of the people wanted experimentation and change. They would not have been content with less. F. D. R. sensed this and responded to it. He did not have all the answers—in fact he had only a few of them—but he saw no point in admitting this and doubtless hoped that some among his advisers would produce good new ideas.

Wide World Photos

F.D.R. BEGINNING HIS RIDE TO FAME
He was accompanied by an unpopular predecessor

Certainly F. D. R.'s was the popular course, as was made plain in the years to come.

To those of us who had loved T. R. the temptation to compare the two Roosevelts was constant. Both men were masters of politics, F. D. R. even more so than T. R., in that he was less inhibited by what he had said or promised. Each was a skilled showman, adept at good staging, and deft in dramatizing himself as the champion of righteousness and the friend of the weak and the downtrodden. Both were excellent public speakers, masters of the compelling phrase, and skillful in arousing popular enthusiasm. Both loved the limelight and throve on personal acclaim. Both men were physically brave to a rare degree. Each overcame serious physical handicaps—T. R. in his childhood and youth when he built his puny asthma-wracked frame into a powerful body, and F. D. R. when he overcame his infantile paralysis. Each man had, in turn, served in the legislature in Albany, then as assistant secretary of the navy, and finally as governor of New York before going to the White House.

But there the resemblances end. Intellectually T. R. was the abler. The range of his reading was extensive and covered several foreign languages, whereas F. D. R., except in the field of naval history, was not noted as a wide reader. While in college T. R. had been elected to Phi Beta Kappa, then as now a mark of excellence in undergraduate study. It is not without significance that F. D. R. in later life was made an honorary member of Phi Beta Kappa and that he usually displayed his key, apparently willing to give the impression that he had earned it through his scholastic standing.

Those who knew T. R. were struck with his integrity. What he promised he performed. F. D. R., in contrast, had a convenient way of canceling one promise with another and of encouraging visitors to think that he agreed with them or supported them when, as a matter of fact, he did neither. T. R. was a militant moralist—an active supporter of the traditional American traits of self-reliance and individual initiative. F. D. R., in contrast, fostered the spirit of dependence. In a time when the revival of individual initiative and courage was all-important he sanctioned

[229]

the widespread preaching by the New Dealers of the doctrine that society owes every man a living and that, if he cannot get it as easily as he wants, it is the duty of government to help him. Thus an entire generation of crisis-shocked youth grew to manhood imbued with social defeatism. "Security" was proclaimed as a "right." Implicit in this was disparagement of self-reliance. In fact, the old ideals of the American people were widely and continuously derided and mocked.

In many ways more enlightening than the contrasts between F. D. R. and T. R. is the comparison between F. D. R. and England's Tudor queen, Elizabeth. F. D. R. shared many of her more mercurial qualities and, like her, was adept in sailing over uncharted seas. John Richard Green, analyzing her character in his *Short History of the English People*, shows how her defects were as useful as her gifts:

"Of political wisdom indeed in its larger and more generous sense," says Green, "Elizabeth had little or none, but her political tact was unerring. She seldom saw her course at a glance, but she played with a hundred courses, fitfully and discursively, as a musician runs his fingers over the key-board, till she hit suddenly upon the right one. . . . Her notion of statesmanship lay in watching how things turned out around her, and in seizing the moment for making the best of them. . . . Had Elizabeth written the story of her reign she would have prided herself, not on the triumph of England or the ruin of Spain, but on the skill with which she had hoodwinked and out-witted every statesman in Europe during fifty years. Nor was her trickery without political value. Ignoble, inexpressibly wearisome as the Queen's diplomacy seems to us now, tracing it as we do through a thousand despatches, it succeeded in its main end. It gained time, and every year that was gained doubled Elizabeth's strength. Nothing is more revolting in the Queen, but nothing is more characteristic, than her shameless mendacity. It was an age of political lying, but in the profusion and recklessness of her lies Elizabeth stood without a peer in Christendom. A falsehood was to her simply an intellectual means of meeting a difficulty, and the ease with which she asserted or denied whatever suited her purpose was only equalled by the cynical indifference with which she met the exposure of her lies as soon as their purpose was answered. . . .

"The diplomatists who censured at one moment her irresolution, her delay, her changes of front, censured at the next her 'obstinacy,' her iron will, her defiance of what seemed to them inevitable ruin. . . . But the greatness of the Queen rests above all on her power over her people. We have had grander and nobler rulers, but none so popular as Elizabeth. . . . Her worst acts broke fruitlessly against the general devotion. . . . Her finger was always on the public pulse. She knew exactly when she could resist the feeling of her people, and when she must give way before the new sentiment of freedom which her policy unconsciously fostered. But when she retreated, her defeat had all the grace of victory."

Had Elizabeth been less flexible she might well have been less successful. The uncertainty of the times made it hard to pursue a course without wavering or backtracking. In our own time F. D. R. was faced with equally uncertain conditions, at home and abroad. A man less ready to change, less pliable in pursuit of his objectives, might have been stymied by conditions beyond his control. The very fact that F. D. R. had no clear idea of where he was going was an advantage. In the crises through which he served as president it was almost impossible to plot a straight course and adhere to it rigidly. His genius, like Elizabeth's, lay in mastery of the art of politics and in ability to hold the love of the people. A president lacking either of these gifts would have had a hard time in the years between 1933 and 1945.

Many persons have lamented the fact that his life was not spared long enough for him to play a major part in the shaping of the peace. But if he had gone abroad to negotiate peace instead of discussing the prosecution of the war—if, instead of planning with Churchill and Stalin moves for furthering their common aims of defeating Hitler, he had to pit America's interests in a new world order against those of Britain and Russia—he would, for the first time, have faced men who were more than his equals, working in fields in which they were the masters and he the neophyte. It must not be forgotten that in his dealings with Congress as well as in his four campaigns for the presidency he was up against political inferiors—men less astute, less skilled, and less cynical. But to outwit Churchill forcefully and shrewdly fighting for British interests to which the United States might well be opposed would be something quite different from working with Churchill, the military ally. Even more so, to face Stalin ruthlessly seeking to sabotage not only world peace but everything that F. D. R. and the peoples of the Western world believed in would be vastly more difficult even than obtaining concessions from the hard-bargaining, tough Stalin of Yalta, then still bound to the United States and Britain by the common need of victory. Finally, the technique which had worked so well in domestic affairs, of making blithe promises to be broken as lightly as they were made, would be fraught with dangers in the ruthless struggle for power that underlies the maneuvers at a peace conference. To "arrange" and smooth over the internecine quarrels in the Democratic party is child's play compared with trying to compose bitter national rivalries which stem from generations of hatred and jealousy. The supreme danger would have lain in his natural confidence that he was as much a master in this less familiar field of world political rivalries as he was in domestic politics. Instead of "outsmarting" Churchill and Stalin, as undoubtedly he believed he could, it is more than likely that they would have used his unfamiliarity with the larger world field to their own advantage.

To say this does not detract from F. D. R.'s fine record as a war president. Against the many appointments of second-rate persons to political positions which he made before the war must be set the fact that he named George C. Marshall to be chief of staff of the Army, Dwight D. Eisenhower to head the forces in Europe, and Ernest J. King to head the naval operations, and that, as our entry into the war became more and more inevitable, he chose as secretary of war an outstanding man of wide experience, Henry L. Stimson. It is immaterial whether the Republicans were right in believing that the appointments to his cabinet of Stimson, the most distinguished Republican "elder statesman," and of Frank Knox, who had been candidate for vice-president on the

Landon ticket, announced scarcely a month before the Republican convention of 1940, were made largely with a view to embarrassing the Republicans at that convention. Both men served the country ably and helped establish F. D. R.'s record as a war president. Only the most partisan hater of F. D. R. would deny him credit for using these men so effectively in building up the magnificent war machine which was America's contribution as a war ally. Only the most crabbed isolationist could remain blind to the fact that his policy, before we finally became an active "shooting participant," of helping the British in every way short of war was of enormous value to us as well as to the British, on whom fell the burden of holding back the Germans until the Russians and ourselves took our share of the burden.

Greatly loved and greatly hated, this complex personality will long fascinate historians. Few Americans loomed so large in world affairs. None so completely dominated the American scene for so many years. And yet, all the while that he wielded this vast influence and shouldered these massive burdens he remained virtually helpless from the waist down, scarcely able to move without assistance. Rarely, if those near him report truthfully, did he lose his resiliency or cheerfulness, or, even in the worst days of the war, his confidence in our ultimate ability to defeat the enemy. Too often his critics were blind to this noble side of his character.

It was F. D. R.'s good fortune that his mother, whom he adored and who worshipped him, lived even into his third term in the presidency, and was in full possession of her faculties to the end despite her advanced age, rejoicing in his successes and giving him the strength of her great love. This lends point to an incident which is said to have occurred in the winter of 1940–41, shortly before the old lady died. Among her friends and childhood contemporaries was a Mrs. Post, who had spent most of her adult life in France until she was forced out of Paris during the German invasion in June of 1940. In New York, where Mrs. Post had many relatives and friends, she and her old playmate, Mrs. James Roosevelt, met at tea. Both ladies were in their mid-eighties. After the expected round of questions and reminiscences between them there was a pause in the conversation. Then Mrs. Post said to Mrs. Roosevelt: "By the way, Sally—when I last saw you in Paris about twenty-five or thirty years ago, you had a very charming young son of yours with you. What's ever become of him?" Cousin Sally remarked a little tartly that he had been president of the United States for the last eight years. But Mrs. Post, not to be thus lightly put off by her old school friend, came back with: "But, after all, Sally, I'm sure you don't know who the president of France is, do you?" To which the honest Sally ruefully admitted that she did not.

CHAPTER TWENTY-SIX

REPUBLICAN LEADERS

IN THE autumn of 1933, Jay Darling (better known as the cartoonist "Ding") and I joined Herbert Hoover as guests of Milton H. Esberg to fish for steelhead on the Klamath River in northern California. I had never been a member of the little group of Hoover intimates, but from my first contact with him in 1919 I was an admirer of his. In the early twenties I had met him numerous times, largely through the intercession of friends of his, such as Mrs. William Brown Meloney, the editor of *This Week*, and George Barr Baker. I had shared their enthusiasm for him as a presidential candidate when the 1928 convention approached. We felt that his firsthand knowledge of Europe would be of great value and that his demonstrated ability as an efficient executive would stand him in good stead in the presidency. Furthermore, we were eager to see in the White House a man of action, unafraid of responsibility, and experienced as an engineer and a promoter of great enterprises. He seemed the ideal man—as the country obviously believed when it elected him by an overwhelming majority in November of 1928.

It was Hoover's misfortune to have come to power only a few months before the world plunged into the worst depression of modern times. The dislocations in the European economy caused by World War I had begun to make themselves felt here in 1928. Our own machinery of production, overstimulated by the war demands and by the needs of postwar Europe, continued to turn out goods of all kinds, agricultural as well as industrial, in increasing quantities. Businessmen and farmers were convinced that there would be no end to prosperity. They did not realize that Europe's capacity to buy from us had reached a saturation point, and that this would cause a piling up of goods in America in larger quantities than we could consume. No man in the White House—or elsewhere—could have checked the ensuing economic paralysis. Because Mr. Hoover was no wiser than anyone else in foreseeing the depression or in anticipating its intensity, and yet was head of the nation, people began to blame him for their troubles. By 1932, his name had become synonymous in the public mind with hunger, unemployment, and financial disaster.

Mr. Hoover's lack of political experience made his four years in the White House more difficult and burdensome for himself. A president's every act, and even his every hope, is conditioned by politics and by his past, present, or future relations with politicians. If he by-passes or ignores a senator, or shows his impatience with a congressman, he is laying up potential trouble for himself when next he needs congressional support. To an expert administrator like Hoover it must often have been exasperating to be hampered or thwarted or delayed at every move by the need for considering the feelings or political ambitions of a legislator.

During this fishing expedition Mr. Hoover told us about his experiences with F. D. R. in February, 1933, in connection with the growing banking and gold panic. The main outlines have since been published by William S. Myers and Walter H. Newton in their study, *The Hoover Administration* (1936). Mr. Hoover was doing his utmost to avert the nationwide closing of the banks. His sole concern was to try to steer the ship of state through the ever worsening storms to avert disaster. Rightly or wrongly, he believed that assurances from the President-elect that there would be no tinkering with the currency and that the budget would be balanced would stem the incipient panic. He wrote a personal longhand letter to F. D. R. urging him to make such a statement, and sent it by the head of the Secret Service to be delivered personally into the hands of the President-elect. This was February 17, 1933.

Common courtesy, let alone concern for the fate of the country, justified Mr. Hoover's expectation that Mr. Roosevelt would

[236]

Wide World Photos

HERBERT HOOVER
Better at catching steelhead trout than fishing in troubled
political waters

give this extremely urgent appeal from the President of the United States prompt attention. Mr. Roosevelt did not even acknowledge receipt of it for twelve days, and then expressed regrets that the intended reply, which had been dictated a week earlier, by an oversight had not been sent. It proved to be an evasive rejection of Mr. Hoover's plea. During these critical twelve days the panic had been growing. Mr. Hoover therefore made a new appeal to the President-elect for some sort of assurance about credit and currency and offered to work with him in any way possible to try to stem the tide of disaster. But F. D. R. took the constitutionally correct position that he could do nothing until noon, March 4, and that, until then, to use Ray Moley's phrase, "the baby was Hoover's, anyway."

It is open to question whether a statement from the President-elect such as Mr. Hoover wanted him to make would have restored confidence and halted the closing of the banks. But there can be little doubt that F. D. R. was shrewd enough to appreciate the political advantages to the incoming administration which his more cynical advisers foresaw if he declined to follow Hoover's suggestion—the worse the mess on March 4, the greater the credit which the new administration could take when the panic subsided and the inevitable recovery was resumed. The full responsibility for the panic and the depression could then be riveted on the Hoover administration. To the Roosevelt administration would go all credit for recovery. This attitude seemed to Mr. Hoover and his associates not only utterly cynical but shockingly callous towards the millions of persons who, as a result of it, were added daily to the list of depression victims.

While we were fishing for steelhead on the Klamath River an incident occurred which dramatized the conflicting elements in Mr. Hoover's character. On the third afternoon, while he was in the river and the rest of us were at the Esbergs' camp, the local schoolteacher called to ask if Mr. Hoover would visit her one-room school the next morning, saying that it would mean a lot to the children to be able to see and meet a former president of the United States. Mr. Esberg, who knew his Hoover well, said that he thought it could be arranged. Accordingly, when Mr. Hoover returned and had had a good supper, Mr. Esberg remarked casually: "By the way, Chief, I've ordered the car tomorrow morning and thought we might go upstream a bit."

"What for?" Mr. Hoover interrupted gruffly and suspiciously.

"I thought we might have better fishing up there, and it would give us a chance to stop off at a school," said Mr. Esberg.

"I won't do it," Mr. Hoover snapped.

"It would mean a lot to the children," Mr. Esberg explained soothingly, "and would take only five minutes of our time."

"I won't do it," Mr. Hoover repeated stubbornly.

"Ding" interposed with a plea that the children would greatly appreciate it, and I remarked that such things were a part of the role of a former president. None of us made any impression, so the matter was dropped until the next morning, when, after breakfast, Mr. Esberg announced that the car was waiting. Mr. Hoover growled but got in, and in a few minutes we arrived at the little schoolhouse near the river.

Not knowing him as well as did Mr. Esberg, I had misgivings. They proved unfounded, for not only did Mr. Hoover speak gracefully and graciously and show a deep personal interest in each of the children and in the teacher, but when he left the school he turned to Mr. Esberg and said: "Do you know that nearly all the children in this school are undernourished, and that the teacher is taking five dollars a month out of her own small salary to furnish them an extra snack at lunch?" Mr. Esberg had not been aware of it. But Mr. Hoover was not content to let the matter drop. "It would only take about a hundred dollars to provide a decent meal for the kids for the rest of this year," he said. "If you and your friends will help out, I'll underwrite the balance." There spoke the real Hoover. Few other people visiting that school would at once have discovered the need. It was typical of him that, having discovered it, he at once took steps to meet it appropriately and effectively.

The association of Hoover's name with the depression was still such a liability as the campaign of 1936 approached that it was obvious to all except himself that he was unacceptable. I was

[238]

therefore interested, when I visited Kansas City in 1935, to find Roy Roberts, the rotund and dynamic managing editor of the Kansas City Star, and his scholarly associate, Henry J. Haskell, head of the editorial page, hopeful about the presidential possibilities of Alf Landon, then governor of Kansas. When I reported this on my return to New York, Mrs. William Brown Meloney, editor of the *New York Herald Tribune's* Sunday magazine, *This Week*, suggested that on my next visit to Kansas I write a piece for her on Governor Landon. This I was soon able to do, and it was published just a year before he was nominated—one of the first articles about him in any Eastern newspaper. The fact that the *Herald Tribune* was regarded as the leading Republican journal in the East naturally resulted in this article's receiving wide attention in Republican circles.

I found Governor Landon an intelligent, modest, effective citizen, with a remarkable record of balancing his state's budget at a time when nearly all other states were going heavily into debt and when the federal government was piling deficit on deficit. In type and manner as well as in his official record Landon was the antithesis of F. D. R. He was unostentatious and simple where F. D. R. was flamboyant and complex. He was sincere and modest where F. D. R. was a master showman. Landon was a believer in thrift and saving where F. D. R. spent lavishly. Landon was orthodox in economics. F. D. R. was fascinated by economic nostrums and novelties. Landon was an excellent administrator and chose his subordinates for their ability rather than their politics. F. D. R. paid much attention to a potential appointee's politics and, in particular, to whether a candidate for a post had been for Roosevelt before Chicago.

Unfortunately the antithesis between the two men was so complete that, where Roosevelt had one of the great magic radio personalities of our times, Landon was a master at making people tune in on another program. A stumbling speaker with a monotonous voice, lacking in histrionic training, unable to read a manuscript so that it sounded alive, he yet found himself one of the principals in a contest which was being decided largely by radio listeners. Furthermore, he stood for economy and retrench-

[239]

ment against an administration which was supporting millions of voters on government relief rolls. In theory the people should have voted for him overwhelmingly on this score alone. But in fact only a minority was interested in curtailing government spending. Certainly the heart-warming promises of the charmer in the White House had a much wider appeal than the cold common sense of the pay-as-you-go governor of Kansas. F. D. R. not only promised—but provided—bread and circuses. He made each voter feel that he, F. D. R., was personally interested in his—the voter's—welfare and was his personal friend. Better political skill than this has rarely been exhibited.

In 1938 I saw much of Landon when he was a member of the United States delegation to the Pan-American conference in Lima, Peru. On closer acquaintance I found him to be shrewd yet unpretentious, reserved yet genial,—an admirable type of American public man. Conscious of his unfamiliarity with Latin-American affairs, he worked hard to understand the problems and welcomed help and suggestions. He enjoyed his associations with the Latin-Americans—except the Peruvian custom of eating the evening meal at nine or ten o'clock at night, or even later, which left him with an inner void in the early evening. As my wife and I had rented a small house in a suburb of Lima for the duration of the conference, we kept a supply of what we called "Landon snacks," which were always available when he dropped in towards the end of a busy afternoon, as he often did.

Another Republican presidential possibility of whom I saw much during these years was Ogden Mills. He was not an avowed candidate, but that his was the outstanding intellect in the Republican party is apparent from the fact that his speeches between 1933 and 1936 were usually printed in full by the *New York Times* and the *New York Herald Tribune*, which is more than was done for any other Republican leader of the period except former President Hoover. In Ogden's case the recognition of his abilities was well merited. He had a first-rate intelligence, great courage, and absolute integrity. He had thought much about political and economic problems and had taken pains to master them in detail. His essentially orderly mind presented complex problems in a simple, analytical, easily understandable form. A gift for pungent phrases helped him in his presentation.

Mills was, of course, a conservative, but far from the reactionary which he was charged with being. He believed that our dual system of representative government, leaving to the smaller units those functions which they best could handle, was the most truly liberal form of government yet devised. He opposed the encroachment of the administration in Washington on local affairs. He fought government planning in the field of economics except as an emergency palliative in great crises like war. He was a staunch upholder of the free-enterprise system. More, even, than Governor Landon, Ogden Mills was the outstanding antagonist of everything that the New Deal stood for. His opposition not only was vocal but was highly intelligent. Yet it proved as futile against the charm and promises of F. D. R. as did Landon's more pedestrian approach. Ogden was fully aware of the hopelessness of the contest, for on several occasions he remarked to me ruefully that the real trouble with the conservatives in politics was that they were too honest—that they refused to promise the moon, whereas the New Dealers never hesitated to promise anything to anyone, regardless of whether they had either the ability or the intention of fulfilling these promises.

In the 1936 campaign Ogden, like a good many other Republicans, hoped that Landon would make a good showing. His faith in the good sense of the American people led him to believe that they would welcome a man of Landon's constructive, conservative point of view and that, even though they might not elect him, they would give the Republican ticket enough support to act as a brake on F. D. R. Ogden came to the *Herald Tribune* on election night to follow the returns, and as the evidence continued to pile up that F. D. R. and the whole Democratic ticket were winning by a landslide he became more and more depressed and morose. On one occasion I brought in a bulletin indicating a slight gain for the Republicans in Vermont and Utah—the only two states carried by Taft in 1912—and, thinking to cheer him up, I called out to him: "Well, Ogden, I see we still have those great Republican strongholds, Vermont and Utah!" He turned on me somberly and almost angrily. "This is no joking matter," he said. "It is a great national disaster." He felt deeply that F. D. R. was undermining our form of government and that, with an over-whelming majority, he would be emboldened to new and more destructive courses.

Ogden's death a year later was a loss to the Republican party. His gifts probably never could have been used in the presidency. But his clear mind and his fearlessness in saying what had to be said, regardless of whether or not it was popular, were a whole-some influence in a party which had been stunned into uncompre-hending inertia. Ogden may have been wrong about many things. His conservatism may have been outmoded and impractical. But at least he stood for something definite and positive, where most other Republican leaders followed the uninspiring and unintelli-gent course of opposing anything which the New Deal advocated, regardless of whether it was good or bad. They let F. D. R. do their thinking for them—in reverse. Ogden Mills preferred to think for himself.

As the 1940 campaign approached and it became apparent that F. D. R. would ignore the anti-third-term tradition, the Re-publican party leaders spent much time trying to decide whether the uninspiring and obstructive Senator Taft, of Ohio, or the un-prepossessing but aggressive district attorney of New York, Tom Dewey, would be the better vote-getter. It never occurred to the party solons that, with Hitler approaching Paris and with F. D. R. trying to help the Allies while assuring the American people that he would keep us out of war, neither of these unquestionably able and ambitious Republican politicians might be what the people of the country wanted.

At this stage a phenomenon rare in American politics occurred —the appearance of a meteor on the Republican horizon. Wendell Willkie had few friends among the leaders of the state delegations to the Republican convention in 1940. Here and there a delegate spoke out for him. A little group of his warm supporters inside and outside the convention worked diligently but quietly in his behalf, strengthened by the realization that, although only re-cently in the public eye, he had fired the imagination and hearts of millions by his integrity, his courage, and his frankness. With the exception of T. R. and F. D. R., I know of no one in public life in our time who had greater magnetism than Wendell Willkie. Furthermore, he was a hard fighter, feeling deeply about national and international affairs and unafraid to say what he thought.

In the eyes of the professional politicians Willkie was guilty of the cardinal sin of politics—party irregularity. His only political experience had been as delegate to a Democratic national convention. He was further handicapped by the fact that most of his supporters had come to the Republican convention over the opposition of the machine organization. Among them were political amateurs—and not a few wealthy contributors to party funds, who felt that their generosity entitled them to a say in organization policies. Such men were always disliked by the professionals. Hence Willkie's chances seemed small indeed and would have remained such had not his popularity overflowed the convention floor and finally broken the deadlock between the Taft and Dewey forces.

I was among many who were delighted with Willkie's nomination. My contacts with him until then had been confined to a few lunches and dinners at the Century Club, but I admired his good sense and courage. His charm stimulated enthusiasm and dulled the critical faculties. He was, in a sense, an inspired as well as an inspiring leader, with a large mind capable of expansion and growth. In comparison, Taft's seemed like a constricted and crabbed intellect and Dewey's like that of a pert but meticulous bookkeeper. Willkie knew that the world was on fire. Taft would only have accepted it as a fact when the blaze burned the chair on which he was sitting. Willkie knew that a great leader must have imagination to foresee, skill to dramatize the foreseeable, and courage to do so even at the risk of unpopularity. Dewey was almost as eager to avoid courting unpopularity as was F. D. R.

Under the circumstances Willkie seemed the ideal man to replace F. D. R. Where Landon had been merely the antithesis of Roosevelt, Willkie was a positive and vital new leader, with a personality almost as vivid and distinct as F. D. R.'s and with dramatic skill and an excellent radio personality. Yet, as the campaign got under way, signs appeared that Willkie, like Wood and Hoover before him, was being handicapped by his lack of political experience. He listened to the political amateurs among his intimates more than to the professionals. True, he fought hard, tirelessly, and vigorously—almost too much so for his own good, as he strained his voice and came near exhausting his robust vitality. But Willkie was by nature slow in appreciating the infinitely complex interrelations of petty personal ambitions which are so important in party organizations. He did not realize that to the organization leaders he was an outsider and that, as a result, it was all the more important for him to pay particular attention to the leaders personally and to seek their advice and satisfy their sense of their own importance. Instead, he concentrated on his own efforts in the campaign.

No one knows whether, if he had followed a different course, he would have had enough votes to win the election. Roosevelt, in 1940 as in 1936, and again in 1944, had the advantage of controlling an army of patronage and the handing out of billions of dollars. He was at the crest of his popularity. He had only to ask and it would be given him, only to smile and the people would applaud rapturously. Not even Willkie, with his great charm and rugged leadership, could do more than unravel a few strands of the ties with which F. D. R. had bound the voters so closely to him.

Willkie came to lunch at the *Herald Tribune* the day after the elections in 1940. He was frank, cheerful, fair, and appreciative. He showed no bitterness toward F. D. R., nor did he seek to blame anyone in his entourage for his defeat. He admitted mistakes of political judgment. He had warm praise for all who worked for him. His was the reaction of a big man in adversity.

In subsequent months Willkie seemed to grow in stature and to gain in wisdom—with the possible exception of wisdom in political matters. So, for example, he opposed Dewey for governor of New York in 1942 before the latter was nominated—which seemed to me foolish and unwise. For saying this to him I was for a while in his bad graces. As the spring of 1944 approached, he was determined to plunge head-on into the campaign for the presidential nomination, despite the fact that he had little strength

WENDELL L. WILLKIE

He shone like a meteor but could not win the voters away from F.D.R.

among the political leaders and was no longer a great popular favorite.

I remember very well one of the last talks I had with him. It was shortly before the primary election in Wisconsin. He had asked me to meet him at the Century, where he recapitulated the situation as he saw it in that state and elsewhere with regard to his own support. He assured me that his chances in Wisconsin were of the very best, and he expressed confidence that numerous party leaders in New York were for him. I happened to know that some, at least, of these men were lukewarm in their support and that others would be liabilities rather than assets. But his confidence was so serene that I did nothing more than to express mild surprise and gentle doubts. A few weeks later he came in a poor fifth in the Wisconsin primaries and, largely due to the good advice of Gardiner Cowles, Jr., of the *Des Moines Register*, withdrew from the race. The meteor of 1940 was no longer even a flash on the Republican horizon—which was the party's and the nation's loss, for Willkie embodied great forces for good and was, in fact, even in defeat a greater influence in this country than many of the lesser men who sought to prevent his nomination in 1940 and to force him out of the running in 1944. His early death was a tragedy, and was mourned by all who had known him and loved his rugged, bear-like, warm-hearted personality.

CHAPTER TWENTY-SEVEN

ON THE LECTURE FRONT

THE *Herald Tribune* had agreed to give me time off each winter for a number of lecture tours. I discussed current events, usually the problems of the Pacific, or the coming resumption of war in Europe. Mine was the unpopular side—that the Japanese and the Germans were planning war; that unilateral disarmament would leave us at the mercy of gangster nations; that if there was to be some sort of world order it must rest on force.

Whenever I discussed the possibilities of war I met with polite incredulity. The local newspapers condensed the gist of what I said and quoted some of the high spots, but neither they nor the audiences would believe that trouble was imminent. I have fat volumes of clippings covering several hundred lectures from 1934 to 1940. Typical is one from the *Indianapolis Star*, on March 26, 1935, which headlined a report of a talk of mine in that city: "EXPECTS WAR IN EUROPE IN FIVE YEARS," and mentioned the fact that I listed the annexation of Austria by Germany as the likely first step in Germany's inevitable expansion—as it turned out to be. In an analysis of Japan's plans to master the Pacific, I said in California in October, 1935, that "unless unforeseen circumstances intervene, we shall see, before another generation, the Japanese flag flying over the Philippines." This was picked up by a news agency and widely reprinted as an oddity. Several West Coast papers added—correctly—that I had also said that "Japan's plans encompass the rich Dutch East Indies" and that "in the event of war Japan would act swiftly to carry out her expansion plans."

In this same year, at the end of a lecture in Scranton, Pennsylvania, about the German menace, I was asked if I thought that the United States would be involved in a new European war. My answer was that if Japan should use the occasion of such a war in Europe to further its imperialist ambitions in Asia "the United States might find itself pulled into the war by the back door." What I said about the German menace received editorial notice, but neither Scranton paper commented on our possible entry into the war.

In May, 1938, the *Oklahoma City Times* reported at length, a talk of mine in that city in which I summarized the events leading inevitably to a resumption of the war in Europe. It quoted me as saying that "the war may start when Hitler tries to seize the German sector of Czechoslovakia [which he did a year later]. When that happens, a Pandora's box of conflicting Balkan nationalities will be let loose to plunge Europe into a blood bath"— a forecast as accurate as its metaphors were mixed. The story ended by saying that "the United States, Mr. Roosevelt believes, will keep hands off unless Japan should drag us in." While there was no editorial comment, the news story seemed to disparage what I had said.

Even in such magazines as *Asia*—in its day well regarded by all interested in Far-Eastern affairs—articles warning against Japan's warlike ambitions were either ignored or resented by the good people who devoutly hoped that there would be no war. In the February, 1935, issue of *Asia*, for example, I discussed Japan's denunciation of the Washington Treaty for the limitation of naval armaments, and said that "Today we find not only that Japan is bent on a policy of military expansion on the Asiatic mainland but that Japanese big navy men speak openly of duplicating on the sea the successful policy of the Japanese army on land, which means that Japan is planning to expand southward toward the Netherlands East Indies and perhaps even farther. There is no other possible interpretation of her denunciation of the naval treaties and her demand to increase her naval strength to such a point that her navy is as large as, or larger than, that of Great Britain or the United States." I then asked the question whether the United States was prepared to face war and added: "In view of the great disparity of resources of the United States and Japan there can be no doubt of the ultimate outcome of such a war, provided the American people are willing to see it through. But there is equally little doubt that such a war would be of long duration and in the early months, or even years, it would be marked by a succession of Japanese victories in the waters of the western Pacific. The fact remains that, either to hold or to regain the Philippine Islands or to bring about an effective blockade of Japan, the United States Navy would have to be able to operate far from its home bases. Inasmuch as the effective cruising range of the average naval vessel is comparatively short, the task of basing a fleet within striking distance of Japan is almost insurmountable. One of the reasons for this is that Japan now controls all of the approaches to the Asiatic mainland and the Japanese waters with the exception of the Aleutian Islands off Alaska. Thanks to her possession of the mandated islands, which she obtained from Germany, she could easily harass the lines of communication of any fleet attempting to operate in the neighborhood of the Philippines. Through her bases and her submarines and airplanes operating from the mandated islands, she is, in fact, even with her present navy, completely dominant in the Pacific west of Hawaii." This also brought me reproaches from self-styled "liberals" who regarded the article as "provocative" and "unfriendly" to Japan.

Fortunately, crystal-gazing is only an incidental function of a lecturer. He is, of course, expected to be informative and, if possible, amusing. He must know how to hold an audience. He must have a "name"—that is, he must have written books that have been well reviewed, or he must have held important offices. And he must have the stamina of an ox. When a lecturer signs up for a lecture tour he is at the mercy of two relentless masters—the lecture bureau and the local committee. It is to the interest of the lecture bureau, which exacts exorbitant commissions, to book a lecturer for as many engagements as can possibly be sandwiched into the agreed time limit. It is the determination of all local committees to make the most of the lecturer by overwhelming him with demands on his strength, patience, and courtesy. This means that the lecturer is usually busy until long after his lecture and that he must travel at night by the most uncomfortable methods

N. Y. Herald Tribune Syndicate

CARLISLE'S "ALL ASIA IN THE BAG"
The Japanese militarists thought they had won a continent

[249]

of locomotion, usually boarding a train or bus in the small hours and arriving at the next destination before dawn, having slept fitfully or not at all.

In fairness to lady chairmen throughout the country it is only right to recognize that they suffer more acutely during the forty-eight hours preceding the actual laying of hands on the contracted lecturer than does anyone other than a young girl facing her first party. I am told that even a chairman who has handled lecturers for years undergoes steadily mounting blood pressure until her lecturer is safely deposited in the back of the hall a good twenty minutes before he is scheduled to speak. This may explain why, on one occasion when I was to address a large group of women in a Los Angeles theater and had been told to appear at the stage door "only a few minutes" before the lecture was scheduled, a coldly furious madame chairman, with lorgnette and high dog collar, in the traditional Helen Hokinson style, met me in such a state that she did not even acknowledge my greeting. Instead she snapped, "Follow me!" and rapidly led me down a dark corridor to the back of the stage. Pointing to a chair on the stage behind the drawn curtain, she said: "Do you see that chair?" Meekly I said, "Yes." "You will go and sit in that chair," she said to me as she might have addressed an insufferable child, "and in just two minutes the curtain will go up, and you will introduce yourself!" And she turned her back and disappeared. In just two minutes the curtain was rung up, and for the first and only time in my lecturing career, I had to introduce myself. Apparently I had cut the schedule so close that the good lady was almost out of her mind. Fortunately, instead of being embarrassed, I made some joking remarks about what I had put the chairman through —and was being put through myself—and so got off to a good start.

Every lecturer has been torn between boredom and interest as he has heard one lady chairman after another rehash his criminal record. In theory the ordeal should be fairly simple for the chairman. Inevitably she is furnished with a biographical sketch. But in practice her task is complicated by her fear of making a mistake—a fear so strong that often it is distracting. Several times I have listened to my own biographical notice in *Who's Who in*

America repeated either verbatim or barely paraphrased, only to have the chairman at the climax introduce me as Nicholas Longworth. I have also had a chairman completely forget my name and have to check on it on the program.

On one occasion, madame chairman, whose amplitude was only with difficulty constrained within a tight and strong gown, opened the meeting by saying that before introducing the speaker she wanted to pass on a piece of personal good news—she and her husband were going around the world on a cruise. She recited their itinerary in detail and with excited relish—Japan, China, India, Palestine, Italy, France, England, etc. She explained that they were leaving just after Christmas but begged the ladies not to worry about the rest of the lecture course because she had arranged with Mrs. Jones to handle the engagement of speakers during her absence. She extolled Mrs. Jones's many abilities, and then, glancing at me in the front row immediately before her, she added with fervency: "And I sincerely hope Mrs. Jones will have *much* better luck getting speakers than I have."

As she realized how this sounded, she was so appalled that she was almost speechless. Fortunately the ladies began to chuckle —which relieved the tension—and I laughed. When I reached the platform I made an appropriate reference about luck in getting speakers, but seven years later, when I met this lady again, she was still so embarrassed that it was only with difficulty that she forced herself to greet me.

On another occasion in Los Angeles I had an experience of the kind that whitens the hair of a lecturer. It was an afternoon meeting in a large hall. The house was full, and I was steaming along with the self-confidence which a lecturer, like an actor, has when he is holding the attention and interest of the audience. Glancing at my watch, I saw that I had about twelve minutes left and planned the balance of my talk to fit into that time. Suddenly one woman after another in the audience—it was a ladies' current-events club—got up and walked out—perhaps as many as forty. While I concentrated with one part of my brain on finishing the lecture, with the other I kept asking myself: "What under the sun could I have said to make so many women so annoyed or disgusted or bored that they couldn't sit it out?" This same part of my brain recalled tales of professors unconsciously misusing words. The harder I tried to think what I might have said, the hotter and more bothered I got. When the time was up I was soaked and haggard. The applause was partly reassuring, although in my then confused state I thought it somewhat restrained. As I left the platform madame chairman came up to me saying that she owed me an apology. She had forgotten, she said, to warn me that the reception committee, which included about forty women, made it a practice to leave their seats about ten minutes before the end of the lecture so as to powder their noses before serving tea. She always told speakers of this lest they be disturbed to see so many leave at the same time, but she had overlooked it in my case.

The capacity of women audiences to listen to lectures without showing signs of boredom is, I think, greater than that of men. Most men lack the urge for intellectual uplift which is responsible for a large part of the attendance at women's club lecture courses. If the lecturer is able to amuse them, men will remain attentive. But they seem less disciplined in their reactions. Often as I watched men in an audience trying to pull through a lecture evening I was reminded of an experience which I had shortly after returning from Hungary in 1933. At the local private school I was persuaded to give a talk about representing the American government abroad as minister or ambassador—a difficult assignment for an audience ranging between the ages of 8 and 15. In the school gymnasium where the reluctant pupils were assembled they were grouped by ages, those from 8 to 11 on the left as I faced the length of the gym, and those from 12 to 15 on the right. I soon saw that the moment I lost the interest of the younger group they began wriggling and squirming in their chairs. The older ones were more controlled—though probably no less bored. The youngsters would not stop wriggling until I recaptured their interest. But as soon as I lost it the group would again squirm. This was the signal for me to try to think of some new incident which might catch their attention. Many times, afterwards, I recognized the signs of loss of interest among adult audiences and realized that only adult discipline prevented them from squirming and wriggling in their seats—although it did not stop them from going to sleep.

At a men's club in a Pennsylvania town before which I was lecturing, an elderly man in the front row slept comfortably and quietly throughout my entire talk. When I later joined my wife, who was with the wife of the chairman of the club group, I remarked, in reply to the question about how the lecture had been received, that only one man went to sleep. Instantly the local lady cried out with incredulity: "What? Only *one?*" Nothing that my wife or I could do thereafter salved her embarrassment, as she realized how her remark must have sounded. Apparently it was prompted by her knowledge that about a half-dozen members of the club were notorious for sleeping through such lectures. Hence her surprise when I reported only one sleeper in the group.

Usually the arrival of a lecturer is treated as a social "event," especially if the community is small. Sometimes he finds himself a prize in a local social war, one group trying to snatch him away from another. If he is wise he defers to madame chairman—at least until after all the formalities have been completed, which nearly always includes a meal before and a reception after the lecture. Often, also, he is taken to see the local sights. West of the Mississippi these are admired in terms of size, which may explain why, when I landed in St. Joseph, Missouri, at five in the morning, unshaven, unwashed and only half-awake, I was met by a committee of local businessmen who were to drive me to the hotel for an early breakfast, and who insisted that we see the sights on the way. I was shown the packing house, which, they said, was the largest packing house west of the Mississippi, and the stockyards (also the largest) and various other enterprises, likewise characterized in the same manner. Finally, as the climax of the sight-seeing tour, I was shown the lunatic asylum, which they proudly and solemnly assured me was the largest lunatic asylum west of the Mississippi. I kept a straight face until I was deposited at the hotel. On this same visit an enthusiastic Missourian, whom I had asked about Missouri's governor, praised that gentleman and his family extravagantly and ended by saying that Missouri had the handsomest governor's wife of any state in the union.

Time and again, as I traveled about the country, I was struck with the immense kindness of those whom I met. It is an outstanding American trait—one which is notably lacking in Europe. Courtesy and politeness of a formal sort are the rule on the Continent. But in the United States I found everywhere a genuine desire to be friendly, helpful, and considerate. This was true on the part of men as well as of women. There seemed no bounds to their hospitality other than the ability of the visiting lecturer to take it. Each time I went on a lecture tour I came back exhausted but with renewed faith and pride in the American people —something which one loses if one remains too long in New York. True, I failed to convince the audiences of my points. Some of them resented my acceptance of the resumption of war as a fundamental postulate. But the genuine friendliness of their reception was as heartening as it was satisfying. Whether or not the ladies felt that they got their money's worth—one tactful chairman told me just before introducing me that she hoped I would be worth the fee which was to be paid me—I, for my part, enjoyed these opportunities of getting around the country and was sorry when our entry into World War II made it virtually impossible for any but a military expert to talk intelligently about current events.

CHAPTER TWENTY-EIGHT

BATTLING BRASS

IN OCTOBER, 1942, I received a telegram from Elmer Davis, head of the Office of War Information, reading: "Will be in New York tomorrow. Can I see you." Thinking that he wanted to protest about recent criticism in the *Herald Tribune* of the government's war-news policy, I telegraphed him to meet me at lunch at the Century and said that I would bring our fellow-Centurian, Geoffrey Parsons, the editor of the *Herald Tribune*.

With characteristic directness, Elmer opened the conversation by saying: "I have come to New York to ask if you will take over the job of deputy director of the Office of War Information in charge of relations with the Army and Navy."

"What would my duties be?" I asked.

"To do what you can to induce the Army and Navy to get out fuller and more accurate news about our war effort, with less delay."

"That's quite an order," was my comment.

"Yes. It's the toughest job we've got in the O. W. I.—and the most thankless."

Parsons—my boss at the time—said he felt that I had to accept, that the job needed doing, and it was up to me to try to do it. As I had wanted to help in the war effort but lacked my Roosevelt relatives' ambition to return to soldiering in my fiftieth year, I signed up for this, the most frustrating and futile job in my life.

It was frustrating and futile through no fault of Elmer's. He was a valiant, shrewd, and tireless chief, giving me the benefit of his advice and help and the full support of his office. But in

[255]

dealing with the Navy, he and I were up against the prejudices of a long-entrenched, bureaucratic hierarchy dominated by a man who, because he was one of the greatest naval strategists and organizers in American history, was convinced that he was an expert on public relations. Admiral Ernest J. King will go down in the annals of American naval history as the man who, although handicapped by a badly crippled fleet operating in waters entirely in command of the enemy, outplanned, outbuilt, and outfought one of the world's greatest naval powers. Had anyone suggested to him that Elmer Davis, because he was an expert in public relations, would make a good commander of a battleship in action, the Admiral would have been incensed. Yet it never occurred to him that a training as a fleet admiral did not *ipso facto* fit a man to form sound opinions about public relations in time of war. It used to be said of him that he would have liked it best if only two communiques had been issued by the Navy during World War II. The first, dated December 8, 1941, would have read: "Following an attack by the enemy, the American fleet put to sea yesterday." The second, after the capitulation of Japan, would have read: "Having defeated the enemy, the American fleet is returning to its home ports." What transpired in between those dates would have been published months or years later, after the most careful editing and censoring by an entire board of admirals.

As a reluctant concession to public opinion the Navy, after Pearl Harbor, had issued occasional reports about its activities, but these reports were so lacking in candor and information that the country had come to believe that the Navy was not telling the truth about its part in the war. People felt that it had been hiding bad news in order to "cover up," and that it had delayed the publication of important actions, successful or unsuccessful, so as to be able to hand-feed the American public such news as it thought would best protect the Navy from criticism. The conviction that the Navy had been holding back the truth was so widespread that confidence in the whole war effort was shaken. It was largely to help restore confidence that F. D. R. appointed Elmer Davis director of the O. W. I. The press, radio, and the public had faith in him. When in November, 1942, he gave his word to the American people that, at least at that time, the Navy was telling the public the truth, people began to put credence in the communiques and statements issued by the Navy Department.

Under the executive order setting up the O. W. I., the Navy bureau of public relations was directed to consult with Elmer on matters touching publicity. But O. W. I.'s very existence was resented by the Navy because it was quite obvious that there would have been no O. W. I. if the public had not become convinced that the Navy was holding out information about the war. In other words, the creation of the O. W. I. was a reflection on the Navy's conduct of public relations. As the mismanagement of the Navy's publicity was directly traceable to Admiral King's prejudices on the subject, the resentment of the Navy's public relations bureau against the O. W. I. was shared—if not inspired—by the high command. But with the finesse of a long-entrenched bureaucracy, the Navy, faced with the mandatory nature of the executive order creating the O. W. I. but determined to adhere to its own ideas of publicity, developed the most perfect form of run-around of any bureau in Washington. The technique was simple: to listen to every suggestion from the O. W. I. with cordial appreciation and gratefulness; to promise prompt and enthusiastic support in submitting the suggestion to the high command; and, after a more than reasonable delay, designed to give the impression that the high command was studying it from every possible angle, to report regretfully that the suggestion had been turned down.

The lot of the officers in the Navy's bureau of public relations was not a happy one. They lived in constant fear that their careers would be ruined if they incurred the ill will of their able but arbitrary commander-in-chief. Furthermore, they had been indoctrinated with the conviction that what the highest authority decrees may not be questioned. Even if some of them believed that Admiral King's attitude about public relations could profitably be modified, they would have been helpless to do anything had they so desired. Their function was to act as buffers between the press, which was seeking legitimate information (with the support of the O. W. I.), and the high command, trying to placate the former at the same time that they feared the latter. The head of the bureau was sufficiently well padded, both outside and in, to withstand pressure from both sides.

The situation was further complicated for us in the O. W. I. by the fact that the Naval Academy at Annapolis, at the same time that it turns out excellent naval officers, inculcates in them the idea that the graduates of Annapolis stand apart from, and above, the rest of the people of the country. My immediate predecessor, a Bostonian born in the inner circle of the most exclusive clique of old Boston society, remarked to me that at Harvard he had been a member of the Porcellian Club and, subsequently, of the Somerset Club in Boston, and that he had thought that he knew all there was to know about the innate conviction of superiority over the rest of mankind which a group of Americans might hold. He had found, however, that the assumption of such superiority on the part of his Boston friends was as nothing compared to the unshakable conviction of Annapolis graduates that no outsider was the equal of those who had attended that institution. I mention this not in a derogatory sense, for the graduates of Annapolis have been able as naval officers and compare favorably with the officers of the British or any other navies. But it created a state of mind which established a barrier between all Annapolis graduates and all civilians for the simple reason that Annapolis graduates knew that no civilian could possibly have any ideas about anything which could by chance be as good as, or better than, those of Navy men. Translated into the specific, this meant that no civilian expert in public relations could understand the Navy's public-relations problem as well as the Annapolis graduate who for the moment happened to be in charge of the bureau of public relations, even if the officer had had no experience in this field.

Both Elmer and I naïvely thought that, as Secretary of the Navy Frank Knox was a newspaperman and an old friend of ours, he could help. But we soon learned that, fine and fearless as he was, Colonel Knox had little influence in this matter. In my fairly frequent contacts with him he was always friendly and responsive, but not only did he stand in awe of Admiral King but he was reluctant even to make suggestions to him. King was not open to reason or to argument from any man not a graduate of the Naval Academy at Annapolis—including the Secretary of the Navy. None of his associates or subordinates dared to tell him that his ideas of public relations were hurting the Navy.

Under the circumstances, our only hope—short of direct intervention by the President, which Elmer naturally was reluctant to ask—was to seek out every possible approach to the high command of the Navy through which the stubborn Admiral might be influenced. The aim was to reach officers close to Admiral King and unofficially and informally explain to them the nature of the problem. As this work fell to me, it did not endear me to the chief of the Navy's bureau of public relations, who naturally resented my unwillingness to accept his refusals and my readiness to contact higher-ups on my own. When, metaphorically speaking, I had been tossed out of the door of the Navy Department, I crept in through a window. When I had been thrown out of the window I came down the drain. Direct approach, as I have indicated, was fruitless.

Fortunately Admiral King, when I called on him officially, turned me over to a member of his staff whom I found to be wise, helpful, understanding, and frank, and who, as he faced imminent retirement due to an unexpected physical disability, was not as afraid of the Commander-in-Chief as were other naval officers. In a quiet way he was able to help create a favorable reception and full consideration of a number of ideas about public relations which the head of the bureau of public relations did not dare even to pass along to the high command. Furthermore, I found Admiral King's chief of staff, Admiral Edwards, a reasonable and responsive individual. The same was true of Vice Admiral Horne and of Admiral Cooke, both of whom were in constant close association with King. From Admiral Richard E. Byrd I also had valuable help, for, although his influence in Navy circles was weakened by the fact that he had been named admiral for work as an explorer rather than as a man of the sea, he had useful contacts and understood public relations. Furthermore, he dared to say what he believed even to those who resented plain speaking.

In fairness to Admiral King it should be said that his antagonism to fuller and freer information about the Navy was grounded in his awareness of the desperate plight of the Navy following Pearl Harbor and in his realization that the Japanese did not know how bad it was. He was determined to prevent the Japanese from learning this until the losses had been made good. If, in the process, he withheld information from the American people, that was, comparatively speaking, unimportant. Many naval officers felt at the time that if, before the Battle of Midway in June of 1942, Japan had realized how vulnerable we were, the Japanese Navy might have inflicted irreparable damage to our forces. Fortunately, the Japanese attack on the American fleet in the Battle of Midway was a defeat for Japan—a defeat which lifted a load of worry from the shoulders of our naval leaders. Thenceforth, however long and hard the war in the Pacific, the American Navy would become progressively stronger in proportion to the Japanese, and the danger of Japan's invasion of the American continent would decrease. A turning point in the war had been reached. Victory was still far away, but defeat was no longer imminent.

Because of the Navy's previous unsatisfactory publicity record, even the news of the Battle of Midway was received with skepticism. Too often before—specifically, in the Battle of Macassar Straits, the Battle of the Java Sea, and the sinking of the *Langley*—the Navy had initially given the impression that our forces had met with success, only later to admit defeat or disaster. A similar policy had been followed in the case of the Japanese attack on the Aleutians. Word of the landing in the Aleutians first came through the Tokyo radio early in June, 1942. A few days later a spokesman in the Navy Department was quoted as saying that "certainly none of our inhabited areas, islands, or rocks are troubled with any uninvited visitors up to this time." Forty-eight hours afterward, Japanese landings on Attu and Kiska were admitted but were characterized as "small." On June 14 the Associated Press reported that "in Army and Navy circles the Japanese landings were viewed as nothing to arouse concern." Yet the fact was that the Japanese had landed thousands of soldiers and that the occupation of the Aleutians was a serious blow to us and gave the Japanese valuable bases in the Western Hemisphere.

"Security" was Admiral King's main preoccupation—quite rightly. When he lectured me bitterly about this, and with open animus against all who, like Elmer and myself, were trying to get him to take the American people more into his confidence, I pointed out that it would help the Navy's public relations if the people could be told the whys and wherefores of security, and I suggested that he have someone on his staff indoctrinate me on the subject. This he did, and when I prepared a brief summary of the Navy's reasons for withholding certain types of information, we arranged to have Vice-Admiral Horne use it in his testimony before the Naval Affairs Committee of the Senate, and then had this summary reprinted in the *Congressional Record*.

From this statement it was apparent that if the enemy, after a naval action in which he knew he had scored a hit, could receive prompt and accurate information about the extent of the damage which he had done, he could so shape his subsequent maneuvers as to profit by our losses. If, on the contrary, he knew only that he had made a hit and did not know whether the vessel was lightly or severely damaged, he was likely not to risk his own vessels in further action lest he find himself overpowered. Often a vessel which had been damaged in action limped away at night and had to steam slowly for several days before it could reach port. If the enemy could get accurate information that a crippled vessel was trying to get away he could send fast ships of his own in pursuit and sink the crippled vessel before it could reach port.

So, also, if the action had been on a more extensive scale and a good many vessels had been involved, it could be of vital value to the enemy to have specific information about the number and types of our ships which were incapacitated so that he could take advantage of our losses. It followed, therefore, that in many cases the policy of delaying the publication of information was sound. Certainly no American, whether an editor or broadcaster or a man in any other work, would want news given out which might endanger the lives of our men in the armed forces. All that they ever asked was that the reason for withholding news be valid and that security be not used as an excuse to keep things from the American public which the enemy already knew.

After the Battle of Midway, the public relations of the Navy Department improved a little because of the fact that the high command, as I have indicated, realized that thenceforth the strength of the American Navy relative to that of Japan would increase until final victory was achieved. Nevertheless, in Europe the German submarine campaign threatened to present serious publicity problems—especially if the Navy withheld factual information. Those of us who had been in World War I knew how near the Germans had come to victory in 1917 and 1918, thanks to their submarine campaign. In the winter of 1942–43 there was reason to believe that the Germans would greatly increase the effectiveness of their submarine campaign. As our antisubmarine vessels would not be in operation in sufficient numbers by the summer of 1943 to prevent the Germans from seriously crippling the transport of American troops and supplies to Europe, we feared that a successful raid on a convoy, or a series of such raids, might be made public by the enemy in such a manner as to shock the American people. If the Navy were again to be vulnerable to the charge of withholding facts from the people, it might not only shake confidence in the leadership of Admiral King to such an extent that he would be forced out, but it might once more weaken the faith of the people in the whole conduct of the war. We felt that the best way to forestall this was to take the people into the Navy's confidence by issuing periodic statements setting forth the truth about the progress of the submarine campaign.

The Navy Department was reluctant to discuss the potential public-relations problems which we might have to face. Admiral King was opposed to giving out any information about submarines. He and other high officials were of the opinion that not only was it unnecessary to tell the public about submarine warfare but that it was no business of the Office of War Information to interest itself in the problem. Knowing from my contacts with members of Admiral King's staff that he would not allow the publishing of the figures of the tonnage of merchant vessels sunk by the submarines each month, because he felt this would help the enemy, I set about working out various formulae through which the public could be given an idea as to whether the antisubmarine campaign was going well or badly. I presented these formulae informally to one of the ablest and most broad-minded officers in the department, who told me that nothing could be done without the consent of the British. The Secretary of the Navy took a similar point of view.

Accordingly, we got in touch with the British, only to be told that nothing could be done except by direct contact between the President and Winston Churchill. Weeks passed in all these discussions, to no purpose. Then, fortunately, Mr. Churchill came to Washington. Elmer placed on the President's desk a memorandum setting forth some of the formulae which might be used to give the public an idea of the submarine war. The *New York Herald Tribune* and the *New York Times* came to our assistance with editorial comment urging the President and Mr. Churchill to deal with the problem.

Several persons took up with Mr. Churchill the importance, from the American point of view, of loosening the restrictions on publicity about the submarine campaign. He was adamant against the publishing of monthly tables of losses. We had exhausted all means to have a more sensible policy adopted.

Fortunately, by the month of June the antisubmarine campaign became so effective that submarines ceased to be a major threat to the Allied war effort. But it was a satisfaction to us when, in August, Mr. Churchill and President Roosevelt finally issued a joint statement about the submarine campaign which gave a clear picture of what was happening. Even though this statement did not mention the tonnage of vessels sunk, it at least mentioned the number of submarines sunk in the previous three months. Here was a case in which we had worked for six months to educate the higher-ups to the need for fuller publicity, at last to meet with a certain measure of success.

To the end of my tour of duty with the O. W. I. Admiral King remained as impervious to reason in matters of public relations as he was responsive and brilliant in his all-important duties of winning the fighting war. If it seems ungracious, and perhaps picayune, to dwell so extensively on his shortcomings, I do so only because knowledge of his failure in this field may encourage some future commander-in-chief of the Navy to entrust the conduct of the Navy's public relations to men who are experienced in this line.

Shortly before I left the O. W. I., in the autumn of 1943, the Navy had another relapse in its public relations because of its failure to use experienced men. Elmer, in his matter-of-fact Indiana twang, muttered to me as he looked up mournfully from his desk: "They just don't understand. They just don't understand." And then he added: "With a few changes Mr. Churchill's famous words about the Battle of Britain apply to the Navy Department's public-relations policy: Never have so few withheld so much from so many."

Ours was, of course, a professional and interested reaction. As I look back I wonder only at one thing—not that naval officers failed so dismally in public relations, but that men who were so competent in their own specialties were not smart enough to recognize their limitations in this field, and to put in charge of public relations the best expert in the country. Perhaps, if World War III comes, they will do so.

CHAPTER TWENTY-NINE

GLIMPSES OF THE *TIMES*

MY NEWSPAPER work alternated between the *New York Herald Tribune* and the *New York Times*. Perhaps because of the persistence of the tradition of the dominant Horace Greeley the *Herald Tribune* was more personalized than the *Times*. In fact, I often had the impression that the "H. T." managed to get itself out each day by the momentary and more or less haphazard co-operation of a number of disjointed, independent editors and writers, whereas the *Times* regularly was masterminded with precision. One of the results of this was that the *Herald Tribune* had —and continues to have—a greater variety of individualistic writers. Men like Heywood Broun, Franklin P. Adams, Henry E. Krehbiel, and Lawrence Gilman wrote with an originality and personal tang rarely shown by *Times* writers. Furthermore, when a reporter on the *Herald Tribune* brought in a story to which he had given a distinctive or humorous twist it was likely to be run as written (always provided he had not prejudiced its accuracy), whereas the *Times* preferred conventional coverage.

Yet my respect and admiration for the *Times* was—and is— great. The paper has been criticized as being too much of an institution. This, I think, is a mistaken judgment. The editing, let alone the gathering, of the million words which come to the office of the *Times* each day impose tasks which can only be efficiently performed by a large staff of specialists, acting under carefully co-ordinated direction.

There were two reasons for the success of the *Times* after Adolph S. Ochs took it over. The first was the formula to which he and his successor adhered so rigidly and insistently, that *Times* news reports must be not only complete but fair and as accurate as possible. The second was Mr. Ochs' skill in picking and backing able assistants. In other words, at a time when journalism in New York was intensely personal, reflecting the prejudices and restricted interests of the owners, Mr. Ochs made the *Times* a paper which could be relied upon to be impersonal, impartial, and receptive to news of all kinds. This was his contribution to the *Times*—and to American journalism. So great was the success of this simple formula that standards set by the *New York Times* were valued and adopted by newspapers throughout the nation.

In implementing this policy Mr. Ochs gave full power to the ablest managing editor in the history of American journalism— Carr Van Anda. The two men differed in character and personality, but worked well together. Mr. Ochs was warm-hearted, almost exuberant, full of ideas, with limitless curiosity and an excellent "front." The fact that he had begun to support himself so young that his education had suffered helped him to understand the lacks and needs of men and women who were similarly handicapped. He sensed that things which were not clear to him would not be clear to millions of others. He had a passion to know the whys as well as the whats. Van Anda, in contrast, was a man of prodigious learning, who delighted in the solution of abstruse intellectual problems in higher mathematics and astronomy and who perceived the whys instantly and almost instinctively. His mind operated like a highly efficient precision instrument. Except in his relations with his friends, he was cold and detached, essentially just and fair, but unswayed by personal considerations. So sharp were his reasoning powers that he foresaw the probable sequels and implications of a current news story, and often guessed correctly on mere shreds of evidence when and where a story would break. His staff and associates viewed this capacity with awe. Lacking a better explanation, they attributed it to a sixth sense. But to Van Anda his flair for anticipating news was merely a normal exercise of the intellect. Furthermore, he knew that unless it was implemented with the best possible news coverage it had little value. Accordingly he mastered the mechanics of or-

[266]

ganizing the gathering of the news, which meant not only the training of a corps of experts in many fields but also making effective provisions for the transmission of their stories as quickly as possible—not an easy task half a century ago when long-distance telephoning was limited to a few hundred miles and there was no radio.

Like all editors, Van Anda was on guard against persons who wished to plant or twist news stories for their own ends. Infallibly he recognized special pleading and would spot the kernel of truth in a story or discard it as not newsworthy. Mr. Van Anda listened with an open mind and asked blunt and unmasking questions. Mr. Ochs, in contrast, was more inclined to accept people at their own valuation. To say that Mr. Ochs was gullible would be to misinterpret his fundamental kindness. He was receptive to plausible new ideas, especially if they were in fields in which his knowledge was limited. Anything new, anything unusual, aroused his interest. His curiosity had an appealing boyish quality.

I remember that, at one of the daily editorial conferences over which he presided, Mr. Ochs told us that, walking down Broadway to the office of the *Times*, he saw a crowd outside the window of a corner store staring at an elderly man in an abbreviated gym suit flexing his muscles as he lectured to a roomful of people. Going in, Mr. Ochs found that it was Bernarr Macfadden, at the time publisher of the tabloid *New York Graphic*, which Mr. Ochs deplored as an example of everything a newspaper should not be. Macfadden, in addition to boosting the *Graphic*, was selling for a dollar a pamphlet on health development. Mr. Ochs, as he described the scene to us, became warmly indignant at this sort of showmanship, and at the gullibility of New Yorkers who not only would buy the *Graphic* but actually would pay a dollar for one of Macfadden's pamphlets. Van Anda, who had been listening without comment, at this point interjected dryly: "Did you buy one of the pamphlets, Mr. Ochs?" Sheepishly Mr. Ochs admitted that he had, which brought laughter from the editorial council. With characteristic honesty and generosity he added that he thought the pamphlet was pretty well done.

One of Mr. Och's best and most endearing qualities was the

way in which he welcomed having his suggestions, ideas, and opinions ripped to pieces by members of his staff. None was more relentless in this than Van Anda, yet Mr. Ochs neither showed resentment nor yielded unless Van Anda convinced him that he was mistaken. At the daily editorial conferences Mr. Ochs would often come up with a dozen or more ideas. Nine out of ten, on examination, were dropped, but the tenth was likely to be so valuable that it more than counterbalanced those which had proved fruitless. His great alertness, his buoyancy, and his warm humanity were a constant stimulus to his associates and encouraged them to be more receptive and broader in their own interests. His energy, imagination, and urge to know made him the dynamo of the *Times*—and one of the great newspaper publishers of the century.

Like so many successful men, Mr. Ochs had not only ability but also luck. So, for example, it was his good fortune that his son-in-law, Arthur Hays Sulzberger, had qualities of character and intellect which enabled him to take over on Mr. Ochs' death and continue the Ochs traditions to fresh triumphs. Mr. Sulzberger brought to the office of publisher an extensive and detailed knowledge of every step in the operation of the *Times*, together with a balanced judgment and a large measure of personal kindliness and sympathy. Furthermore, he was wise enough to know that everything he did would be weighed in comparison to how Mr. Ochs might have done it, and that, if he allowed this to influence him too greatly, he would himself be constantly thinking in terms of Mr. Ochs, without being able to benefit from the man's experience and wisdom. He had to be himself, and as he was modest, fair, and just, he disarmed criticism and won the affection as well as the respect of his staff.

For managing editor, Mr. Sulzberger kept Edwin L. James, who had taken over from Frederick T. Birchall, the acting managing editor since the retirement of Carr Van Anda. James, whose capacity to growl was a protective mechanism to compensate for his short stature, became an able managing editor, shrewd, courageous, well informed, and hard to impose upon. "I'm just a hired man," was one of his favorite forms of self-deprecation when he

ADOLPH S. OCHS
He raised American journalistic standards and created a great
institution

was using with the completest freedom the full initiative which the publisher had long given him because of his proved ability. "Jimmy" liked to pose as a tough character, forever chewing the end of a cigar and talking out of the corner of his mouth. In defense of the *Times* he could be pugnacious and relentless. But under this pose, which he carried in and out of his office, was a basic sympathy for his staff and an intense loyalty to them. For this they liked him, and for his unquestioned ability as a newspaperman they respected him.

Another of Mr. Ochs' key men whom Mr. Sulzberger kept on was Lester Markel, who took over the *New York Times Sunday Magazine* in 1923, and, in recent years, also supervised the *Book Review* and other special features of the Sunday paper. Where a managing editor has to deal primarily with the day-to-day development of the news and can, up till the small hours of the morning, change the make-up of his paper if news developments demand it, the Sunday editor is hampered by the fact that the magazine goes to press on the Wednesday before it appears on the newsstands. This is why Mr. Markel once described his work as more hazardous than tightrope-walking or flagpole-sitting. The articles which go to press on Wednesday deal, almost without exception, with the background of current news, but by Sunday something may have occurred to make one or more of these articles completely out of date. As a result the Sunday editor has to try to see the news ahead—which requires a streamlined and efficient form of crystal gazing. Yet the number of times when Lester Markel was misled in using the crystal ball of his own clear head are surprisingly few. I never asked him how often he had guessed wrong, but I doubt if it would run to as much as 5 per cent of the time.

Someday Mr. Markel may write his autobiography or a thesis on what makes a Sunday editor tick. I suspect that such men are born, not trained. Certainly I doubt that the Columbia University School of Journalism, of which Markel is a graduate, deliberately set about preparing him to be a great Sunday editor, or that it could so prepare some other of its students. The Sunday editor's process of seeing the news ahead involves pure reason. It was

Markel's—and the *Times'*— good fortune that, like Van Anda, he had a steel-trap mind, clear, precise, coldly efficient.

Markel and James, together with Charles Merz, head of the editorial page, functioned under Mr. Sulzberger as the general staff of the *Times*, and rarely did an abler quartet run any institution. It was characteristic of the *Times* that its foreign-news service, which was and is, without question, the best of any newspaper in the world, and its Washington bureau, of which the same may be said, operated as almost autonomous units. The Washington bureau, so long headed by the highly competent and un-self-assertive Richard V. Oulahan, was taken over in 1933 by Arthur Krock, whose shrewdness and wit were matched by his detailed knowledge of national affairs acquired through personal observation during several decades. Krock was criticized for being too human in his signed column on the editorial page of the paper because he often spoke well in it of his friends. But this amiable weakness was compensated by the fact that the over-all news coverage of the national capital under his direction was as full, fair, and unprejudiced as the rest of the news stories in the *Times* —which is another way of saying that the *Times'* Washington coverage was unsurpassed.

One of the reasons why Krock had critics as well as many friends is that he was one of the few Washington correspondents who frankly enjoyed social life in the national capital. Most newspapermen believe that correspondents should not establish too close personal relations with men and women in public life lest, consciously or otherwise, they allow these friendships to color their handling of the news. Krock's enjoyment of these contacts was tempered by his shrewdness and common sense, both of which warned him when prominent individuals sought to use him for their own ends. The fact that his wit and his fondness for *bon mots* was as celebrated as Alice Longworth's meant that many persons feared him at the same time that they enjoyed his company. Other Washington correspondents may have known as much as he about the current scene, but few if any had his encyclopedic background and his keenness in evaluating the news, and none was better company.

The catalog of outstanding *Times* personnel could be prolonged for many pages. It includes the late Simeon Strunsky, whose warm and whimsical humor radiated not only from the "Topics of the Times," which for so many years he wrote, and from his books, but also in his conversation. It included, at least during part of my first tour with the *Times*, the hardheaded, flatspoken, and witty Elmer Davis, and, during my second tour, the immensely able and balanced Anne O'Hare McCormick. Elmer left the *Times* to free-lance, and with the rise of radio commentating he capitalized his Indiana twang to present his condensed analyses of national and international events in simple phrases enlivened by a gift for dry paradox.

For Mrs. McCormick I had, as did all her associates, respect and admiration. Hers is a penetrating intelligence. Like Van Anda, Markel, and "Jimmy" James, she has an unerring quickness in detecting sham and propaganda. At the same time, she has a thorough knowledge of world affairs and a gift of inspiring confidence in all with whom she speaks so that they open their minds and hearts to her. Being sensitive, and having high integrity, she never embarrasses her informants by indiscreet use of what they have told her. As an interviewer she is welcomed by Europe's—and America's—leading figures because they value her judgment, know the thoroughness of her information, and like her simplicity, directness, and understanding at the same time that they respect her shrewdness. More, even, than de Blowitz and Wickham Steed of the *London Times*, who, in their day, were heeded with special attention in the chancelleries of Europe, Mrs. McCormick is noted for what she gives in return, as well as for what she does with the information which she has received. I was told that many continentals feared de Blowitz. Many Englishmen distrusted Wickham Steed at the same time that they recognized his extraordinary knowledge of the forces that led to the outbreak of World War I. But I know of no one who has feared or distrusted Anne O'Hare McCormick—unless it was Stalin.

Characteristic of her quick perceptions was an answer which she gave to a question from the audience at a meeting in Times Hall over which I was presiding in the winter of 1945–46, at which she had made one of her periodic reports about conditions in Europe. Among other things, she had described seeing in Austria the Russian troops take away with them every animal and every stick of furniture and every implement as they evacuated parts of Austrian territory, leaving the Austrian peasants with only the shells of their houses. When she sat down, a tall man, obviously of Russian or eastern European origin, rose and with ill-controlled anger and in a strong foreign accent, asked Mrs. McCormick what the difference was between this sort of action by the Russian troops in Austria and the "shameful" looting of Germans by Americans which had been reported in some of the newspapers. Mrs. McCormick jumped to her feet and said that she would be very glad to explain the difference. "I'll tell you just what it is," she said. "It's the difference between planned economy and free enterprise." For a moment the audience didn't quite grasp her point, so she elaborated that in Austria the stripping of all usable articles from the farms had been done by the Russians under orders. In Germany the few cases of looting by Americans had been the acts of individuals, and had been punished by the authorities. During that particular meeting we had no more heckling from Communist sympathizers.

While these individuals—and many others—helped to make the *Times* great, the fact that it is an institution gives strength to the men and women who work for it. On the *Times*, once an affirmative decision is made, it is backed to the limit at every level. The telephone operators take no less pride than do reporters when they are able to help contact someone urgently needed in order to complete a story or verify a bit of information. In the illness or absence of a key person on the *Times* someone else takes over promptly and efficiently.

It is no reflection on the editorial writers of the *New York Times*—of which I was one for seven years— to say that, as I look back on the *Times*, its news service stands out as its most distinguished contribution to journalism. The reason is obvious—that, as the name implies, the *Times* is a *news*-paper, and not a journal of opinion or a magazine of background. It is to read the news, rather than to read editorials, that most persons buy it. Editorials

[272]

on occasion influence men in public life. But they are far less influential than most publishers like to believe. Certainly it is now an accepted fact that the editorial opinions of the American press as a whole carry little weight in political elections.

News stories, on the other hand, even though they may be exclusive, reach many more readers. This is particularly true of the front page. In this connection I had a pertinent experience as a result of discovering by chance, when I was on a vacation in Yosemite National Park in 1928, that the National Park Service was planning to turn over to one of the California lumber companies a large stand of exceptionally fine sugar pines on the western border of the Yosemite. The surrender of this sugar-pine area was to be in the form of a trade for other property inside the park boundaries held by this lumber company—that is, the Park Service would receive title to the lands further inside the park in exchange for lands on the border where they could be easily lumbered.

As a lover of trees and of the national parks, this seemed to me a betrayal of public trust. The director of the National Park Service, Stephen T. Mather, and his assistant, Horace M. Albright, happened to be in Yosemite while I was there. I checked this story with Albright, who was an old friend. He explained that in none of the national parks did the government own all of the land within the park boundaries. The reason for this was that the parks had been established long after the Homestead Acts, and that many individuals legally owned land within the park boundaries that had been homesteaded prior to the creation of the parks. Under existing laws these homesteaders or their legal successors could do with their own lands what they wanted. No power of condemnation for park purposes existed. In Yosemite several thousand acres of land which the Park wanted to use had belonged for years to one of the big lumber companies. The Park Service had no funds to buy this land even if the owners would be willing to sell. But the Park Service could exchange park lands for private lands if the owners were willing to accept the exchange, which, in this case, they were.

My reaction was simple and direct—to sound the alarm. I told Albright that I was sure that if I, who had long been interested in national parks, had not known that there were privately owned areas within the parks, the overwhelming mass of the people in the country would be equally ignorant and that they would be as resentful of the condition as I was, and as eager to see it remedied. Accordingly I suggested that, instead of taking the negative attitude of reducing the area of Yosemite in order to obtain title to lands within the Park boundary owned by the lumber companies, the Park Service should take the offensive and state publicly that, unless this exchange could be prevented and the threatened lands bought by government funds, Yosemite would be endangered. I added that I was sure that there would be widespread popular support for such a position. He agreed to speak to Mather, the director of the Park Service, about making a statement to that effect, and I telegraphed the *New York Times* asking if it wanted a story about it. Mather was reluctant, but when the *Times* asked for a thousand-word story I suggested that I write a statement for Mather to make and that he and I use that as the basis of an interview. This we did, and the next morning the *Times* carried on the front page the story which Mather and I had agreed upon, headlining the threat to Yosemite and to the park system as a whole. The press of the country took it up—as I knew it would—and within a few weeks Mr. John D. Rockefeller, Jr., had offered to put up one and one-half million dollars for acquisition of these and other privately owned lands in Yosemite and other parks, provided the federal government matched his gift dollar for dollar. The necessary legislation was introduced in Congress. I enlisted the interest of the Sierra Club and of influential Californians so that the bill in Congress would have adequate local support from the California delegation, and before the year was out the money was voted, the lands were acquired, and the splendid sugar pines on the west border of Yosemite were preserved from destruction and kept in the Park. Here, certainly, was a case when a news story on the front page of a great daily paper accomplished much.

Because the tradition is still strong, particularly in the field of politics, that it is the privilege of a newspaper publisher to use his editorial columns to support his own political predilections and criticize opposing views, it is often assumed that a publisher dictates his editorial policy. It is quite true that most publishers would be reluctant to see their editorial columns express views on important problems of national or international policy at variance with their own opinions on these matters. In practice there is— or should be—a high degree of harmony between the opinions of the publisher and his chief editorial writer. But in my own experience as editorial writer on the *Times* and on the *Herald Tribune* never once was I directed to write an editorial that ran counter to my own beliefs. This does not mean that I concurred with all the policies of the editorial page on all matters. Far from it. If a change of policy was contemplated in one of my chosen fields I had the opportunity of arguing against it, but if I failed to convince, the phrasing of the new policy fell to the editor or to some other member of the staff. This was the accepted practice on both papers.

Mr. Ochs, whose concept of the role of a newspaper in the community was broad, early envisioned the services which a paper like the *New York Times* could render by printing the full texts of important speeches and state papers. He realized that these would be invaluable in libraries, universities, and schools, and in the offices of other newspapers throughout the country. He also realized that the kind of index which the *Times* published first in an annual, then in a quarterly, form would be as useful as the texts—or even more so. While he appreciated the value of these services as circulation-builders, I have little doubt that he inaugurated them because he thought that the *Times* thus was performing an important historical function. Newspapers are, obviously, primary sources of history. Mr. Ochs was aware—and proud—of the fact that the *New York Times*, under his leadership, had become the best single source of recorded history in the country, if not in the world.

This interest in the public-service functions of the *Times* was carried on after his death, largely under the impetus of his daughter, Iphigene Ochs Sulzberger, who shared his vision of the *Times* as an educational force in the community. It was due primarily to her that the *Times* investigated the study of American history in the colleges of this country and published a series of articles which shocked the nation's educators. She also was influential in planning courses on the making of a newspaper and on its role in the community, given for the benefit of the schoolteachers of New York City. For two years I worked closely with her on this phase of the *Times'* public relations, and was interested to see in her not only her father's sense of responsibility to the community but his keen awareness of what people ought to be interested in.

When I rejoined the *Times* in 1944 as assistant to the publisher, it was just embarking on a new public-relations venture—the acquisition of radio station WQXR. The purchase of the station had been the result of Mr. Sulzberger's broad interests, for he, more than the members of his staff, had the vision to see that a good radio station could be a good investment for a newspaper. Some of the higher-ups on the *Times* never completely shook off their traditional concept of radio as a rival for the press. He saw that it could be, in fact, an auxiliary. Mr. Sulzberger believed that broadcasting of news bulletins was a proper function of a newspaper, and he had previously had an arrangement with station WMCA for a three-minute period every hour on the hour.

I was appointed vice-president of WQXR, and throughout my term on the *Times*, I served as principal liaison agent between the two. The transfer of the *Times* news bulletins to WQXR involved long and delicate negotiations with WMCA and a good deal of readjustment in the programming of WQXR. Fortunately the executive vice-president, Elliott M. Sanger, who was the active manager of WQXR, was a man of vision, ability, and sensitivity. I was in constant contact with him, and in my two and one-half years' association with him I found him invariably helpful, understanding, shrewd, constructive, and co-operative. Although WQXR was primarily a music station—and Sanger was deeply interested in this phase of radio work—he realized the great possibilities of tying a newspaper like the *Times* into radio, not only in news but also in other fields. He and I spent many hours canvassing all sorts of possibilities. Often it fell to my lot to endeavor to convince men on the *Times* of the possible radio advantages in certain proposals. At other times my task was to help

CARR V. VAN ANDA
His mind worked like a machine and he foresaw the news

the radio station understand the interests of the newspaper. Fortunately Mr. Sulzberger never for a moment forgot that the popularity of WQXR was the result of its music programming. He was alert to any suggestions which might strengthen this phase of the station's operations.

My liaison work with WQXR, together with other duties as assistant to the publisher, brought me into close association with Orvil E. Dryfoos, who had married Mr. Ochs' granddaughter Marian Sulzberger. Once more I was struck with Mr. Ochs' luck, for this young man, whom he had probably never seen, turned out to have to a high degree those qualities of judgment, shrewdness, and intelligence so essential in the publisher's office, and to have, besides, an engaging manner and personality. It was unusual enough that, as I have already indicated, Mr. Ochs' own son-in-law filled the bill so well. To find in his son-in-law's son-in-law also exceptional ability was something hardly to be hoped for. I do not know what the plans are for the succession to the office of publisher when Mr. Sulzberger retires. But so long as "Orv" is close to the man at the helm—even if not himself the helmsman—the management of this great institution will be in good hands.

To some, these glimpses of the *Times* may seem to give an exaggerated impression of that newspaper's strength. I know of no more effective confirmation of the standing of the *Times* than came in a conversation with one of the leading men of the *Times'* Washington bureau, who, during World War II, had been lured away by one of the nation's largest weeklies, and whose new association had received much publicity and advertising. A few months after he had taken up this new position I met him at a cocktail party and asked him how he liked it. His immediate response was full of formal enthusiasm, but after his third cocktail he said to me: "You know, it was not until I left the *Times* that I appreciated the enormous influence of that paper. When I was on the *Times* staff I could see anyone, anywhere, at any time, without any delay. Now I'm just another editor imposing on the time of overbusy officials." Within a year he was back on the *Times*, and greatly relieved to enjoy once more its power and prestige.

[277]

CHAPTER THIRTY

THE DUST OF NEW YORK

INTERESTING as was the work on the *New York Times* and with WQXR, a bout of pneumonia in 1946—my third—called for taking stock. I could probably stay with the *Times* until run over by a taxi or until I had a fourth and final attack of pneumonia. But this meant accepting the ever increasing strain, discomfort, and barbarity of life in New York. The alternative was to move out to our vacation home at Big Sur, on the California coast, there to write books and to enjoy living. This promised health, release from overstrain, the satisfaction of becoming independent of the ministrations of others, an end to the stultifying routine of professional and social demands, and a chance to do the writing of history which I had long looked forward to. On the debit side would be the loss of contacts with stimulating people, the separation from friends and relatives, the time-consuming chores of maintaining a house and garden forty miles from the nearest town. For my wife, more gregarious than I, the isolation would be more trying. Due to the impossibility of getting help in this remote wilderness, the amount of work in keeping the house up to the standards to which she was accustomed would at times be overwhelming. I knew that I should miss my frequent lunches at the Century Club, where authors, artists, publishers, lawyers, bankers, doctors, architects, professors, and editors came to seek good company. One day one's neighbors at the luncheon table might be Arthur Train, the author of the "Tut" stories, and Walter Damrosch; the next they might be William Adams Delano, the architect, and Wendell Willkie; again they might be Elmer Davis

[278]

and Horace M. Albright, the former head of the National Park Service, or Henry Seidel Canby of the *Saturday Review*, or the landscape architect Charles Downing Lay, or the sculptor Mahonri Young, or any one of dozens of interesting and amusing companions. These contacts were irreplaceable. Not without reason had William Makepeace Thackeray considered the Century as the most civilized spot in America. So it was when he was in New York eighty years ago, and so it still is. For this there would be—and is—no compensation.

Thanks to the ability and thrift of my great-grandfather, old C. V. S. Roosevelt, a century ago, my share of his estate, when added to what my wife had, was enough to enable us to live at Big Sur even if the projected books did not sell well. We listed the pros and cons and, in October, 1946, moved to California. Many friends thought that to leave an important job in New York at the age of fifty-three was a renunciation of all that was worthwhile. They looked on us as fugitives from reality, seeking escape on the wings of the morning. Yet those who visited us at our mountain home high above the blue Pacific marveled at the fullness and satisfaction of our existence. Where they had feared that, cut off from accustomed stimuli, we would stagnate and shrivel, they found us alert and happy as never before, enjoying to the full the advantages of beautiful surroundings, good music, and good living, and keenly interested in what was happening in the world. The more discerning understood that there are compensations in the fruits of self-reliance and satisfactions in the doing of chores in a beautiful environment. When, sometimes, one of us would gag at the unremitting demands of housework, we would recall that in New York we spent hours daily doing things which we disliked, mostly under adverse conditions in an ugly setting. Here we had but to glance out of the window or step out of the door to realize our good fortune.

With the ocean spread out a thousand feet below and the mountain barrier behind us, we were conscious as never elsewhere of sun and sky. The colors on hill and sea changed each hour of the day. At night the brilliance of the stars—the air above us is desert dry throughout most of the year—continually amazed us. So did the antics of the moon, forever shifting the places of its rising and setting. Sometimes we saw, against the sunset's afterglow, the new moon and the evening star, side by side, each with a reflection so bright as to make a path of light across the still ocean. Often the morning star cast shadows as it beaconed over the mountain's crest when the first streaks of green in the east presaged dawn. We found that clouds not only have form but meaning, foretelling weather. We have seen fog born and die. Out of an impenetrable mist patches of ocean or mountain have suddenly emerged, as quickly to be blotted out, as if in the first days of the creation the Lord was testing land and water to see if they were good. Those who have felt the full fury of a Big Sur storm know why the Bible speaks of God answering Job "out of the whirlwind."

By day and night these things brought ceaseless satisfaction. So also, we marveled at the way of the eagle in the air, and at the red-tailed hawk riding as if at anchor in the updraft of the trade wind until ready to plummet down upon a pack rat. We have never tired of the sickle-billed thrasher's melodious overflow of song, giving full-throated thanks from a sunny treetop for another sparkling morning. On still days in winter we have heard the whish of the whales as they blow, and watched their barnacled bodies breach the surface before they sound. We have even seen whales jump clear of the water, and heard the boom of their bodies as they fall back. One morning, just after we had bought the land and had camped on it overnight, there was a succession of explosions as if the road crew were dynamiting a slide. Below us we saw three whales cavorting, slapping a ton of whale tail on the water with such force as to sound like blasting. Whether these were whales in love or merely whales stunning a school of fish for food we never learned, but the occasion inspired the name which we gave to our headland home—Point of Whales.

I soon found that, despite a lifelong habit of devouring newspapers, it was unimportant if I read about something in the paper tomorrow instead of today. What counted was the significance of the event. I saw how many news items could be passed over, either because they were trivial or because subsequent events which had been reported on the radio had superseded the stories in my outdated newspapers. This, in turn, freed for more rewarding things many hours previously devoted to the reading of newspapers.

My yearning for time to think had been one of the decisive factors in leaving New York. I had realized the advantages of working under pressure—that one concentrates more effectively when an article has to be finished by a deadline. Yet I knew that too many such articles represent reactions rather than thought, prejudices rather than sound judgment. The process of thinking may be stimulated by the fulfilling of a commitment to an editor, but if it is to be truly fruitful there must be time to reflect, to compare, to appraise, to question, to analyze, to test. Mere observation and recording is not enough, nor is the amassing of facts. Without understanding they are sterile, and understanding comes to most of us only as the result of study and experience, ripened by reflection.

Now, with time to look back on what I had seen from my front row seat and what I had read of history, politics, and economics, it was clear that the most important development since 1900 had been the transformation of the United States from a comparatively small, unimportant member of the international community into the most powerful nation in the Western world (including Europe west of Russia). This change had come about not alone through the increased population, economic strength, and military power of the United States but also through the relative decline of the British Empire and the nations of western Europe resulting from two world wars. Fifty years ago Americans could safely ignore foreign affairs. Today what happens in distant parts of the globe—in Korea, in Indo-China, in the Near East, or in Africa—has far-reaching repercussions on American activities and hopes. We are irretrievably enmeshed in world affairs. The isolation which so many Americans treasured is a thing of the past.

One other nation has made a comparable growth—Soviet Russia—and thanks to its ruthless dictatorship, its plans for expansion, and its geographical position dominating the continents of Europe and Asia, it is a menace to world peace. Not only has traditional Russian imperialism been revived with larger and more extended goals, but the Communists have launched an ideological campaign which has as its purpose the extinction of freedom and democracy everywhere. The reason for this is that the leaders of Soviet Russia live in constant fear of the ideas of free men. They dread the possible contagion to their own people of the conviction shared by all the Western world that the individual—every individual—has rights which are inalienable, and which are, in fact, a denial of the right of government to tell each citizen what he may or must do. They know that only by suppressing and rigidly excluding such ideas can they perpetuate the political system which they control. Communism cannot survive unless it stifles initiative, crushes originality, and forbids independence of thought. To doubt, to question, to disbelieve, to deny the rightness of authority and the sanctity of official pronouncements, is to strike at the very foundations of the state. Like the Nazis and Fascists, the Communists accept as axiomatic the power of the rulers to decide, dictate, compel, coerce, punish. This authoritarian premise is the complete antithesis of our traditional concept that men are free agents, independent personalities, more important than society, and superior to the state.

Being realists, the Soviet leaders think in terms of the ultimate use of force. This means that their first objective is to make Russia by land, sea, air, and atomic energy the most powerful potential aggressor in the world. Their second objective is to produce disunity among the nations of the free world so as to weaken them as a defensive force. Their third objective is to foster dissension and, if possible, disorder within the more powerful nations of the West, so as to make it more difficult for each of them to take its effective part in military operations. The encouragement of racial hatred, industrial strife, and widespread strikes is part of the standing orders of Communist agents throughout the Western world. Anything which weakens the productive economy of a nation handicaps its military potential. As long as twenty-five years ago the Soviets, as I have already indicated, fostered nationalism and racialism among the peoples of Asia, not because they believed in nationalism or racial tolerance, but because they wished to embarrass and impoverish those European nations which had colonial outposts and important trade interests in Asia. Today they are following a similar technique in Africa. The objective is the simple one of causing Great Britain and France to divert troops and money from the defense of Europe to these overseas areas. The Soviets figure that the weaker the nations of the West and, in particular, the more reluctant they are to pool their resources in a common defense effort, the easier it will be for Russia to expand. By the same token they have planned a sequence of incidents in the more remote parts of the world to lure European and American troops away from their home bases. Korea, Indo-China, Iran, Morocco—all these have been carefully mapped out or encouraged expressly to weaken and disunite the nations of the North Atlantic Alliance.

It is because, in the pursuit of these divisive and subversive ends, the Communist agents in the United States and elsewhere are acting in the sole interest of Russian imperialism that they present such a serious problem. It would be bad enough if the Communists in this country were merely engaged in an effort to win converts for their particular form of reactionary authoritarianism. But as they are the agents of a foreign nation which can only achieve its goal by crushing or changing the political and economic system through which the United States has grown great and powerful, their activities are of grave concern.

The second outstanding development in the last half-century derives from the changed concept of the function of government in the United States. Before 1900 the Jeffersonian tradition was still strong—that the least government is the best government. Today the trend is clearly towards a welfare state. Since the passage of the Interstate Commerce Act in 1887—and more particularly during the last two decades—government at one or another level has:

imposed regulations on the shipment of goods within the United States; fixed freight rates; fixed passenger rates on railroads; fixed the rates of electric power, telephone service, and telegrams; es-

[283]

tablished minimum wages; controlled interest rates; regulated radio channels and the operation of radio stations; prescribed conditions for the practice of medicine and other occupations; through tax provisions, acquired a substantial degree of supervision over many businesses; provided old-age pensions; furnished relief; advanced loans to businessmen, farmers, and would-be home-owners; paid farmers for improving their soil; bought surplus farm products to help keep up farm prices; furnished free lunches for school children.

The list of services now being performed by government would fill a book. They are sure to increase, for the reason that most of these measures have been popular, and politicians will be inclined to devise new means of assistance by government in the hope of winning more votes of a grateful electorate.

The question at issue is not the desirability of the kind of government services so far provided, but rather the fact that when, as has happened in the last two decades, the powers of government over the economic activities of the people are greatly increased, new instruments of authority are created. In the hands of evil or corrupt men these can be used to restrain human freedom. Economic controls, to be effective, must be obeyed by those on whom they are imposed. Even though most of the controls to date have been negative—that is, they have set quota limits beyond which production is not to be pushed—it is but a step from telling people what they may *not* do to telling them what they *must* do. Furthermore, the popularity of the concept of security has led to increasing demands that government be given all the powers which it may need so that people may be assured steady work (not too hard), a modest wage, short hours, and benevolent protection against old age, unemployment, and ill health.

How this can be done short of imposing a form of planned economy is not clear. But what is clear is that, of all labels for reaction, planned economy is the most deceptive because of its plausibility. The underlying theory is that the nation is to produce what it can consume and sell abroad. There is to be a balanced plenty. This calls for a plan. A plan, in turn, calls for planners. These must be all-knowing and all-wise, and never make a

[284]

mistake. They must foresee all contingencies, foretell the weather a year or more in advance, correctly appraise changing tastes, forestall or make allowances for new techniques and inventions, prevent strikes, control imports and exports, and impose their plan. Under such a system each person will have his function as part of a vast machine. Obviously there will have to be machinery for enforcing compliance. Thus we are back to the concept of the master state.

The bland assumption that the solution of our ills lies in empowering government agents to plan our lives for us is one of the strangest delusions of our times. There is nothing to show that the average man elected or appointed to office in this or any other country is, *ipso facto*, endowed with sufficient omniscience to know what we should do and how we should do it. In fact, too often men seek political office because they have not been very successful in other lines. And yet, implicit in the attitude of "let Uncle Sam do it" is the assumption that the men who work for Uncle Sam know all the answers. The history of human freedom, as Woodrow Wilson so truly said, is the history of the struggle to limit the powers of government, not to increase them. Implicit in modern political liberalism is the God-given right of individual independence—which means the right to be free from governmental compulsion. No fair-minded man can deny that the great achievements in industry, commerce, the sciences, and the arts in the last two centuries have been the products of individual initiative working either on its own or in co-operation with other free men, and that the great advances in social thought—the spread of humanitarianism, the alleviation of suffering, the improvement of public health and morals, the impetus towards more widespread education—have come not from government, but as a result of the initiative of free men and women, untrammeled by government dictation or restrictions.

The list of problems could be prolonged for pages. It may not be possible to find solutions for them by gazing out over the Pacific from a promontory. But I am not sure that solutions will —or could—be found in New York. As one of the ninth generation of Roosevelts born on Manhattan Island, I may claim the

[285]

right of questioning the traditional New York conceit that it is the center of the world. It is a great city, and yet, the more I have lived elsewhere, the more I have come to sympathize with the foreman of the cattle ranch in West Texas belonging to the father of Mrs. Eugene Holman, the wife of the president of the Standard Oil Company of New Jersey. This foreman was an ardent Presbyterian of the old school, as rigid in his standards of conduct as in his morals. Not only was he as fanatically opposed to liquor as Carry Nation, but he looked on swearing as a sin and never himself used an oath or took the name of the Lord in vain. To him every one of the Ten Commandments was sacred and to be taken absolutely literally, and any breach of any of them, no matter how small, was not to be tolerated either in others or in himself.

Despite this somewhat stiff attitude, he was highly regarded on the ranch and greatly liked by all the children. Mrs. Holman told me that, when she made her first visit to the ranch after marrying and moving to New York, the old foreman greeted her warmly and, after answering questions about himself and his family, asked her how she liked living in New York. She replied that she liked it very much. For a few seconds he looked at her in silence. Then, with asperity, he said: "I'd rob a bank, if that was the only way I could keep my family from starving. I'd kill a man, if I had to in order to protect my family. But I'll be God *damned* if I'd ever live in New York!"

I don't feel quite as vehemently as this Texan, but I am glad to have shaken the dust of New York off my feet and to be able to be in the Big Sur country, where people enjoy the art of living and have time to think, and where the neighbors' traditional toast is "Kindness!"

APPENDIX

ROOSEVELT GENEALOGICAL TABLE

abbreviated

Claes (immigrant) arrived in 1649

Nicholas 1658-1742 (trader)

Johannes 1689-? (merchant) founder of the Oyster Bay branch

Nicholas 1687-? (silversmith)

Jacobus 1692-1776 (merchant)

Jacobus 1724-? (merchant)

Cornelius 1731-?

Christopher 1739-93

Isaac 1726-94 (banker) founder of the Hyde Park branch

Nicholas J. 1767-1854 (steamboat inventor)

James J. 1759-1840 (hardware & glass)

Elbert 1767-1857

James C. 1770-?

James 1760-1847 (banker)

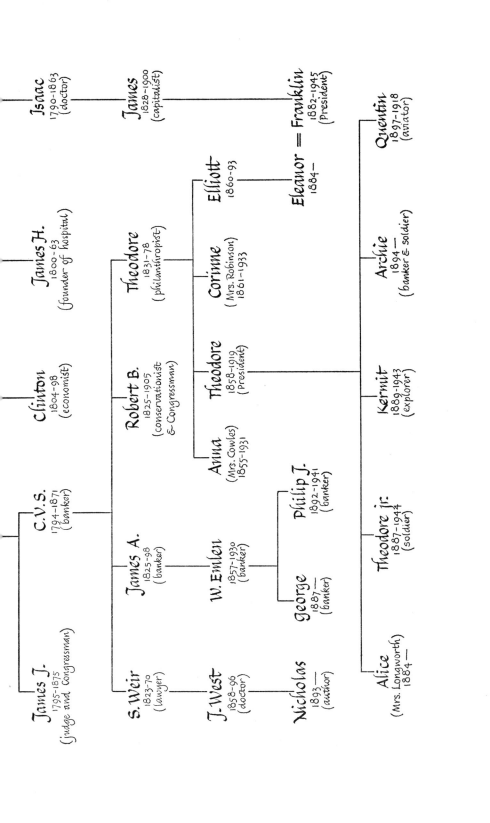

Isaac
1790-1863
(doctor)

James
1828-1900
(capitalist)

Eleanor = Franklin
1884—   1882-1945
              (President)

James H.
1800-63
(founder of hospital)

Theodore
1831-78
(philanthropist)

Elliott
1860-93

Corinne
(Mrs. Robinson)
1861-1933

Clinton
1804-98
(economist)

Robert B.
1825-1905
(conservationist
& Congressman)

Theodore
1858-1919
(President)

Archie
1894—
(banker & soldier)

Quentin
1897-1918
(aviator)

C.V.S.
1794-1871
(banker)

Anna
(Mrs. Cowles)
1855-1931

Kernit
1889-1943
(explorer)

James J.
1795-1875
(judge and Congressman)

James A.
1825-98
(banker)

W. Emlen
1857-1930
(banker)

Philip J.
1892-1941
(banker)

Theodore jr.
1887-1944
(soldier)

S. Weir
1823-70
(lawyer)

J. West
1858-96
(doctor)

George
1887—
(banker)

Nicholas
1893—
(author)

Alice
(Mrs. Longworth)
1884—

INDEX

Adams, Franklin P., journalist: 265
Adams, Henry, historian: dislike of T. R., 56, 62; characterization of Robert Lansing, 112
Albright, Horace M., conservationist: incident of Yosemite National Park, 273 f; at Century Club, 279
Alexander, king of Yugoslavia: author's interview with, 213 f
Alfonso XIII, king of Spain: receives Major Case and author, 84 ff; discussion with Ambassador Willard, 86 ff; at funeral of Archduchess Isabella, 88 f
Allen, Henry, editor; later governor of Kansas: and Wood campaign, 130
Allizé, French diplomat: and counter-revolutionary intrigues in Hungary, 114 ff
Alsop, Joseph W., Jr., journalist: 7
Alsop, Stewart, journalist: 7
Amai Manabilang, Moro leader: voices Moro grievances, 158 ff
American International Corporation: activities in Spain, *see Chapter Eight*
Apponyi, Count Albert, Hungarian statesman: characterization of, 202 f; opinion that nothing is finite in European politics, 219
Augusta, Archduchess: 198 f

Baer, Joseph A., military attaché in Hungary: and Austrian Nazi movement, 211
Balfour, Arthur, British statesman: at Washington conference, 1921, 133 ff
Banzai, Japanese military leader in China: 173
Barnes, William, Jr., New York Republican boss: 51

[291]

Freeman, Commander, member of British mission to Hungary: and Communist seizure of British gunboat, 106f

Gabrielle, Archduchess: 197
Garfield, Secretary of the Interior James R.: 51
Garrett, Alice (Mrs. John W.): education of embassy secretaries, 79f; portrait by Zuloaga, 80
Garrett, John W., diplomat: heads mission in Bordeaux, 69f; arranges interview for author with Mussolini, 215
Geoffrey, Mme de, wife of French ambassador: 83f
Gibbs, Laura Wolcott, author's great-grandmother: active in U. S. Sanitary Commission, 27
Gilman, Lawrence, music critic: 265
Gottschee, Yugoslavia: petition for annexation to U. S., 97
Government, U. S., changes in: 224ff, 283ff
Guttierez, governor of Cotabato province: 157f

Hadley, Herbert, governor of Missouri: 50
Hammond, Paul: 130
Hanfstaengl, E. F., musician and friend of Hitler: 212
Harding, Senator W. G.: nominates Taft in 1912, 49
Haskell, Henry J., editor: supports Landon, 239
Havas, Eugene, Hungarian financial expert: 187
Herter, Christian A., diplomat: 110f
Hioki, Japanese leader: presenter of the Twenty-one Demands, 173
Hitchcock, Frank H., Republican political leader: manages Wood campaign, 125ff
Hitler, Adolf: and Austrian Nazi leaders, 211f; friendship for Hanfstaengl, 212
Holleben, Dr. von, German ambassador: and Venezuelan incident, 60
Holman, Mrs. Eugene: 286
Holmes, Judge Oliver Wendell: opinion of T. R., 62
Hone, Philip, mayor of New York: criticizes J. J. Roosevelt, 3; 12
Hooker, E. H., civil engineer: 51
Hoover, Herbert, head of Inter-Allied Food Mission, later president of U. S.: and Hungarian revolution, 113f; fishing on Klamath River, 235ff; plea to F. D. R. to stem bank panic, 236f; visits Klamath school, 237f; unacceptable as candidate in 1936, 238f; Republican spokesman, 240
Hopper, Franklin, librarian: story of J. P. Morgan, 4f

UNIVERSITY OF OKLAHOMA PRESS

NORMAN